ECONOMICS:

*Examination
questions
answered*

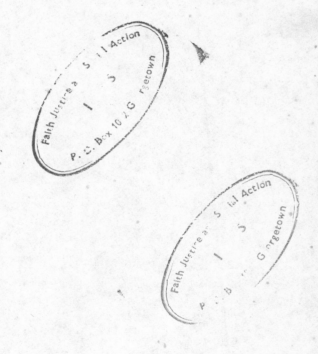

ECONOMICS:

Examination questions answered

Maurice W Jones *B Com (Hons)*
Formerly Lecturer in Economics,
Mid-Essex Technical College Chelmsford

PITMAN PUBLISHING
128 Long Acre, London WC2E 9AN

© Maurice W Jones 1971

First published in Great Britain 1971
Reprinted 1974, 1975, 1976, 1977, 1978,
1980, 1981, 1982, 1983, 1984, 1987

Printed in Great Britain at The Bath Press, Avon

ISBN 0 273 31473 4

Preface

This book is intended to help students who are about to take examinations in Economics, whether at "A" level or as one of the subjects included in their intermediate or final professional papers. It does not pretend to offer a complete and systematic course in the subject, but experience has shown that students benefit greatly from having their attention focussed on the kind of topics which they are most likely to encounter in their examinations, instead of having to devote an equal amount of attention to every page of a conventional textbook.

The author has therefore selected a wide-ranging assortment of essay questions from Economics papers set in recent years, and provided answers to them of a content, length and style suitable for examination purposes. Thus not only is the student provided with a valuable adjunct to the subject matter of his main textbook, but he is initiated into a technique of dealing with the kind of questions with which he will be confronted — many of the topics chosen occur with some degree of regularity over the years, as will be seen by the supplementary questions taken from other papers which have been listed after each essay. These could either be answered in exactly the same way as the preceding essay, or with minor modifications as called for by the particular form of wording in each case.

The following examining bodies have been kind enough to give permission for their questions to be used in this way, and both publisher and author would like to thank them for their willingness to co-operate; needless to say, no responsibility of any kind attaches to the examiners for the content of the answers.

The University of London (U of L).
The Associated Examining Board (AEB).
The Institute of Chartered Accountants in England & Wales (ICA).
The Chartered Institute of Secretaries (CIS).
The Corporation of Secretaries (CS).
The Institute of Cost & Works Accountants (ICWA).
The Institute of Bankers (I of B).
The Association of Certified and Corporate Accountants (ACCA).

v

The first nine sections of the book contain essay questions, classified under the kind of headings adopted by most textbooks, although of course they do not always fall neatly into one or other of these categories. Moreover, the questions have been chosen in such a way as to cover the main topics of the various syllabuses with the minimum of overlap, so that students should not only benefit from reading this book of answers in parallel with their main textbook, but derive added benefit from going through it again when the time comes for revision.

Finally, there is a tenth section containing a selection of "objective test" questions of the type now being introduced into "A" level examinations, and which will no doubt find their way into those of the professional bodies before long. No attempt has been made to arrange these in any particular sequence, as it seems that examination papers of this type will be set in similar random fashion. The probability is that examinees will be called upon to sit for one paper of the traditional type requiring essay answers, and one containing about the same total number of "objective test" questions as that included in this section; it is hoped that the examples chosen will provide the student with a valuable insight into the kind of question he may expect to see, and give him the necessary practice in dealing quickly with them. Answers to these questions will be found at the end of the section.

M. W. J.
Chelmsford 1971

Contents

1
Basic economic concepts

The typical examination paper, especially at intermediate level, often contains a question which simply asks the student in a more or less direct fashion to say what economics is all about. Variations on the same theme quote a definition of economics and invite comments on it, or deal with some other general aspect of the subject, e.g. the nature of economic laws, the significance of opportunity cost, the notion of the "margin", etc.

It is not unusual for students to feel somewhat confused at first by the conflict of views expressed by different economists and the variety of definitions which it is possible to give of quite elementary concepts, but no one should be at a loss to deal with the kind of question set on this part of the syllabus by the time he has reached the end of the course. All that can be said by way of general guidance at this stage is that scarcity of resources lies at the heart of the subject, and that every question in every section of the book is related in some way to it. Scarcity implies the need for making choices, choices are usually made at the margin, marginal decisions explain the shape of demand and cost curves, and so on right through to the organization of finance and industry — both producers and consumers are trying to stretch resources as far as they will go, and economics attempts to analyse the ways in which they go about it.

In writing about these rather broad topics, it is perhaps even more necessary than usual to have a clear idea of what one is going to say at the outset, otherwise there is a distinct danger that the answer will emerge as a series of random observations which get less and less relevant as they go on. The student who will therefore do best with questions of this kind is one who has not only acquired a good understanding of economic principles, but who also has the ability to communicate this understanding in an interesting and convincing manner.

1.1   *Give a definition of economics. Why do economists sometimes disagree with each other on matters of interpretation? (I of B Part I, September 1965.)*

1

Definition

Economics could be defined as a social science which studies man's
behaviour in trying to reconcile his unlimited material needs with the
relative scarcity of available resources. The objects of the study are
(*a*) to arrive at certain generalizations which will serve as the basis
of laws governing man's reactions to problems involving resource
allocation at any given time, (*b*) to examine the means whereby he can
augment the supply of resources at his disposal in the future, and (*c*) to
predict what the consequences of these alternative courses of action are
likely to be.

Why economists disagree

Although there is broad agreement among economists as to the principles
which operate in their chosen field, it is not unusual for them to disagree
on the diagnosis of various economic ills, and still more on their treatment.
Such conflicts of view are not, of course, unknown in what may be termed
the exact sciences, but they are more prone to occur among economists
by the very nature of their subject.

(*a*) *What is "best"?* It has been said that economics is concerned with
means, not ends; in other words, the economist should be prepared to
leave all policy decisions to politicians, and confine himself to investigating
different ways of putting these policies into effect. Even if economists
were content to accept this definition of their rôle, however, they would
still find themselves stepping outside the field of pure logic as soon as they
had to give practical advice. The root of the difficulty lies in the essentially
subjective nature of the word "best" as applied to human welfare: whereas
a pure scientist is able to calculate, and if need be measure, variations in
output of a machine resulting from different ways of designing it, the
economist cannot apply any such yardstick to welfare. What is "best"
must remain in the end a matter of individual judgement, and it is
inevitable that the opinions of economists will reflect their different
personalities and backgrounds.

(*b*) *"Opportunity costs" and "value judgements".* The extent of such
disagreements will, of course, depend largely on the nature of the problem
under consideration. A high degree of unanimity might be anticipated on
a purely technical point, assuming that it could be considered in isolation,
but in practice such simple cases hardly ever occur. By definition,
economic problems involve making choices which affect people, and the
exercise of choice implies that certain opportunity costs have to be
incurred, so that making economic decisions almost inevitably involves
making value judgements once one gets outside the realms of textbook
theory.

(*c*) *Lack of experimental data.* Not only are economists unable to
measure the amount of welfare likely to result from different policies,

but they are also unable to test their respective theories by experimental research; thus it is not merely possible for economists to disagree on what should be done at any given moment, but to argue forever afterwards about what would have happened if some other course of action had been adopted at the time.

(*d*) *Experience unreliable.* Even experience is not a very reliable guide in deciding what should be done in the field of economic policy. The social environment is changing all the time, so that the success or failure of decisions made in the past will not necessarily be repeated in the future, nor will the lessons learned in running the affairs of one country always be applicable to the economy of another.

Summary

In view of all the circumstances, it is hardly surprising that economists are continually at variance with one another, even to the extent of lending their support to opposing political parties. However, these disagreements usually arise from their different concepts of what course of action is desirable or practicable rather than from any conflict over basic economic principles.

SIMILAR QUESTIONS

(i) "Economics is concerned with the fact of scarcity and the need for choice." Explain and amplify this statement. (ICWA Part I, June 1965.)
(ii) "Economics is the practical science of the production and distribution of wealth" — J S Mill. Criticize this definition, making clear the nature and scope of the subject. (ICWA Part I, December 1968)

1.2 *"Economic laws may be defined as statements of tendencies." Discuss this statement. (I of B Part I, April 1964.)*

It is true to say that economic laws can only indicate what is *likely* to happen in certain circumstances for a number of reasons, the first of which concerns the nature of the object being studied, namely Man himself.

Human beings are inconsistent

It is a comparatively simple matter for the chemist or physicist to define and isolate the substances he is interested in, and if he takes the necessary precautions he can be reasonably sure that every time he wants to use them they will have the same characteristics. By contrast, the economist's raw material consists of human beings in all their infinite variety and complexity. Not only is it impossible to find two men who are exactly alike, but the same man is changing all the time because of things which are happening in and around him; having a mind and will of his own, he will not always react in the same way even in the same set of circumstances.

"Economic man" does not exist

Unfortunately for the economist, the difficulties with his raw material do not end there. Unlike "economic man", who has been aptly described as "just a clothes horse for the theorist", any real man is subject to all kinds of emotional pressures which may at times far outweigh any rational calculation of material gain or loss. A man in love might go short of food to buy a trinket for the object of his affection; a man will spend his life in contemplation and poverty if he is convinced that there will be benefits in the after-life; a man who disapproves of alcoholic drink will refuse to hold shares in a brewery, and so on.

Individual v. group behaviour

There is yet a further complication which arises when dealing with the behaviour of human beings. If one pint of water is added to another, the result is a quart of water, without any change in the properties of the substance; put two or more people together, however, and the group will acquire characteristics of its own, perhaps quite different from those of the individuals who comprise it. The most obvious example of this is the way in which members of a community develop competitive urges — we are all familiar with the social phenomenon known as "keeping up with the Joneses", but it is not always easy to predict what form it will take next.

"Cause-and-effect" difficult to isolate

To continue the comparison between economics and the physical sciences, the chemist who wishes to investigate the way his materials behave in various kinds of situations can conduct his experiments under closely controlled conditions, so that the only variables are those which he introduces himself. Again, the contrast with life for the economist is most marked; he can only stand helplessly by and observe the course of events as it develops, and then try to decide which of the countless things that are happening are relevant to his enquiries. Even the simplest kind of theory is extremely difficult to test — he may reason, for example, that a fall in the price of a commodity will result in more of it being sold, only to find that in the case he decides to investigate the reverse has happened. If, nevertheless, he still thinks that his hypothesis is a reasonable one, he can do two things, (*a*) try to discover whether there were any influences operating in the case in question sufficiently powerful to outweigh the influence of the lower price, and (*b*) investigate other similar cases to find out whether the results show any significant degree of correlation. He may eventually decide on the evidence available to him that his original theory was valid, but there is no way of knowing whether the evidence is wholly reliable and complete. The most he should be prepared to say, therefore, is that if the price of a commodity falls, more of it will be sold, and vice-versa, *other things being equal*. It is, indeed, necessary to add this qualification to the statements of economists so often that the phrase is commonly abbreviated to "O.T.E.".

Significance of economic laws

However, the fact that no great degree of precision can be attached to economic laws does not mean that they can be dismissed as unimportant. While their operation may be counteracted or obscured by many other influences, they can always be relied upon to exert pressure in a given direction, e.g. the quantity of ice cream sold may have fallen after a reduction in its price because of the simultaneous onset of cold weather, but it would have fallen still further if the price had remained the same. Certainly, any business man or Government planner who chose to disregard economic laws altogether when formulating his policies would be inviting failure.

SIMILAR QUESTIONS

(i) What is meant by describing economic laws as inductive or as deductive? (CS Intermediate, June 1967.)
(ii) Is Economics a science? (CS Intermediate, November 1967.)

1.3   *What do you understand by the term "opportunity cost"? How is it related to the problem of scarcity? (U of L Advanced, Summer 1967.)*

Definition

The term "opportunity cost" is used by economists to indicate the fact that when one is forced to make a choice between two alternative ways of using scarce resources, the real, as distinct from the money, cost of the preferred alternative is the utility which would have resulted had the other alternative been chosen instead.

Infinite needs v. finite resources

Were it not for the fundamental fact that resources are scarce, the necessity for choice would not arise, and the enjoyment of one satisfaction would not involve the sacrifice of another. As it is, scarcity of resources is continuously forcing us to choose between one course of action and another. As individuals, we are made most keenly aware of this when we consider the endless variety of our personal needs in relation to the comparative smallness of our incomes; we must always weigh carefully the satisfaction we should gain by spending our money on A as against the satisfaction we should lose by going without B. As a community, we entrust the spending of part of our income to the Government, who in turn are faced with the necessity of choosing between defence and welfare, roads and houses, education and health, and so on.

Opportunity cost and marginal utility

In practice, we are usually able to adjust the pattern of our expenditure so as to be able to avoid rejecting one alternative completely in favour of another. More often than not, what we are considering is whether we shall make do with a little *less* of A so that we can have a little *more* of B, or vice versa. In other words, choice is exercised "at the margin", and calculations of opportunity cost involve comparing the satisfactions obtainable from marginal units of different commodities. In order to accommodate our needs in the best possible way to the scarcity of our resources, we must try to equate the marginal utilities of all our various purchases, i.e. the opportunity cost of every marginal pennyworth must balance exactly.

Opportunity cost and time

The problem of scarcity applies with particular force in connection with the allocation of time, as this is one resource which cannot be stored or increased. Man must divide his time in some way between sleeping and waking, leisure and work, every day of every year of his life. The sum total of his decisions will go far towards determining whether he is rich or poor, happy or miserable; while he may often wish that there were more than 24 hours in a day, or that he could live certain periods of his life over again, these possibilities must remain forever closed to him.

Opportunity cost and entrepreneurial decisions

There is yet another way in which opportunity cost is involved in economic decisions, namely those of entrepreneurs in determining the use to which productive resources shall be committed. A plot of land, a unit of raw material, a man's labour or a pound's worth of capital can be used in countless different ways to satisfy human wants, but once the entrepreneur has decided to employ them in one way society has lost the opportunity of employing them in another, at least for the time being. In some cases the decision is quite irrevocable, as for example when what was originally a lump of iron ore finishes up as thousands of razor blades, but in others the commitment is less final, e.g. a man trained as a turner can be retrained as a welder. The fact remains that entrepreneurs determine the week-to-week allocation of all factors of production, and the cost of using them to produce one thing is the opportunity which might have been taken of using them to produce another.

1.4   *What do economists understand by utility and value? How does utility affect exchange value? (CIS Intermediate, June 1962.)*

Definition of utility

Economists use the word utility to describe the satisfaction which people get from consuming various kinds of goods and services. As satisfaction is a subjective thing, utility as such cannot be measured in absolute terms, but for practical purposes the utility of a good to a particular consumer can be gauged by how much he is prepared to pay for it as compared with other things. Of course, this method of assessment does not extend to the comparison of utilities conferred by a good on different consumers — a rich man may be prepared to give much more than a poor one for a certain article, but it does not follow that he will get greater satisfaction from it.

Utility not synonymous with benefit

To say that a thing has utility for a consumer does not necessarily mean that he will derive benefit from it. There are many products which satisfy consumers' desires and yet undoubtedly do them harm, e.g. addictive drugs, and many more which have undesirable effects if consumed to excess, e.g. fattening foods. Economic usage of the term utility makes no distinctions of these kinds, however; willingness to pay is the only criterion of satisfaction obtained.

Definition of value

Value is usually expressed in terms of money, but price is not the same thing as value. If the price of a chair is £5 and the price of a table is £20, this means that, on the community's scale of relative values, four chairs will be a fair exchange for one table, but the same would be true if the price of chairs were £10 and the price of tables £40. When the economist uses the word "value", he always has in mind this idea of "value-in-exchange", but money performs the useful function of enabling us to compare the values of all kinds of goods with one another, i.e. prices are a common measure of "value-in-exchange".

Value determined by marginal utility

To explain the connection between utility and value, it is necessary to introduce the concept of diminishing marginal utility. Given a suitably short time scale, a person's desire for any good decreases as the amount consumed increases, and hence his willingness to pay for additional units of it falls progressively to zero as the point of satiation is reached. Thus the situation can exist where one good which is a vital necessity, e.g. water, sells at an extremely low price, while another which is *not* vital, e.g. perfume, sells at a very high price; it is not *total* utility but *marginal* utility which is measured by the price, and sellers must fix this at a level calculated to sell the entire quantity of a good being produced. It follows, of course, that there is a difference between what consumers would be prepared to pay for units before the marginal one and what they are actually called upon to pay (called "consumers' surplus"), but sellers have no means of knowing whether consumers are buying their first or their marginal units, and are obliged to assume it is the latter in order to avoid being left with unsold stocks.

Summary

Utility simply means usefulness, or the ability to satisfy a want; value means value-in-exchange as reflected by price, and price is a measure of marginal utility.

SIMILAR QUESTION

(i) "Economic goods have prices because they are useful and scarce". Explain and illustrate. (CIS Intermediate, June 1966.)

1.5   *What do you understand by the term wealth in economics? Explain the difference between personal and other ownership of wealth. (ACCA Section 1, June 1969.)*

Definition of wealth

The term wealth is used by economists to denote the stock of economic goods existing at any given time. Economic goods include anything which (*a*) has utility, (*b*) is in some degree scarce, and (*c*) is capable of being transferred from one ownership to another. All such goods have one feature in common, namely value-in-exchange, which implies the possession of all three of these attributes. For example, air has great utility, but is not scarce in normal circumstances; bad eggs are relatively scarce, but have no utility; good health is certainly valuable to the man who is lucky enough to enjoy it, but he cannot sell it to someone else. Therefore none of these would qualify for inclusion as part of a country's wealth, although the latter is an example of personal wealth.

Wealth created by man

A primitive country's wealth consists for the most part of its natural resources, and the income which arises from it does so without a great deal of help from man. With the growth of knowledge and human control over nature, however, the most significant part of a country's wealth consists more and more of assets like factories and machines, roads and houses, artificial harbours and airfields, museums and parks, and a technologically advanced society now derives most if its income from various forms of wealth created by man himself. At the same time, there is a steady increase in personal wealth; not only do the members of an advanced society normally enjoy good health, but between them they possess a vast store of knowledge and range of skills, the fruits of which serve to increase the income of individuals and community alike.

Ownership of wealth

While personal wealth is by definition inseparable from the individuals who possess it, the ownership of other forms of wealth can be divided broadly into two parts, namely that which is in private hands and that which is the property of the state. Privately-owned wealth may again be sub-divided into that possessed by individuals, e.g. their houses, cars, household durable goods, etc., and that owned by business units, such as partnerships and limited companies, comprising mainly capital equipment of various kinds. Publicly-owned wealth now includes a large amount of directly-productive equipment under the control of the nationalized industries, the BBC, local and port authorities, etc., as well as the more traditional sector comprising schools, hospitals, roads, libraries and other institutions which do not aim to cover the cost of their services out of the revenue which they may obtain.

Claims to wealth

When assessing the total value of the community's wealth, care must be taken to distinguish between wealth and representative wealth, otherwise double-counting will occur. For example, share certificates would be counted by an individual as part of his wealth, but it would be wrong to include both their value *and* the value of the assets which they represent in the total wealth of the country. Similarly, the individual would regard his stock of money, including balances with banks and other financial institutions, as part of his wealth, but these too are really only *claims* to wealth, and they could be multiplied a hundred-fold in the aggregate without adding one iota to the value of the country's assets.

1.6   *" 'Laissez-faire' should be the general practice; any departure from it, unless required by some great good, is a certain evil." Examine this statement. (CIS Intermediate, December 1960)*

Definition of "laissez-faire"

This statement epitomizes the view held by most economists in the nineteenth century that the best way to run a country's economy was for the Government to restrict its activities to the provision of law, order and defence, and to leave the conduct of all commercial affairs to those who were engaged in them.

The price mechanism

The basis of the case for laissez-faire was as follows. If individual members of the community were allowed complete freedom to pursue their own course of action, the price mechanism could be relied upon to co-ordinate their activities for the good of all. Entrepreneurs seeking the most rewarding outlet for their abilities would survey the many possible ways of making profits, and would be automatically guided towards those products which were in greatest demand, as evidence by people's willingness to pay high prices for them. Resources of all kinds (land, labour and capital) would therefore be drawn into production of the goods in question

through the ability of entrepreneurs to offer them higher rewards than
they were getting in their previous employment; simultaneously, the
increase in supply of the same goods·would tend to reduce their price
until rewards for producing them reverted to a normal level, whereupon
the movement of resources would automatically cease. The reverse
tendency would operate, of course, with products experiencing a decrease
in demand, so that overall there would be a constant movement of
resources into products where demand was increasing and away from
products where demand was decreasing, profit being the automatic
indicator guiding entrepreneurs' decisions in all cases.

The pursuit of self-interest

The great appeal of this system for the proponents of laissez-faire was the
complete absence of any need for decisions about resource allocation to
be made by any central authority. They argued that self-interest was a
powerful motivating force common to all men, and that it would manifest
itself in (*a*) determinantion to seek out the lowest offer for whatever they
wanted to buy, and (*b*) desire to part with what they had to sell to the
highest bidder, without regard to the identity of the other party to the
bargain, or what objects he had in view. Thus, through the beneficent
influence of what Adam Smith called "an invisible hand", the pursuit of
self-interest would lead to an overall harmony of interests; for example,
the vicar would not refrain from employing an atheist to print the parish
magazine provided he gave a lower quotation than anyone else, nor would
the printer refuse the work because he was antipathetic towards the
Church. In the absence of any intervention by the authorities, there would
be no limit to the ways in which relationships between buyers and sellers
could be formed and reformed according to the changing dictates of
consumer demand, and competition would see to it that these were satisfied as cheaply as possible.

Defects of "laissez-faire"

Coming as it did after a prolonged period of detailed Government regula-
tion which threatened to suffocate the economy, the doctrine of laissez-
faire swept all before it, and in view of Britain's emergence as the world's
greatest industrial power in the century which followed there were few
who were inclined to challenge its validity. Even so, some people were
perturbed by the great inequalities in wealth which the system seemed
to generate, and these doubts were reinforced by the appearance of
recurrent bouts of inflation and deflation as time went on. By the end
of the century, these and other defects of unrestrained laissez-faire were
widely recognized, and now a considerable "departure from it", far from
being thought a "certain evil", has come to be accepted as desirable
in many circumstances.

SIMILAR QUESTIONS

(i) How are basic economic wants satisfied in an economy based on private enterprise? (ICWA Part I, June 1967.)

(ii) How are the problems of scarcity and choice solved in a free enterprise system? (I of B Part I, April 1968.)

(iii) What is the meaning of the term "price mechanism", and what economic functions are performed by prices in a free enterprise economy? (ICWA Part I, May 1968.)

1.7 *What are the disadvantages of a free price system as the only means of allocating resources? (U of L Advanced, Summer 1964.)*

Inequalities in wealth

Perhaps the most serious drawback of the price system is that it generates and perpetuates extreme inequalities in wealth among the various members of a community. This leads directly to a misuse of resources, as the production of goods and services responds only to the pull of purchasing power; when this is very unevenly distributed, the satisfaction accruing to rich people in being able to cater for relatively minor wants is less than the satisfaction denied to poor people who may be unable to command more than the bare essentials for human existence. From the point of view of maximizing satisfaction from a given quantity of resources, there is little doubt that a roughly equal distribution of the national income would be best, but to secure this considerable intervention by the State would be necessary.

Unemployed resources

A free price system would also waste resources in that production and consumption are only very loosely co-ordinated through the profit motive. Almost all production is undertaken in anticipation of demand, and entrepreneurs are bound to be more or less astray in their forecasts of future events, so that surpluses occur from time to time, and factors of production are thrown out of employment. Moreover, there is a pronounced tendency for imbalances between supply and demand, and the price changes which result from them, to be self-aggravating rather than self-correcting: a rise in the price of a commodity acts as a signal for entrepreneurs to direct resources to its production, but the sum total of their individual decisions to do this may lead to overproduction. This results in a fall in price and a switch of resources away from the commodity with consequent underproduction leading to another rise in price, and so on.

"Booms" and "slumps"

Instability of prices, coupled with waste of productive resources, also tends to occur across the whole range of commodities at intervals of a few years, with "booms" and "slumps" alternating in something like regular sequence. Again, the process is inclined to be self-aggravating; confronted with the same gloomy forecasts about demand and prices at the onset of a slump, for example, all entrepreneurs will reach similar conclusions about the advisability of cutting back production, thus creating unemployment, which reduces demand and causes production plans to be further curtailed, and so on. Whenever instability of any kind develops, the expectations of entrepreneurs turn out to be justified because of their own reactions to the situation; hence the pursuit of individual self-interest on which the free price system is based may well conflict with the community interest.

Goods with no effective demand

Another marked defect of the price system is the lack of effective demand for certain kinds of goods and services which are nevertheless of great value to the community. This is either because the goods are of a kind which people cannot purchase as individuals, e.g. law and order, national defence, or because people tend to place them far too low on their scales of preference for their own and the country's economic welfare, e.g. health and education services. Unless the state intervened so as to improve the operation of the price system in these areas, therefore, the long term effect on the national interest would be extremely serious.

Tendency towards monopoly

State intervention may also be necessary to ensure that one of the theoretical advantages of the price system is in fact realized, namely the benefit arising from competition between producers. While consumers operate for the most part as individual bargaining units, sellers tend to form themselves into larger and larger groupings until they are in a position to use the monopolist's power of forcing up price by restricting output. The State is therefore obliged to keep a constant vigil to ensure that "free enterprise" really remains free, and that the allocation of resources conforms with the pattern of consumer demand.

Economic growth

Finally, the unrestricted operation of the price system cannot ensure any particular rate of growth in the economy, or indeed be relied upon completely to produce any growth at all. Freedom of choice in the matter of resource allocation extends to freedom in choosing between present and future satisfaction; if the forces, economic and otherwise, acting on a community favour consumption rather than saving, then the national product will tend to consist of consumer rather than capital goods, and the basis for increasing productivity will be undermined. It may therefore become necessary for the State to intervene in some way to stimulate investment for the sake of its citizens' future prosperity.

SIMILAR QUESTIONS

(i) "The free working of a price mechanism will ensure a better distribution of economic resources than any system of economic planning can achieve." What is meant by this statement? Indicate, with reasons, whether you consider it be justified. (ICA Final, November 1965.)

(ii) Does unrestrained competition necessarily lead to the most efficient allocation of resources? (C of S Final, June 1968.)

1.8 *"Economic planning is suited to backward countries, but not to advanced ones." Discuss. (U of L Advanced, Summer 1965.)*

"Planning" v. "free enterprise"

The rival merits of planning and free enterprise have become something of a political issue since the emergence of nation states organized on communist principles, but from an economic point of view the only question that matters is how a community can achieve maximum utility from the use of its resources. Neither planning nor free enterprise can lay an exclusive claim to superiority in this respect, and in fact countries at all levels of development plan the working of their economies in various ways and to different degrees, so that the terms "planned economy" and "free enterprise system" cease to have any precise meeting. One can, however, make a broad distinction between countries which favour planning as a basic principle and those which do not, and it is therefore possible to discuss the question in this context.

Planning in backward countries

When a country's total resources are very slender, the theoretical problems of resource allocation are comparatively simple. Needs which are truly vital must obviously have priority, and if there is little or nothing to spare after these have been met the central planning authority has the minimum difficulty in deciding what should be done. Even so, the following practical problems connected with formulating and implementing a national plan in a backward country must not be underrated.

(*a*) First, the planning authority must be able to call upon the services of a considerable number of *people* sufficiently well qualified to understand the techniques involved, and who are moreover prepared to work towards the fulfilment of the plan without regard for their own economic and social interests.

(*b*) Second, the ability to plan presupposes the availability of *data* on which to base a plan, and such data are extremely difficult to come by in a country whose population may consist largely of illiterate peasants with an inherent distrust of officialdom.

(*c*) Finally, it is one thing to draw up a plan, and another to ensure that it is carried out; poor *communications* and lack of the necessary *enforcement procedures* may mean that the plan, however well conceived, simply fails to "get off the ground".

Planning in developing countries

In many ways, the success which a backward country may have in overcoming these difficulties creates new kinds of problems for planners, for example—

(*a*) As available resources increase, so consumers are inclined to put a higher premium on *quality* or *variety* in the production of goods rather than mere quantity, but no system of planning based on a physical allocation of resources can hope to cater adequately for a wide range of individual preferences.

(*b*) Increasing productivity usually involves the adoption of more complex and roundabout *methods of production.* Greater efficiency is secured by increasing specialization, so that more and more firms are drawn into the scope of the production plan for every product, and it becomes a very difficult problem indeed to integrate the activities of all of them. Not only must the quantities of components required at each successive stage of production be analysed as far back as the raw materials, but the timing of each operation must be such that no temporary shortages occur to hold up progress once the plan is set in motion. This kind of control is difficult enough for a single large firm making a technically advanced product, but almost impossible when planning the physical allocation of resources for an entire country's production.

(*c*) As production plans became more complicated, the planning authority would also find it more difficult to bring about the kind of *changes* which are necessarily associated with economic progress. Having spent a great deal of time and effort working out all the implications in terms of factor allocation of a production plan based on current technology, the authority would obviously be reluctant to revise its calculations in order to accommodate every improved method as soon as it was devised, especially if it could compel consumers to accept the type of good provided for under the original plan. The tendency would be to postpone changes as long as possible, and then endeavour to incorporate them all in a completely new plan, say once every five years.

(*d*) Another difficulty for planners which is almost bound to be aggravated by increasing prosperity is the need to enter into *international trade* to a progressively greater extent. As the volume and variety of consumers' demands increase, so will it become less likely that the whole range of products required to satisfy them will be available from domestic sources; in any case, much of the potential benefit of specialization is lost if..it is not international in scope. Thus from the point of view of national planning a practically uncontrollable element has now entered into the scheme of things; while it may be possible to regulate the supply of and demand for commodities produced and consumed at home, no such constraints can be applied to foreigners. The prices of imported goods are in effect world prices settled by international bargaining, and the exports which must be sold to pay for them have to compete with other countries' exports in respect of price, quality, etc.

Planning in advanced countries

From these comments, planning in a highly advanced country would appear to be not only unsuitable, but well-nigh impossible. This is by no means the case, however, provided that attempts to direct the use of resources by physical controls, sometimes called *"imperative planning"*, are progressively abandoned in favour of more refined methods. These consist in part of influencing the behaviour of both producers and consumers through the use of the tax system, and in part of involving employers and trade unions in drawing up and following a national plan designed to co-ordinate production, consumption, investment, exports, etc., in the common interest. The latter, now known as *"indicative planning"*, has only enjoyed a limited success so far, but development along these lines would appear to be more suitable for advanced countries than the cruder kinds of physical planning.

SIMILAR QUESTIONS

(i) Consider with examples, whether economic theories evolved in developed countries are applicable also in developing countries. (C of S Intermediate, May 1969.)

(ii) "Economic planning is an obsolete device for achieving faster growth in the modern industrial economy." Discuss. (CIS Final, December 1969.)

1.9   *"The economic development of backward countries depends chiefly on their rate of industrialization." Explain and discuss.(U of L Advanced, January 1966.)*

Dependence on nature

A country whose people lack any kind of technical skill is bound to have a low standard of living. Even under the most favourable circumstances, agriculture offers a poor and uncertain reward to the peasant who merely relies on his own physical effort applied to a few hand-made implements to secure a livelihood; in effect, he is almost completely dependent on Nature, and his production will be highly susceptible to changes in climatic conditions and to the effects of soil erosion.

Control over nature

The fundamental requirement for man's economic advance is greater control over his environment: "industrialization" is only an omnibus word to include all the means whereby he is able to extract a greater and more reliable value of production from the "land" factor. Progress at every stage of evolution, from that of the primitive "collectors" to today's highly developed industrial societies, has depended upon man's finding new ways of exploiting the earth's resources. Indeed, the whole concept of a "resource" depends upon the state of technology existing at the time the assessment is made; oil seeping through the surface of the ground would have been a nuisance to the early North American Indians trying to raise their crops, but to the modern Americans it represents not only a supply of power but a source of raw materials for a vast and growing petro-chemicals industry. Modern man is thus increasingly able to subject the "free gifts of nature" to some complicated process involving much technical skill and costly capital equipment, and thereby transform them into valuable finished products.

Interdependence of agriculture and industry

Even in agriculture, where Nature's contribution to the value of production retains the greatest significance, the rôle of industry as defined above is of growing importance. Yields of crops and animal products can be vastly improved by greater mechanization, the production of more and better fertilizers and pesticides, the development of improved varieties of seeds and strains of cattle, etc., to a point where it becomes difficult to determine where the dividing line between farming and industry should be drawn. Even in prosperous countries whose economies depend mainly on food production, e.g. Denmark, high productivity owes far more to the application of industrial techniques and products to agriculture than it does to the munificence of Nature, and, as in other advanced countries, rising living standards are paralleled by a decline in the proportion of the working population directly engaged in farming.

Versatility of industrialized countries

Finally, not only does greater mastery over Nature increase productivity in highly industrialized countries but it also makes them far less vulnerable to changes in their economic environment. An advanced economy can react to a shortage in the supply of a particular raw material or foodstuff by switching more resources to its production, or by importing it in exchange for greater exports; failing this, the energies of scientists and inventors are focussed on the problem of finding or creating substitute materials. For example, both sides in World War II rapidly developed synthetic rubber to make good the loss of natural rubber supplies, atmospheric nitrogen replaced Chilean nitrate when that country began to abuse its monopoly, and so on. Similarly, a decline in world demand for its products is less serious for an advanced industrial country than for a primary producer: the former should be capable of adapting its technology to the manufacture of other, perhaps more sophisticated, products, whereas the latter must usually accept a deterioration in its terms of trade.

Summary

For these reasons the statement contained in the question is entirely justified; backward countries cannot in fact hope for much in the way of economic progress until the primitive arts of agriculture are allied to the products and techniques of a growing industrial sector.

SIMILAR QUESTION

(i) "Developing economies should concentrate on raising agricultural productivity before investing in industry." Discuss. (CIS Final, 1968.)

1.10 *Discuss, with examples, the use of diagrams in the study of economic theory. (C of S Intermediate, November 1968.)*

Diagrams clarify ideas

Economic theory is concerned with the formulation of ideas, and the development of cause-and-effect relationships. While it is always possible to express these ideas and relationships in words, it is often helpful to present them in the form of a diagram, especially when it is a question of tracing the effect of a change in one of a pair of variable quantities upon the size of the other.

Law of Demand

The most obvious example is the Law of Demand, which makes a statement about what is likely to happen to the quantity demanded of a product (the dependent variable) if there is a change in its price (the independent variable). The economist coins words like "contract" and "extend" to denote the change in quantity demanded caused by a rise and a fall in price respectively, but the idea is conveyed much more readily to the mind through the eye by presenting it in the form of a "demand curve", thus —

Basic economic concepts

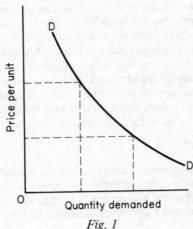

Fig. 1

Equilibrium price

A diagram such as this does not usually pretend to show actual quantities
demanded at various prices, as demonstrated by some piece of experimental research; all it does is to show the *inverse* relationship which is
assumed to exist between quantity demanded and price, and for this
purpose any line which falls from left to right will serve. In a similar way,
a "supply curve" rises from left to right, showing a *direct* relationship
between quantity offered and price, and by bringing the two together
the eye can perceive at once that there is only one price at which the
quantity demanded and the quantity offered will be equal —

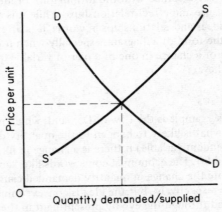

Fig. 2

More complex examples

The more complicated the relationships involved, the more desirable it becomes to illustrate them by means of a diagram. For example, in analysing the way in which a monopoly determines its most profitable output, it is possible to argue in terms of maximizing the difference between total revenue and total cost, in which case a diagram displaying the way in which these change with changes in output will illustrate the point being made very simply. Alternatively, one may argue that output will be increased until the point where the revenue obtained from additional sales (marginal revenue) is overtaken by the cost incurred by producing the additional output (marginal cost), and again the point of intersection of these two curves will display the level of output at which this occurs. The latter diagram can then be extended without introducing too much confusion to show how the firm which had a monopoly in its home market would revise its price and output policy if it went in to the export market as well, simply by adhering to the principle of equating its marginal cost with marginal revenue in each market, thus —

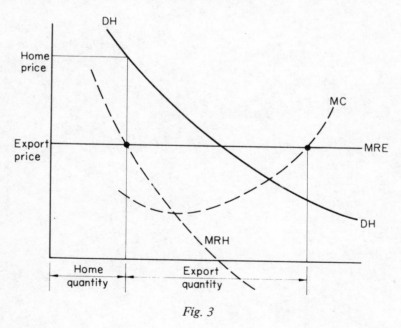

Fig. 3

From this diagram can be seen at once the total output which the firm would produce, the proportions into which this would be split as between home and export markets, and the price charged in each market. Moreover, the effect of changes in the market situation can easily be demonstrated, e.g. a rise in the export price level would increase total output, increase the proportion of the output sold abroad and raise the home market price.

Limitations of diagrams

There is, of course, a limit to the number of interrelated variables which can be shown in two-dimensional form, and extremely complex relationships can only be expressed with the aid of mathematics, but diagrams involving no more than an application of the principle of the simple graph can be usefully employed to illustrate a wide range of economic theories. They do not, of course, "prove" anything, but they certainly serve to clarify the points at issue, and for that reason are invaluable to teacher and student alike.

SIMILAR QUESTION

(i) Discuss the role of diagrams in the study of economic theory. (CIS Intermediate, June 1970.)

2
Factors of production

This section looks in greater detail at the resources, or "factors of production" as they are called, which are referred to in a general way in Section I.

They are divided for the purpose of analysis and discussion into land, labour, capital and enterprise, though in reality it may be virtually impossible to isolate one factor from another. For example, it is easy to say that "land consists of all the free gifts of nature", but in reality the land on which we grow our crops owes a great deal of its fertility to the labour and capital which has been embodied in it over the years. Similarly, the functions of the entrepreneur in production are said to be decision-making and risk-bearing, but it is almost impossible to identify any person or group of people in the real world of business who are exclusively responsible for these functions, and for nothing else.

However, the student should not allow himself to be unduly worried by these practical aspects, as the majority of questions simply ignore them, and concentrate on the parts played by each of the factors in production. By definition, land plays a passive rôle, so that greater productivity can only come about as a result of more effective use of the others. Hence many questions are related to population size, age structure, etc., the effects of division of labour, the problem of mobility of labour, the desirability of increasing the supply of capital, changes in the method of production, and so on.

It is important for the student to understand fully the way in which the Law of Diminishing Returns operates, and how it relates to the concept of the optimum firm. He must also appreciate the full significance of the qualifications to this law, namely that it is only valid providing the state of technology and methods of production remain unchanged, so that larger outputs at lower cost can be obtained through improvements in technique and economies of scale.

All in all, this section can usually be relied upon to provide at least one and probably two questions in the average paper, and if the student has a sound grasp of principles he should have no trouble in answering them. In particular, straightforward topics like the division of labour or the rôle of capital should present the minimum of difficulty, the main problem being to keep the length of the answers within bounds.

2.1   *Examine the reasons why land in different parts of the world will command different market values. (ACCA Intermediate, December 1965.)*

Scarcity relative to other factors

Unlike the other factors of production, the quantity of land available was fixed by Nature when the world began, and will remain fixed whether there is a demand for its services or not. For this reason it is often stated that "land has no supply price", but this is certainly not the same thing as saying that land is freely available to whoever needs it; all the factors are scarce in the sense that there is too little to satisfy all and sundry demands, and in any given circumstances the one which is relatively scarcest will command the highest price. It is true that where there is an abundance of land relative to labour and capital, as in thinly populated underdeveloped countries, the value of a square mile will be very low; on the other hand, in a densely populated, highly developed country like Holland, land is so precious that prodigious efforts are made to reclaim a few acres from the sea.

Differences in fertility

Apart from the scarcity of land as a whole relative to the other factors, the fertility of any particular area will exert an important influence on its market value. Of two plots of land having equal areas, the one which yields the greater crop for a given application of labour and capital will obviously be the more desirable, and competition between would-be cultivators will ensure that its price is the higher.

Relative values of products

Moreover, since different crops have different market values, it is also a question of what kind of crop the particular piece of land is capable of producing, and how the income from selling it fluctuates with changes in the market situation. At one time, for example, land suitable for growing cotton would have been extremely valuable, but competition from synthetic textile fibres has reduced the revenue obtainable from marketing raw cotton so much that land which was incapable of growing anything else would not now be in such great demand.

Proximity to markets

The position of a piece of land also plays a large part in determining its value. Proximity to some densely populated area means that produce can be marketed at low cost, so that even land of indifferent fertility will fetch a high price in the vicinity of large urban concentrations, and vice versa. There comes a point, of course, where the value of land is not related to its agricultural potential at all, but to its suitability for building; in the case of commercial premises, "fertility" would be measured by the revenue obtainable from the site by selling a manufactured product or a service.

Non-agricultural uses

It is, in fact, the development of various non-agricultural uses for land which have produced the most spectacular increases in value. Land in the centre of great capital cities is sold by the square foot rather than by the acre at prices which make it imperative to erect multi-storey buildings on it, and as the cities grow larger so central site values get higher. Similarly, the rapid increase in tourism has produced a dramatic rise in the value of land along the coastal fringes of popular holiday areas, e.g. the Mediterranean, so that again developers are obliged to build multi-storey hotels or flats on land once considered almost worthless by the local peasant farmers. Last, it must not be forgotten that "land" includes "all the free gifts of Nature", and the discovery of mineral wealth, e.g. oil in the Sahara and iron ore in Western Australia, has transformed valueless desert wastes into areas with very high market values indeed.

2.2 *Discuss the advantages and disadvantages of specialization in the case of (1) individuals, and (2) localities. (ICWA Part I, December 1968.)*

Individuals

The main advantages of specialization, or "division of labour", among the members of a group of workers, are as follows —

(*a*) It enables the highest degree of correspondence to be achieved between the different characteristics of individual workers and different kinds of job.

(*b*) By concentrating his effort on the kind of task for which he is best fitted, the worker soon attains proficiency in it, and continues to increase his dexterity and skill by constant repetition.

(*c*) No time is lost in transferring from one task to another.

(*d*) By restricting the range of tasks, perhaps to a single operation, mechanization is facilitated, and the rate of production is greatly increased with less physical fatigue.

(*e*) A greater degree of consistency in the product can be expected as a result of using specialized machine tools, permitting interchangeability of parts and making servicing easier.

(*f*) By adhering to the principle of one man, one task, one tool, a more intensive use of capital is obtained.

(g) Work study is simplified, and systems of "payment by results" made easier to devise, with consequent gains in productivity.

(h) Costs are easier to analyse, so that inefficiency in the use of manpower or plant can be quickly located and corrected.

The main disadvantages are —

(a) Workers are likely to get bored performing a relatively simple task all the time.

(b) The wide gap which opens up between top management and workers on the shop floor makes labour relations more difficult.

(c) There is an increased risk of redundancy arising if changes in technology or the conditions of demand make a particular kind of skill obsolete.

(d) The high degree of interdependence created by minute sub-division of tasks makes production planning more difficult.

(e) A breakdown in one particular sector of a firm or industry, e.g. because of a strike, may lead to widespread dislocation of production.

(f) It becomes more difficult to cater for non-standard requirements.

Localities

Numerous advantages, collectively referred to as "external economies of scale", normally result from many firms in a locality being engaged in the same kind of production. These are —

(a) "Satellite" firms making the appropriate kinds of component parts or performing specialized processes tend to establish themselves in the area. Since they are able to undertake work for all the main firms in their respective fields, they enjoy internal economies of scale which would not be achieved if each main firm tried to cater for its own requirements.

(b) Other satellite firms may find it worth while to set up plants in the locality to utilize by-products of the main firms which would otherwise go to waste.

(c) Specialized transport, banking, insurance and other commerical services evolve to meet the particular needs of the industry.

(d) A pool of labour having the necessary specialized skills is formed, with local educational and training facilities to ensure its continuation.

(e) Efficiency and progress are stimulated by rival firms being in close proximity to one another.

Although such special factors play an important part in reducing production costs, the whole locality becomes extremely vulnerable to changes in the economic environment. Sooner or later most industries experience a change in the demand for their product, or perhaps in the way demand can be catered for, and when this happens the lack of versatility of both plant and workers may prove to be a grave disadvantage. The decline in orders may be the result of competition from foreign producers enjoying greater natural advantages, the development of a substitute for the established product, or perhaps a radical change in the traditional method of manufacture; in any event, the process of adjustment is likely to be accompanied by high unemployment among the workers and subnormal profits for all the firms in the area, including those like shops, public houses, garages and so on whose income depends on the workers' pay packets.

2.3 *What is meant by the "danger of overpopulation"? Discuss its relevance at the present time. (U of L Advanced, January 1964.)*

The Malthusian view

Any discussion relating to the threat of overpopulation inevitably revolves around Malthus's famous *"Essay on the Principle of Population"*, written in 1798, which is still considered by many to contain the essential truth of the matter. His general contention was that there is a constant tendency for population growth to outstrip the means of subsistence: whereas two parents were clearly capable of producing more than two children to replace them in the next generation, and so on ad infinitum, it was equally clear that there was an absolute limit to the amount of food which a fixed area of land could produce, however much the techniques of agriculture might be improved. As Malthus saw it, there were therefore two possibilities —

(*a*) either people must be willing to restrict their numbers voluntarily (the *"preventive check"*), *or*

(*b*) population would be kept down to subsistence level by disease, war or famine (the *"positive checks"*).

Obviously, he advocated the preventive check, which, having regard to his religious beliefs, amounted to no more that late marriage and a consequent reduction in the number of children per family.

Subsequent developments

Since Malthus propounded his theory, the world's population has increased many times over, and it is still going up at a rate of about 1½ per cent per annum. In a broad sense, the mere fact that numbers continue to increase in this way is a refutation of Malthus's ideas — on the face of it, food production must be keeping up with the rising population somehow, even though subsistence level is barely maintained in many areas. Nevertheless, many scientists still think that mankind is headed for disaster if something is not done very soon to check the rate of population growth. They would say that the 19th century increase in European populations was made possible only by the opening up of vast new areas of cultivation in North

America, Australia, and so on, and that the plight of Asia's teeming millions today demonstrates clearly enough that Malthus was right after all.

Balance of births and deaths

Those who argue merely in terms of the overall rise in numbers overlook one very significant aspect of population growth, however; the massive increases which have occurred invariably stem from a fall in the death rate, in particular infant mortality, rather than a rise in the birth rate. Whenever there is a fall in the death rate in the 0–15 age group, it naturally produces a rise in the number of births per 1,000 of the population soon afterwards, but there is no evidence to show that the average number of children born into a family is rising in countries with high rates of population growth. On the contrary, it is usually found that a fall in the death rate is followed after a certain interval by a reduction in family size to a point where birth rate eventually falls to about the same level as death rate, so that a position of something like equilibrium is again arrived at.

The present position

Statistics are even now somewhat lacking in countries like China, but the existence of Malthus's positive checks to population growth would presumably be reflected by a tendency towards a levelling off in numbers accompanied by a rise in the death rate, which is precisely the opposite of what seems to be happening. In other words, it may well be that China and all the other under-developed countries are passing through a cycle of population growth which will lead them, as it has others, to a position approaching equilibrium in the years ahead. For the time being, however, the underlying improvement often tends to be obscured by the fact that falling death rates are manifested first and foremost by a fall in *infant mortality*. This means that (*a*) infants saved from dying are, up to the age of 15 or thereabouts, merely an addition to the burden of dependency, and (*b*) from about the same age they start to produce children of their own, more of which survive than previously and so on. There may thus be a prolonged period during which it is a neck-and-neck struggle between rising productivity and rising numbers, but ultimately the scales are tipped in favour of a higher living standard by a fall in the birth rate, as mentioned above. Why and how this happens may be a matter for conjecture, but it has occurred so often in the past that one may perhaps be permitted to assume that it always will.

Meanwhile many so-called "western" countries seem to have entered upon a further phase of growth which may well turn out to involve an increase in family size, but with living standards already high and still rising this can hardly be said to constitute a threat along Malthusian lines.

SIMILAR QUESTIONS

(i) What are the likely economic consequences of the continuous growth of population in this country? (CIS Final, June 1966.)

(ii) Is Britain being overpopulated? Discuss. (I of B Part I, September 1968.)

(iii) "The short run approach to the population explosion in developing countries, should be to increase food supply rather than to restrict growth." Discuss. (CIS Final, December 1969.)

2.4   *Outline the distribution of the working population of the UK between various types of production (rough proportions only are required). Explain the reasons for this pattern and for recent changes in it. (U of L Advanced, January 1967.)*

Main occupational divisions

It is usual to divide the working population into three main groups, i.e. primary, secondary and tertiary producers. The first group is confined to those who work in agriculture, fishing, mining, quarrying and other extractive industries; the second includes builders and other kinds of construction workers, together with those in processing and manufacturing industries; the third comprises all those who are employed in buying and selling, wholesaling, retailing, banking and finance, transport and communications, the professions, central and local government and the service occupations generally. Very roughly, those in the first group total less than 10 per cent of the working population, and their numbers relative to the rest are falling; those in the second group amount to about 40 per cent, a fairly stable proportion which conceals substantial changes among the different occupations included in it; the third group now accounts for over 50 per cent of the working population, and its relative size is growing.

Increase in tertiary sector

To those who are accustomed to thinking of production solely in terms of manual labour, these figures may present a puzzling and somewhat disturbing picture. How, it may be asked, can a small and relatively diminishing number of workers engaged in the essential occupations of growing food and making goods support a growing army of people who only move things from place to place, or, worse still, do nothing but talk or make marks on pieces of paper? To reason thus, however, is to misunderstand the true nature of production, and the means whereby it is normally increased; any kind of work which contributes, directly or indirectly, to the satisfaction of consumer wants merits the description "productive", and the changing pattern of occupational distribution simply reflects (*a*) the changing nature of those wants, and (*b*) an increasing degree of sophistication in our methods of production.

Changes in the pattern of demand

Taking these two points in turn, a rising living standard is invariably linked with a decline in the proportion of income spent on food, and, to a lesser extent, on the other necessities of life. After all, a man can only eat so much, and even if his needs for clothing and shelter are less easily satisfied than his desire for food he finds that with increasing prosperity more and more of his income is available for spending on entertainment, travel, and other kinds of services. Even in the realm of necessities, he will attach greater importance to variety and convenience in use than mere volume, so that a large proportion of the money spent on food is likely to be absorbed by packaging, advertising and distribution rather than the raw material.

Changes in the methods of production

As for production methods, there is a close connection between greater efficiency, increased specialization and economies of scale. In the days when every town and village had its own craftsmen, making goods from locally-produced raw materials for a local market, society had little need of workers other than those engaged directly in production, but the small scale of these operations and the purely manual nature of the work restricted productivity per man to a very low level. Since the Industrial Revolution, however, advances in technology have tended to raise the optimum scale of production and to increase the degree of specialization, both of workers and plant. Developments of this kind inevitably increase the proportion of people employed in tertiary occupations and, while their contribution to production may not be easy to identify or to measure, the efforts of workers in the primary and secondary groups benefit enormously from it.

Summary

Far from being a cause for alarm, therefore, a relative increase in the number of workers engaged in tertiary occupations may be taken as an indication of increasing material prosperity, and with the further development of automation in manufacturing industry the trend seems likely to continue.

2.5   *What do you understand by "the mobility of labour"? To what extent do you think that unemployment is caused by low mobility of labour? (U of L Advanced, January 1964.)*

Definition and types of mobility

The expression "mobility of labour" is used to denote the movement of workers from one job to another, usually with reference to the various difficulties associated with such movement. Labour is commonly accepted as being the least mobile of the factors, but the degree of immobility depends upon the find of movement involved, i.e.

(*a*) *Geographical,* i.e. requiring the worker to make his home in a different part of the country.

(*b*) *Industrial,* i.e. exchanging one job for another of a similar kind in a firm making a different product;

(*c*) *Occupational,* i.e. changing to another sort of job altogether, involving a different kind or degree of skill.

Reasons for immobility

The first type of movement undoubtedly presents the greatest difficulty for a variety of reasons. People of all ages develop social and economic ties in their own locality, and these become all the stronger with the passage of time, so that older workers in particular find the prospect of moving hard to face. In addition there is the problem of finding suitable new living accommodation, plus the cost involved in moving household goods.

Even if no change of location is involved, transfer from one job to another is discouraged by the trend towards the narrowing of wage differentials, especially between skilled and unskilled work, a factor which is re-inforced by the relatively high rate of taxation on marginal earnings.

Finally, any kind of mobility presupposes both the awareness of better job opportunities and the will to take advantage of them; quite often, immobility of labour can simply be ascribed to a combination of ignorance and apathy.

Mobility of labour and full employment

There are many different causes of unemployment, but immobility of labour certainly makes the number out of work at any given time greater than it otherwise would be. Government full employment policies can normally be relied upon to prevent any general surplus of labour occurring, but the usual state of mobility in the UK results in a situation where the number of unfilled vacancies begins to exceed the number of unemployed as soon as the latter falls much below 400,000, so that any attempt at a further reduction in the unemployment figure gives rise to inflationary pressure.

Transitional unemployment

There is, of course, bound to be some unemployment of a transitional nature in any free society. Entrepreneurs will be obliged to dismiss workers from time to time because of fluctuations in the demand for their products, and although other employment opportunities may not be altogether lacking there is bound to be a time-lag before the people concerned find suitable vacancies in other firms. It might even be argued that the efficient working of the price mechanism depends on the existence of a reservoir of unemployed labour, however small, as some degree of flexibility is essential in order to absorb the effects of random short-term changes in the conditions of demand and supply.

Structural unemployment

The reason why so many people find it difficult to get work in the UK, however, even at a time of so-called "full employment", is that the supply of labour is slow to adjust itself to more radical changes in the pattern of the economy. The industrial revolution promoted the growth of Britain's great basic industries of coalmining, steelmaking, textiles and shipbuilding in the northern and western parts of the country, all strongly orientated towards the export trade, but the events of the 20th century, culminating in the great depression of the 1930's, made this industrial structure and location largely obsolete. Even though a whole new generation of workers has since come into existence, and in spite of the efforts of successive Governments to foster the growth of new industries in them, the percentage of jobless in these areas remains well above the national average, and provides ample evidence of the extent to which immobility of labour contributes to the problem of unemployment.

2.6   *Examine the economic effects on a country of a large-scale emigration of young, working-age people without dependents. (U of L Advanced, January 1966.)*

People are producers and consumers

Labour is unique among economic resources, in that human beings are both an instrument and the end of all productive activity. A change in the size of the population will be reflected by a corresponding change both in the number of workers, and in the number of mouths to feed and backs to clothe; while it is possible to theorize on the optimum population size of a country in the long run, having regard to its area and natural resources, far greater importance attaches to changes in the balance between production and consumption in short-run situations.

Concept of optimum population

Large-scale emigration is sometimes advocated as a cure for the alleged over-population of the United Kingdom; no less an authority than Winston Churchill once said that 25 million would be about the figure to aim at if we wanted to restore a proper balance between numbers and environmental factors, and thus maximize the standard of living. Unfortunately, statements of this kind usually disregard the practical implications of such changes, even supposing that a country wishing to dispose of half its population could devise a means of making them go, and that other countries could be found who were willing to accept them. Whether Government assistance were given or not, the great majority of those who emigrated would be, as the question postulates, young working-age people without dependents, as they would be the most willing and able to move.

Young emigrants – the balance of advantage
Bearing in mind that people are both producers and consumers, there could be no doubt that the net effect on the economy of young people emigrating would be distinctly harmful. Up to school-leaving age, a child is exclusively a consumer of goods and services on a fairly large scale; the State commits about 7 per cent of the national income to education alone, and a sizeable proportion of the National Health and other social services are devoted to promoting children's welfare in one way and another. Add to this the money spent by parents on housing, feeding and clothing their families, and a value of anywhere between £5,000 and £25,000 might be put upon the resources invested in a young person on the threshold of his working life. If at this juncture he leaves the country never to return, the loss of his productive services far outweighs the consequent fall in consumption. If he does not emigrate, and if he achieves an average life span, an individual normally passes through three phases –

(a) up to working age, during which he is wholly dependent on the rest of the community;

(b) his working life, during which he is making a net contribution to maintaining the rest of the community;

(c) after his working life has ended, when he again becomes dependent on the rest of the community. (This is true even if he has contributed in full to a retirement pension, as in real terms he is then producing nothing.)

If the surplus goods and services produced during phase (b) are insufficient to cover the deficits represented by phases (a) and (c), then from an economic point of view the individual has been a net loss to the community during his lifetime as a whole; the best that can be said about the young emigrant is that, providing he stays abroad for good, he at least spares his native country the burden of supporting him in his old age.

SIMILAR QUESTION
(i) Consider the effects of international migration on the economy of a country of net emigration. (C of S Final, May 1969.)

2.7   *How does the economist's concept of capital differ from that of an*
      accountant? (ICWA Part I, June 1966.)

The economist's concept of capital

To the economist, "capital" is a factor of production in the same sense
that land, labour and enterprise are factors of production. All of these
normally contribute in some measure to the creation of values, the
distinguishing feature of capital being that it consists of resources which
have been stored up in some way with the object of increasing the
effectiveness of the others. One writer has defined capital as "produced
means of production", thus emphasizing the purpose underlying the
creation of capital, but it would be wrong to think of the nation's capital
as consisting entirely of various kinds of physical assets — resources used
to provide education and health services for the people also play an
essential part in raising the level of productivity by increasing the efficiency
of labour, and the time and effort devoted to research yields a benefit in
later years in the form of more efficient plant.

The process of capital creation

Thus for the economist, capital represents an investment of resources
undertaken with a view to increasing production in a roundabout way at
some later date, and it follows that the creation of capital can only be
achieved at the cost of diverting resources from the production of goods
and services which satisfy consumers' needs immediately and directly.
The rate at which the stock of capital can be increased, beneficial though
this may be to future living standards, is therefore conditioned by the
extent to which the community as a whole is prepared to accept a
reduction in its living standard in the present; while the economist may
enlarge on the merits of a "high rate of investment", as he would put it,
the final decision whether or not to commit resources to the creation of
capital rests with politicians, businessmen, and ultimately with individual
members of the community themselves.

The accountant's concept of capital

Turning now to the accountant's notion of capital, it is at once apparent
that he thinks primarily in terms of money. When he is considering the
need for a business to increase its capital, he will debate whether it is
better to issue £1 m. worth of ordinary shares or £1 m. worth of debentures, or whether again it might be preferable to borrow the money from
a bank. In any event, the final outcome will appear as an increase in one of
the items on the liabilities side of the firm's balance sheet; capital for the
accountant is therefore defined as the amount the business owes to the
people who have advanced money in one way or another to finance its
operations.

Reconciliation of two viewpoints

Further reflection shows, however, that the difference between the economist's and the accountant's concept of capital is more apparent than real. The balance sheet of a business does in fact provide a valuable insight into the nature of that difference; whereas the accountant thinks first of items which appear on the liabilities side, the economist is concerned with the kind of things which appear on the assets side, viz. buildings, plant and machinery, etc. These are, of course, merely counterparts of one another; the accountant would readily admit that "capital" in his sense of the word was no good to the firm unless it was put to some use, i.e. exchanged as soon as possible for physical assets of some kind. Indeed, when he speaks of "fixed" and "circulating" capital, the accountant is much closer to the economist's viewpoint, in that he is now concerned with the form in which the firm's assets are held rather than the source of the money which was used to buy them.

Ultimately, therefore, the difference turns out to be one of verbal usage rather than basic principle, and the economist and the accountant should have no difficulty in understanding one another provided that they have a rudimentary knowledge of each other's disciplines.

2.8   *What is the function of the entrepreneur and what types of decision must he make? (ICWA Part I, June 1965.)*

The entrepreneur as a factor of production

The function of the entrepreneur is central to a "free enterprise" economy, since it is he who initiates production and decides upon how the other three factors, land, labour, and capital, are to be employed. In so doing, his aim is to maximize the difference between the revenue obtained from selling the product he decides to make and the cost of hiring the factor units he requires to make it. In other words, he endeavours to obtain the greatest profit he can be exploiting his knowledge of the market, but his ability to enrich himself in this way is limited by two considerations —

(*a*) The existence of other entrepreneurs who may be willing to ask less for the same product or pay more for the same kind of factor units, and

(*b*) the incomplete nature of the information available to him about the market situation, and particularly about the changes which are likely to occur in it during the lifetime of his enterprise.

Risk and uncertainty

The entrepreneur's unique contribution to the functioning of the "market economy" is his willingness to shoulder the risks inseparable from forecasting. In the absence of any centrally-directed plan for the allocation of resources, the entrepreneur not only decides what is to be produced, but where, and what the price shall be, and he must also make contractual arrangements with the owners of capital, land, and labour to get the work done, but if at the end of the day the revenue obtained is insufficient to cover the costs incurred then the entrepreneur must pay the penalty for his over-optimistic estimates. If it were not for the possiblity of change, both revenue and costs could be calculated exactly, and there would be no call for the entrepreneur's services, but since change is ever-present there is bound to be some element of uncertainty about the eventual outcome of any business venture, and the entrepreneur can justly claim to fulfil a useful social function in assuming financial the risk arising from such uncertainty.

Insurable and non-insurable risks

It is, however, important in this context to distinguish between insurable and non-insurable risks. Every entrepreneur faces a wide variety of risks in addition to the fundamental one arising from changing market conditions, e.g. there is always the possibility that fire, theft, damage to "third parties" and so on may involve the business in some unforeseeable expense. Fortunately, the losses arising from causes such as these can be estimated within fairly close limits in respect of business enterprises as a whole; what is a random occurrence to the individual firm becomes a matter of actuarial calculation when the operations of all firms are aggregated, so that for the payment of an annual premium the individual entrepreneur can shift the burden of risks of this kind on to an insurance company. In other words, all losses arising from unforeseeable misfortunes can be reduced to a fixed annual cost except the most important one, namely that the business will lose money as a result of a change in market conditions. Not only do these defy any attempt at forecasting by insurers, but the probability is that all the firms in an industry would suffer losses simultaneously from any adverse development, and would therefore all be presenting claims at once, whereas the insurance company's ability to pay relies on claims being made in a purely random fashion.

Distinction between entrepreneur and manager

In the real world of business, entrepreneurs frequently become involved in one way or another with the implementation of their own decisions about the way in which profit can be maximized. In the small business, for example, the owner/entrepreneur usually works harder than anyone to ensure the success of his enterprise, and may also commit a large part of his personal fortune to providing it with capital. When it is remembered that he might have decided to earn a fixed wage by working for someone else, and lent his money to the government at a guaranteed rate of interest, such wages and interest appear as an opportunity cost which ought to be deducted from his net revenue before assessing the reward he has earned in his capacity as entrepreneur. It is not always easy in practice to distinguish his work in managing the business, i.e. co-ordinating the work of the hired factors as efficiently as possible, from his purely entrepreneurial function, but the essential feature of the latter remains his willingness to risk losses for the sake of making profits.

SIMILAR QUESTION

(i) What is an entrepreneur? To what extent can it be argued that everyone fulfils this economic role? (I of B Part I, April 1968.)

2.9 *State, and explain clearly, the Law of Diminishing Returns. Does this law apply to all factors of production? (ICWA Part I, May 1968.)*

Statement of the Law

The Law of Diminishing Returns states that if an increasing number of units of one factor is combined with a fixed supply of other factors, there will, beyond a certain point, be a less-than-proportional increase in total output. It is assumed that there are no economies of scale, and that the state of technology remains the same.

Illustration of the Law

What the Law postulates is in fact a fairly typical short-run situation, in which one of the factors at the disposal of an entrepreneur is fixed for the time being, e.g. the area of a farm, and the only way to increase output is therefore to use more of a factor which can be increased in supply, e.g. labour. Starting from zero, the effect of increasing the supply of the variable factor is to increase output by a more-than-proportional amount to begin with, but after a certain point first the marginal and then the average product of the variable factor will decline, as shown in the following table and graph.

Output of Grain from 1 sq. mile of Land

Number of men employed	Total number of units produced	Marginal product of labour	Average product of labour
0	0	–	0
1	10	10	10
2	30	20	15
3	54	24	18
4	72	18	18
5	87	15	17·4
6	99	12	16·5
7	108	9	15·4
8	115	7	14·4
9	120	5	13·3
10	123	3	12·3
11	124	1	11·3
12	123	−1	10·25

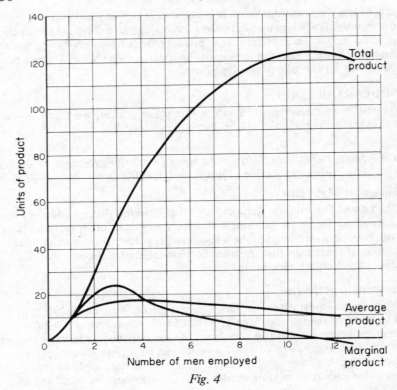

Fig. 4

Significant features of the Law

The points to notice are —

(*a*) That from 0 to 3 men employed there is a more-than-proportional return to additional labour, i.e. the variable factor is working under conditions of *increasing* returns.

(*b*) That from 3 men onwards there is a less-than-proportional return to additional labour, i.e. the variable factor is working under conditions of *diminishing* returns, although the average product per man continues to rise for the time being.

(*c*) At 4 men, the average product of labour is at a maximum, declining thereafter but never falling to zero. At this point, the marginal product and the average product of labour are equal.

(*d*) At 11 men, the total product is maximized, i.e. no further addition to output is possible by increasing the labour force. At this point the marginal product of labour is, of course, zero.

(*e*) Beyond 11 men, the total product falls, and the marginal product of labour therefore becomes negative.

Quantity of variable factor to be employed

The conclusions to be drawn from the above are that in no circumstances would less than 4 men or more than 11 men be employed to cultivate one square mile of land. These extreme positions would in fact only be reached in the unlikely event of either land or labour respectively being available free of cost to the entrepreneur, in the first case because his only object would then be to maximize the product per man and in the second because he wished to maximize the product per square mile. In all other circumstances the number employed would fall between 4 and 11 men, the choice being dictated by the relative scarcity of land and labour.

Substitution of factors at the margin

Although the Law of Diminishing Returns is usually presented in the above way, the fundamental point at issue is that one factor may usually be substituted for another at the margin, but that the substitution is never perfect. The example could equally well have shown the effect of combining an increased area of land with a fixed labour force, and the general result would have been the same; all that the Law is saying in effect is that, given the relative scarcities of land and labour, there is one particular combination of the two which will produce a given output with the least expenditure of resources. Other combinations on either side of the optimum are possible, i.e. the same output could be obtained by substituting a unit of land for a unit of labour, or vice versa, but because land and labour are imperfect substitutes for one another the cost of the output in real terms will always be higher.

Diminishing returns in industry

Although agriculture provides an example which makes it easy to visualize the way in which the Law of Diminishing Returns works, it is equally applicable to any situation where it is sought to increase output without increasing the supply of all the factors. Such a situation commonly occurs in factories, for example, where the size of the plant is fixed in the short run and the only way of securing week-to-week changes in output is to vary the supply of labour. (This could be done without resort to "hiring" and "firing" by working short time or overtime). Precisely the same effects would be observed, i.e. increasing returns to labour at first because of more effective use of the plant, followed after a certain point by diminishing marginal and average returns to labour, and finally a stage where no further increases in output whatever were possible with the existing plant. At any given level of costs for labour and capital, the optimum number of men to employ would be that which resulted in the last pound's worth of labour making the same contribution to the size of the output as the last pound's worth of capital.

Economics of scale and improvements in technology

The argument can be extended to all the factors simultaneously; whenever one of them is fixed in quantity, output can be increased by increasing the supply of the others, but only at the cost of incurring diminishing returns to all of them. The qualifications to the Law are important, however; if increasing the supply of capital, for example, involves using larger as distinct from more numerous units of plant, economies of scale might be more than sufficient to offset the effects of diminishing returns. Similarly, improvements in the design of plant would have the effect of postponing the incidence of diminishing returns. In practice, therefore, as larger units of plant of more advanced design come into use so the optimum combination of factors changes in some industries to a point where thousands of pounds' worth of capital are invested for each man employed.

SIMILAR QUESTIONS

(i) Formulate the "law of diminishing returns" stating carefully the conditions which must be satisfied for it to hold and illustrate the working of the law. (CIS Intermediate, December 1966.)
(ii) How should a firm decide in what proportions to combine the factors of production it employs? (CIS Intermediate, June 1967.)
(iii) "Developing economies should invest more in labour-intensive production and less in capital-intensive production." Discuss. (CIS Final, June 1969.)

2.10 *Explain why, in some cases, average costs may fall with increasing output, (a) in the short run, (b) in the long run. (U of L Advanced, January 1966.)*

Short run average cost

In a short-run situation, any tendency for average cost per unit to fall as a result of an increase in output must indicate that, prior to the increase, the factors of production were not being combined in the best possible way, i.e. at least one factor was being under-utilized. Such a situation commonly occurs at a time when trade is slack; a firm's plant may be operating at well below its designed capacity, so that an increase in output will have the effect of spreading the fixed burden of overhead costs over a larger volume of production, thus tending to reduce average cost per unit without changing the plant in any way. This effect will be particularly marked when capital cost is a high proportion of total cost, as it would be, for example, in a car plant or an oil refinery.

Long run average cost

An increase in output is likely to lead to a fall in average cost per unit in the long run whenever advantages can be taken of the opportunity thus afforded to benefit from *economies of scale.* Industry abounds with examples of plant and processes the cost of which do not normally increase *pro rata* with an increase in output; broadly speaking, these can be analysed into those which are due to (i) lower construction costs per unit, (ii) lower fuel costs per unit, (iii) better staffing ratios, and (iv) better integration of processes.

Both (i) and (ii) are related to the simple facts of solid geometry. A cube measuring 1 ft x 1 ft x 1 ft has a volume of 1 cu ft and a total surface area of 6 sq ft, whereas a cube 2 ft x 2 ft x 2 ft has a volume of 8 cu ft and a surface area of 24 sq ft; in other words, the volume increases as the *cube* of the linear dimensions whereas the surface area increases as the *square.* The significance of this may be seen if the cube is now envisaged as some kind of container in which a process is taking place, e.g. an oven baking loaves of bread; an increase in productive capacity of eight times can be secured for far less than eight times the construction cost.

Still thinking in terms of an oven, the heat which must be put in to maintain working temperature is equal to the heat lost by radiation, which again is a function of the surface area, not the capacity, i.e. eight times as many loaves can be baked at only four times the fuel cost.

Turning to (iii), an eight-fold increase in the capacity of a piece of plant will not normally involve a similar increase in the number of men required to run it as many tasks are "indivisible", i.e. they must be performed whether the effect produced is great or small. For example, one man may be required to turn a switch or watch a temperature gauge; it will not take two men, let alone eight, to perform the same task on the larger of our two ovens.

As regards (iv), some kinds of machine are only available in certain sizes, so that the chances of matching inputs and outputs at successive stages of production are increased by having "banks" of machines at each stage. If for example, Stage A used a machine with a capacity of 3 units, Stage B a capacity of 2 units, and Stage C a capacity of 5 units, then an output of *5 units* would require 2 machines at Stage A, 3 at Stage B and 1 at Stage C, though only the last stage would be fully loaded. If the output were increased to *30 units*, however, stage A would require 10 machines, Stage B 15 machines, and Stage C 6 machines, and all stages would be working to capacity.

In short, when faced with a demand for higher output, production engineers in manufacturing industry can usually find ways of deriving benefit from economies of scale arising from one or more of the causes mentioned, given sufficient time for the necessary changes in plant to be made.

SIMILAR QUESTIONS
(i) Distinguish between fixed and variable costs, and explain how average
total costs for a firm vary with output (*a*) in the short period (*b*) in the
long period. (CIS Final, June 1962.)
(ii) Why are the main British and American producers of motor-cars large
and few? (CIS Final, June 1965.)

2.11 *Can the idea of diminishing returns be used to explain diseconomies
of scale? (U of L Advanced, Summer 1966.)*

Increasing output with a fixed factor

The Law of Diminishing Returns is concerned with attempts to increase
output by the application of successive increments of a variable factor or
factors of production to a fixed quantity of another factor. Starting from
zero quantity of the variable factor(s), there will be first a more-than-proportional increase in total output, then, after a certain point, a less-than-
proportional increase, until finally output stops rising altogether and
starts to fall.

Increasing output with all factors variable

The incidence of diminishing returns to the variable factor(s) of production
after the first part of this sequence indicates the need to increase the supply
of all the factors if average cost per unit is to be prevented from rising, but
with this may come the opportunity of changing the method of production.
With reference to labour, advantage can be taken of large numbers of
workers to introduce greater specialization; in the case of capital, the
introduction of large, indivisible machines results in the more efficient use
of fuel and manpower. For these reasons, manufacturing industries, in
which labour and capital are the predominant factors, usually benefit from
economies of scale, i.e. it is normal for unit costs of production to fall as
output increases.

Elements of fixity (1)

It must no be assumed, however, that the Law of Diminishing Returns can
be ignored altogether in industrial production; while there is any element
of fixity in the supply of any of the factors employed, there will be a
tendency for higher costs to assert themselves to a point where they offset
the gains to be secured by an indefinite increase in the application of
labour and capital. Land at once suggests itself as such a factor, but in
reality it seldom imposes any limitation on expansion; a particular firm's
activities could hardly achieve the scale where they were hampered by
sheer lack of available land space somewhere, nor so press upon the sources
of supply as to raise the cost of its raw materials.

Elements of fixity (2)

An increase in the scale of production does, however, give rise to more difficult problems in the field of management, and it is here that the answer to the question may be found. As the number of people in the organization increases, so the task of co-ordinating their activities becomes more complex, until the capacity of the human mind to grapple with the mass of interconnected relationships involved is stretched to its limit. Although the responsibility for implementing policy decisions made at directorial level can be sub-divided and delegated to any number of people in the management hierarchy, this does not solve the problem; it is one thing to make decisions and give instructions, and another to ensure that the desired results are being achieved. In practice, the success of top management depends upon its ability to obtain and assimilate sufficient facts about the business quickly enough to exercise effective control over what is going on; while the techniques of communication and data processing are being constantly improved, "diseconomies of scale" can usually be traced to the fact that increasing the supply of management does not result in a proportional increase in its effectiveness, i.e. it is working under conditions of diminishing returns.

SIMILAR QUESTIONS

(i) Is there any contradiction between the "law of diminishing returns" and "economies of scale"? (CIS Intermediate, June 1969.)

(ii) (*a*) What are the economies of scale?

(*b*) What factors limit the scale of production, and from what disadvantages does the large firm suffer? (ACCA Section I, December 1969.)

3
Demand, supply, and price

Now we are introduced to the laws which govern demand and supply, and how price operates so as to maintain equilibrium between the two.

Provided he takes care to distinguish between changes in quantity caused solely by alterations in *price*, i.e. movements *along* a given demand or supply curve, and changes caused by new *conditions* of demand or supply, i.e. a movement in the *position* of the whole curve, the student should have no difficulty in handling the stock kind of question based on the simple demand/supply curve diagram.

Elasticity of demand and of supply are also frequently the subject of questions in this section, and again, provided the student has taken the trouble to learn these very straightforward topics, he should welcome a chance to answer them.

Rather more complicated though still quite straightforward questions arise in connection with what are called the "economics of the firm", i.e. how an individual supplier will react to various kinds of market situations. The concept of a perfect market, though somewhat abstract, is easy enough to comprehend, but its implications for the size of a firm's output require a clear understanding of how and why output is invariably fixed at the point where marginal revenue and marginal cost are equal. Once understood, this principle can be then applied to the price and output policy of a monopolist (another perennial favourite with examiners), imperfect competition and discriminating monopoly.

This section therefore offers a wide range of possible questions, ranging from simple to fairly difficult, but they should appeal to the student who prefers a piece of logical reasoning to the somewhat philosophical discussions called for in Section I. In very many cases the exposition will be helped by including appropriate diagrams, even where they are not explicitly asked for.

3.1 *"The amount demanded of a commodity will usually be greater the lower the price, other things unchanged." Why is this so, and what is the significance of "other things unchanged"? (U of L Advanced, Summer 1965.)*

The Law of Diminishing Marginal Utility

The statement contained in the question must be true if one accepts the validity of the Law of Diminishing Marginal Utility. This law states that, during an appropriate period of time, successive equal increments in the supply of a commodity afford less and less satisfaction to the consumer, other things remaining the same. Whilst this law is incapable of formal proof, in that "satisfaction" is entirely a matter of subjective assessment on the part of individual consumers, it is based on an entirely reasonable assumption which is borne out by common observation of human behaviour. If, for example, an individual had to allocate his income between two commodities, A and B, both of which had some positive utility for him, he would clearly fail to reap the maximum benefit if he purchased only A to the exclusion of B, or only B to the exclusion of A. Evidently some intermediate position would be best, such that, given their relative prices, the last penny spent on A yielded the same utility as the last penny spent on B, i.e. the marginal utility of the two commodities would be equal, and any movement to either side would result in a net loss of satisfaction.

Effect of a price reduction

The effect of a reduction in price of one of the commodities, say B, would be to make a pennyworth of it physically larger than before, which would make its marginal utility greater than that of A. The individual's reaction would therefore be to purchase more of B, thus decreasing its marginal utility, and less of A, thus increasing its marginal utility, to a point where they were again equal. This argument can, of course, be generalized to include any number of commodities and the whole body of consumers; starting from a position of equilibrium at given levels of prices, i.e. with all marginal utilities equal on consumers' collective scale of preferences, a reduction in the price of any one commodity will increase the utility of the marginal pennyworth of it relative to all the others, and consumers will seek to adjust to the new situation by buying more of the now cheaper commodity and very slightly less of all the others.

"Other things unchanged" (1)

The foregoing argument is, however, only tenable if, during the period of adjustment, nothing else occurs which has a bearing on consumers' tendency to react in the way described. In fact, a great number of things can, and often do, happen to obscure the working of the Law of Demand, which is in fact what the question is enunciating. One can well imagine, for example, a reduction in the price of ice cream being more than offset by a spell of bad weather; cheaper cigarettes by fresh revelations about the connection between smoking and lung cancer; lower-priced perambulators by a fall in the birth rate, and so on. Indeed, the possiblities of a change in the state of demand (which will be reflected by a shift in the whole demand curve to right or left) are well-nigh infinite — one need only list them under such broad headings as seasonal influences, changes in the size and age structure of the population, changes in the size and distribution of the national income, the effects of advertising, and the vagaries of Government policy, to see that this is so.

"Other things unchanged" (2)

There are, however, less obvious cases of failure of demand to extend when price falls which perhaps account for the inclusion of the word "usually" in the question, and which therefore call for special comment. For instance, it not infrequently happens that a reduction in the price of a commodity causes people to buy less of it because they assume there has been a falling off in quality, even though this is not really the case. From the strictly theoretical point of view, however, the mere fact that people think it is an inferior product has the effect of making it one, and it could therefore be argued that this situation should also be represented by drawing a new demand curve. Similarly, a fall in the price of a commodity may cause people to postpone buying it in the expectation that its price will fall still further; whether or not this constitutes another exception to the Law of Demand depends upon whether one accepts the argument that the time difference creates two different commodities, as in the previous case.

"Other things unchanged" (3)

There is also the well-authenticated example of the "Giffen good", the demand for which varies directly rather than inversely with the price. This is because the total amount spent on the commodity, normally a basic foodstuff in a society living near subsistence level, represents such a large proportion of the average family's budget that a fall in its price is tantamount to a rise in a real incomes, and an increase in national income has the general effect of increasing the demand for superior goods at the expense of inferior ones. It could therefore again be said that what is involved here is a new demand curve, not a movement along the old one, or, alternatively, that income-elasticity of demand is sufficiently negative to overcome price-elasticity.

Summary

The statement contained in the question is therefore correct — indeed, some would say that even the word "usually" is an unnecessary qualification if the definition of a commodity is made sufficiently rigorous. Since price is only one among many other things which could influence the quantity demanded, however, the qualifying phrase "other things unchanged" is highly relevant and very important.

SIMILAR QUESTIONS

(i) As the price of the good increases so the quantity demanded of that good decreases. Discuss the economic reasoning for this statement. Is this reasoning always true? (ACCA Intermediate, December 1965.)
(ii) State the factors that determine the demand curve of consumers for a particular good. (ACCA Section I, June 1966.)

3.2 *What is the justification for drawing the supply curve of a commodity so as to suggest that larger quantities are offered for sale at higher prices? (CIS Intermediate, December 1967.)*

The answer to this question divides into two parts, the first relating to goods already in existence, the stock of which may be regarded as a fixed quantity, and the second to goods being continually produced in quantities which vary in accordance with changes in the state of demand for them.

Goods already in existence

The supply curve for goods of this kind, e.g. the first edition of a book, is simply a "mirror image" of the demand curve for them. At any given moment of time all the books in existence are possessed by someone,

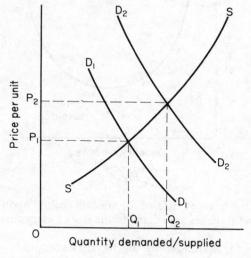

Fig. 5

which means that every book must be valued by its owner at a figure not less than its current market price. This is not to say, however, that every owner would be prepared to part with his copy at the same price, any more than every potential buyer would be prepared to give the same price

to acquire a copy. Every person who is interested in the ownership of such
a book will have his individual estimate of its utility to him. whether he
possesses one of them or not; it is simply that present owners value the
books more highly than the money they could get for them, while non-
owners value the money they would have to pay for them more than they
do the books.

Now, if there should be an increase in demand, some owners who were
previously at or near the margin will be transformed into sellers because
of the rise in price, and after a sufficient number of copies have changed
hands a new position of equilibrium will be reached (Fig. 5)

Goods being continually produced

Now we have the radical difference that the sellers of the goods have no
desire to own them; they only engage in production because they estimate
that the utility of the goods to purchasers is such that a sufficient quantity
will be sold to cover the cost of production with something to spare for

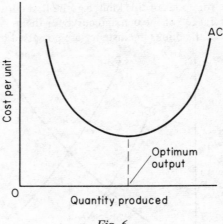

Fig. 6

profit. Hence the quantity offered for sale will depend upon the way in
which costs and revenues are related to the size of every firm's output in
the industry.

In the short run, a firm is only able to vary its output by changing the
quantity of its variable factors, e.g. labour, in relation to the quantity of
its fixed factors, e.g. capital equipment. Given that there is only one combination of variable and fixed factors which will give minimum average
cost per unit, i.e. when the plant is working exactly to its designed
capacity, any other combination must result in higher average cost per
unit; whereas over the initial stages of increased output, average cost will

benefit from a better spread of fixed overhead costs, once the optimum combination of factors has been exceeded, diminishing returns to the variable factors and hence higher cost will supervene (Fig. 6).

What is significant in determining the size of a firm's output is not average cost, however, but marginal cost in relation to the marginal revenue obtainable from the sale of that output, which will be fixed at the point where these two are equal. The arithmetical relationship between average and marginal cost is such that MC is below AC at first with both falling; then a point of minimum MC is reached while AC is still falling; next, MC starts to rise, being momentarily equal to AC at the latter's minimum value; finally, MC exceeds AC and goes on to increase at a faster rate, thus —

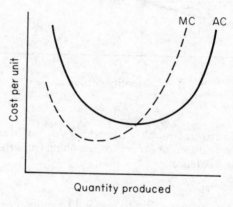

Fig. 7

Different firms in an industry will, of course, have different cost structures; for the sake of simplicity, we will consider no more than two representative firms, one small and one large, operating in a perfectly competitive market, so that while their costs will be different at any given size of output their marginal revenues will be the same (Fig. 8).

It will now be seen that at price OP_1, only the larger firm is able to equate its MC and MR, and is therefore solely responsible for the industry's output OQ_1 (= P_1A); at price OP_2, the smaller firm is now able to make a contribution, while the larger firm's output moves further up its MC curve, and the output of the industry becomes OQ_2 (= $P_2B + P_2C$); at price OP_3, both firms move further up their MC curves, and the industry's output becomes OQ_3 (=$P_3D + P_3E$). Hence we can deduce that the short-run supply curve S — S of an industry is obtained by the lateral addition of the outputs of all the firms comprised in it, such outputs being determined by the slope of their respective marginal cost curves.

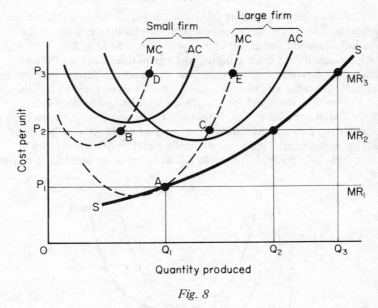

Fig. 8

So we again arrive at a supply curve which slopes upwards from left to right, but by a very different process of reasoning from that applicable to goods already in existence.

SIMILAR QUESTIONS
(i) Why would you expect a firm to respond to an increased demand for its product by expanding its output rather than by just charging a higher price for the same output? (CIS Intermediate, December 1965.)
(ii) Why should a firm respond to an increased demand for its product by expanding its output rather than by just charging a higher price for the same output? (CIS Intermediate, June 1968.)

3.3 *Explain the concept of elasticity of demand and consider its practical significance. Illustrate your answer by diagrams. (ICWA Part I, May 1968.)*

Elasticity of demand
The Law of Demand states that a change in the price of a commodity will cause a change in the quantity demanded: the concept of elasticity of demand relates to the *extent* to which a change in price will cause demand to change. Elasticity is therefore entirely a matter of *degree;* if the change in demand is relatively great compared with the change in price, demand is

said to be elastic, whereas if the change in demand is relatively small it is said to be inelastic. The difference may be shown by reference to two commodities, A and B, the demand curve for the former being steeper than the latter —

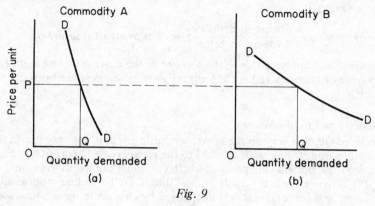

Fig. 9

Clearly, a change in the price level up or down would be reflected by a relatively larger change in OQ in the case of commodity B than it would for commodity A, indicating that the demand for commodity B is the more elastic of the two.

Measurement of elasticity

The slope of the demand curve can be a misleading guide to elasticity, however, as it obviously depends on the scales chosen for the axes of the

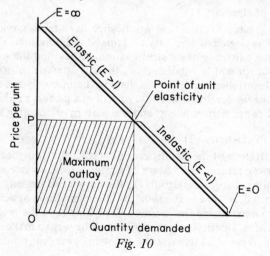

Fig. 10

graph, also on the position of the curve in relation to the axes. Moreover, the change in demand and the change in price are always measured relative to their previous values, so that a "curve" consisting of a straight line of constant slope would have an elasticity which changed throughout its length (Fig. 10).

The expression $\dfrac{\% \text{ Change in demand}}{\% \text{ Change in price}}$ gives a convenient measure of

elasticity, and applying this to the top end of the curve it will be seen that the value of elasticity (E) in the limit is $\dfrac{\infty}{0} = \infty$, whereas at the bottom end it is $\dfrac{0}{\infty} = 0$.

Elasticity and total revenue

The price OP, half way up the curve, is significant, as it not only marks the transition from the inelastic (E < 1) to the elastic (E > 1) part of the curve as price rises, but also the point at which consumer outlay on the commodity is maximized (E = 1). It follows that if a seller had no costs at all to consider, or if his total cost was unaffected by changes in the amount sold, price OP would be the one which would not only maximize his revenue but his profit (total revenue − total cost). Even where total cost varied according to the amount sold, a seller who estimated correctly that the demand for his product was inelastic at the current price would be certain to increase his profit by raising the price; he would not only increase his total revenue, but also reduce his total cost because of the contraction in demand for his product and hence the reduced volume of output required to meet it.

Significance of elasticity (1)

This obviously has great practical significance in so far as monopolies are concerned. The degree of elasticity of demand is determined almost entirely by the existence of substitute commodities, and the monopolist sells a product for which, by definition, there is no close substitute. In the absence of Government intervention, he will therefore always tend to raise his price above the level which would prevail in a perfect market, to the detriment of consumers' interests and the pattern of resource allocation.

Significance of elasticity (2)

Another illustration of the significance of elasticity is provided by the fixing of railway rates. For a system of a given size, railway costs are not very sensitive to changes in output, i.e. the number of passengers or tons of freight carried, so that in the short run the main hope of achieving a surplus lies in maximizing the revenue. For a long time the reaction of the Railway Board to a deficit in one year's working was to make a flat percentage increase in all its rates the following year, but now they are conducting a detailed survey of all their traffic with a view to raising rates only for those services where demand is inelastic, and to reducing those where demand is elastic.

Significance of elasticity (3)

One further example concerns the problem of maintaining production and sales at a more or less constant volume in spite of seasonal or other types of cyclical fluctuation in the state of demand. If the seller could ascertain the elasticity of demand for his product, increases and decreases in demand could be offset by changes in price, thus enabling production and distribution facilities to work near capacity levels all the time. Some attempt is made to do this by transport undertakings with "cheap day" fares, electricity supply authorities with low night tariffs, and the GPO with cheaper telephone calls during "off peak" periods.

SIMILAR QUESTIONS

(i) Define the price elasticity of demand and discuss the use of this concept in the analysis of economic problems (C of S Intermediate, June 1968.)

(ii) Explain what you understand by elasticity of demand. Why in a situation of perfect competition is the elasticity of demand for a product important to: (*a*) a single producer of a good, and (*b*) all producers of a good? (ACCA Section I, December 1968.)

(iii) (*a*) What factors determine the elasticity of demand?

(*b*) What is meant when it is said that elasticity of demand is (i) equal to unity (ii) less than unity (iii) perfectly elastic, (iv) perfectly inelastic? (ACCA Section I, June 1970.)

3.4   *Define "elasticity of supply". Why might one expect the elasticity of supply of a commodity to be greater in the long run than in the short run? (U of L Advanced, Summer 1965.)*

Definition

The term "elasticity of supply" is used to denote the degree of responsiveness of the supply of a commodity to changes in its price. There are two extreme possibilities —

(*a*) Where supply is completely inelastic, i.e. it does not respond at all to changes in price. This situation is represented in Fig. 11(a).

(*b*) Where supply is completely elastic, i.e. an indefinitely large quantity will be supplied at a given price, as in Fig. 11(b).

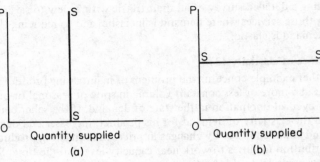

Fig. 11

Degree of elasticity

In all intermediate cases, it is a question of how much supply will change for a given change in price, and the fraction $\dfrac{\% \text{ Change in quantity supplied}}{\% \text{ Change in price}}$ can be used to evaluate the degree of elasticity. Any straight-line "curve" which passes through the point of origin has an elasticity of unity, irrespective of its slope (Fig. 12(a)), whereas a straight-line "curve" which cuts the vertical axis has an elasticity greater than unity Fig. 12(b)), and one which cuts the horizontal axis has an elasticity less than unity (Fig. 12(c)).

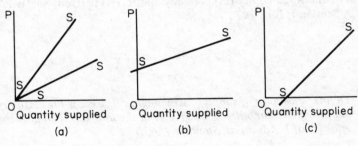

Fig. 12

The time factor

Changes in supply are normally evoked by changes in the state of demand. Speaking in terms of an increase in demand, one can analyse the attempts of an industry to extend its supply in what Marshall called the "market period", the "short period" and the "long period" respectively.

(a) The "market period". This allows only sufficient time for stocks on hand, plus any that could be termed "in sight", to be sold off to the

highest bidders. In such circumstances, the supply is to all intents and purposes fixed, and elasticity tends towards zero.

(*b*) *The "short period".* This is deemed to be sufficient to allow entrepreneurs to increase output by increasing the supply of variable factors, e.g. labour, in their production processes. While capital remains fixed, however, increased output beyond a certain point can only be obtained under conditions of diminishing returns, so that costs are bound to be rising. In other words, the short period response of the industry is simply to move up along its normal supply curve, which is the lateral sum of the marginal cost curves of all the firms which it comprises. Since normal supply curves slope up from left to right, they have a greater degree of elasticity than the near-vertical curve associated with the "market period".

(*c*) *The "long period".* Now the time-scale is long enough to permit existing firms to increase the supply of all their factors, and for new entrepreneurs to enter the industry from outside. It is possible to build new factories and new machines to go in them, to train a new generation of workers, and for the industry's suppliers to raise their capacity to a higher level. Now that the optimum combination of factors has been restored, a lower level of costs will tend to prevail, though there may be an offset if new factor units and new firms are less efficient than the old. On balance, however, it is highly probable that the general level of costs in the industry will be lower in the long than in the short period, i.e. that elasticity of supply will have again increased.

SIMILAR QUESTIONS

(i) Define the elasticity of supply. Consider how far a firm's elasticity of supply may be expected to vary according to whether it relates to the short period or the long period (C of S Intermediate, November 1967.)
(ii) Define the elasticity of supply. Under what circumstances would you expect it to be large and when would you expect it to be small? (C of S Intermediate, May 1969.)

3.5 *Many factors combine to determine the level of demand for one commodity. Set out a number of these factors, and discuss the effect on the level of demand for all goods should one of these factors change. (ACCA Section I, December 1967.)*

Changes in the sales volume of a commodity may be caused either by changes in its price or by changes in the state of demand for it. Changes of the former kind, called extensions and contractions, are governed by the Law of Demand, and are outside the scope of this question. Our attention is therefore directed to changes in the state of demand, called increases and decreases; what we are discussing is not simply a movement up or down a given demand curve, but the establishment of a completely new curve ($D_2 - D_2$), either to the right or left of the original curve ($D_1 - D_1$), thus —

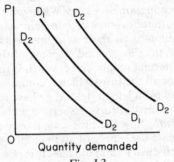

Fig. 13

Size of real national income

There is normally an increase in the amount of purchasing power which people have from year to year, arising mainly from increased productivity. This is obviously going to influence the level and pattern of demand across the whole range of commodities, and it is the effects of changes in this factor which are discussed further at the end of the question.

Redistribution of the national income

In this context, redistribution usually implies a more equal distribution, the effects of which are also very widespread. In general, the national income is more equally distributed in the UK now than it was 100 years ago, but still not as equally as it is in some other countries.

Population changes

An increase in the size of the population, such as that which occurred in Britain during the 19th century, must increase the demand for all kinds of goods. The pattern of demand is also influenced to a significant extent by the age structure of the population, bearing in mind the great differences which exist between the needs of young and old people.

Taste/fashion/convention

Sweeping changes in the state of demand can occur as a result of developments in this field. These may range from long-term changes in conventional attitudes and behaviour to rapid variations in women's fashions. In Victorian times, for example, it was usual for both sexes to wear a hat out of doors, but nowadays people go bareheaded most of the time; the vogue for mini-skirts decreased the demand for cloth, but increased the demand for tights, and so on.

Cyclical changes

Many products experience a regular and largely predictable variation in the state of demand. This may occur on —

(*a*) A daily basis, e.g. the increase in demand for transport during the "rush hours" of the morning and late afternoon;

(*b*) A weekly basis, e.g. the increase in demand for retail goods on Fridays and Saturdays by wage earners;

(*c*) A monthly basis, similar to (*b*) but emanating from salary earners, and

(*d*) An annual basis, e.g. the increased demand for holiday accommodation in July and August.

Advertising

A well-conceived advertising campaign has enormous power to generate an increase in demand. Much of its success will depend upon whether it can create a distinctive "image" for the product in question, which involves allied policies in relation to branding and packaging.

Government policies

There are many ways in which Government policy decisions can affect the state of demand. For example —

(*a*) A credit squeeze will decrease the demand for most products, especially durable goods.

(*b*) Agreement to a reduction in tariffs will extend the demand for imported goods because of lower prices and hence decrease the domestic demand for home-produced goods.

(*c*) Legislation to improve road safety has increased the demand for new car tyres and seat belts.

Substitutes

The appearance of substitutes for established commodities will decrease the demand for the latter, e.g. the advent of nylon, terylene, etc., has made inroads on the market for cotton goods. A similar effect is produced by changes in the price of another good forming part of a composite supply, e.g. a rise in the price of beef will increase the demand for chickens.

Effect of a change in national income

Reverting to the first category above, the effects of an all-round increase in purchasing power on the demand for different products will differ according to what is called their "income-elasticity of demand". Broadly speaking, goods in the luxury class will experience a more-than-proportional increase in demand, goods which come into the category of everyday purchases will show a less-than-proportional increase, while so-called "inferior" goods

will actually suffer a decrease in demand. There is no doubt that manufacturers of cars, for example, have benefited more than most from the rise
in national income per head over the last 50 years, but over the same period
the consumption of bread per person has tended to fall.

The explanation for the latter phenomenon is that when people are able
to afford a more varied and attractive diet there is simply less room left
for what was once the staple item in their food supply. Similar effects can
be observed on the demand for other products which were only bought
previously because people could not afford anything better, e.g. margarine,
cheap cotton clothing, etc.

SIMILAR QUESTION
(i) What factors, other than a change in the price of the commodity may
cause the demand for the commodity to change? Show by a diagram, how
such a change would affect the demand curve. (ICWA Part I, December
1965.)

3.6 *Is the apparent tendency for cigarette prices to increase by the full
amount of an increase in tax consistent with supply-demand analysis?
Argue your case. (U of L Advanced, January 1964.)*

Outlay taxes — the general case
The effect of an outlay tax on the basic supply-demand diagram is to raise
the supply curve by a vertical distance equal to the amount of the tax per
unit, thus —

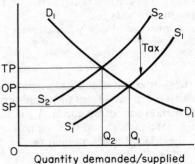

Fig. 14

Although the Government collects the full amount of the tax, namely
the taxed price, TP, minus the supply price, SP, consumers are only called
upon to pay the difference between TP and the original price, OP, leaving
suppliers to pay the difference between OP and SP. In other words, buyers

and sellers share the payment of the tax, meeting it out of their consumers' and producers' surplus respectively.

The influence of elasticity

These shares will not necessarily be equal, however; buyers will pay most of the tax when supply is more elastic than demand, and vice-versa. If one accepts the view that the demand for cigarettes is very inelastic, therefore, this provides sufficient explanation for the ability of sellers to pass on *most* of the increase in tax to consumers; having become more or less addicted to smoking, the latter are for the most part unable to go without cigarettes altogether, or even to curb their consumption to any great extent. Since there can be no such thing in reality as a completely inelastic demand, however, the ability of sellers to pass on the *full* amount of the tax increase still needs to be explained.

Changes in the state of demand

To do this is it necessary to remember that supply-demand analysis is only valid on the basis of "ceteris paribus", i.e. all things affecting the situation other than price are assumed to remain unchanged. During the years that the tax on cigarettes has been going up, however, a number of other developments have been taking place which could account for a sustained increase in demand, which, taken in conjunction with inelastic demand, would tend to raise price, thus —

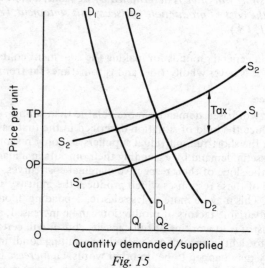

Fig. 15

Now instead of the taxed price settling at the intersection of D_1-D_1 and S_2-S_2 as before, it is pushed higher to the point where D_2-D_2 and

$S_2 - S_2$ intersect, and the difference between TP and the original price OP could well be as great as the amount of the tax, if not more.

Possible reasons for an increase in demand

While one cannot be certain of the factors which may have contributed to such an increase in demand, a number of possiblities suggest themselves. For example, cigarettes are typical of the kind of "conventional luxury" for which demand is income-elastic, so that every increase in the community's purchasing power causes a more-than-proportional increase in demand for it. Further, the ranks of smokers have been swollen in recent years by (*a*) the spread of the habit amongst women, and (*b*) the influx of a disproportionately large number of teenagers as a result of the "baby boom" in 1946/47. Last, the increasing efforts of the advertisers must have played their part in counteracting the effect of higher prices, so all things considered it is not surprising to find that cigarette manufacturers have succeeded in passing on every increase in tax which has taken place.

There are signs however that these influences may now have worked themselves out and may even have been counteracted to some extent by the effect of anti-smoking propaganda.

3.7   *"In the short run price is determined by demand, and in the long run by the cost of production". Discuss this statement. (ACCA Section I, June 1968.)*

There are good general grounds for making the statement contained in the question, but it is never wholly true, and is sometimes far from being true.

Short run price

In the majority of cases, demand is more volatile than supply, and this tends to produce the kind of situation described in the first part of the statement. In the short run individual suppliers can only respond to a sudden increase in demand by extending their outputs in a manner governed by the slope of their respective marginal cost curves, and it is the sum total of these responses which produces the industry's short-run supply curve. This may be more or less elastic, depending upon how easily the supply of variable factors of production can be increased, and how near the industry is to working at full capacity, but it will certainly slope up from left to right in accordance with the prevailing conditions of supply whatever they may happen to be. In other words, an *increase* in demand, which can and often does occur overnight, can only produce an *extension* in supply in the short run, with the result that price rises to an extent which depends mainly on the displacement of the demand curve as shown in the diagram, where S–S is the supply curve, D_1–D_1 the original demand curve, D_2–D_2 the new demand curve, and the increase in output from OQ_1 to OQ_2 is accompanied by an increase in price from OP_1 to OP_2. It will be noted, however, that the degree of elasticity of the supply curve also has some effect on the price; while the increase in demand makes it certain that the price will rise, conditions of supply determine to some extent the amount by which it will rise.

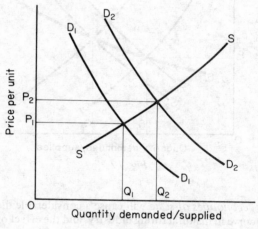

Fig. 16

Long run price

If the increase in demand seems likely to persist, then suppliers will start making plans to increase output by increasing the quantity of all the factors of production, in particular the amount of fixed capital they employ. In the long run, therefore, new conditions of supply will be established in the industry, and the whole supply curve will be displaced to the right. The amount of this displacement will depend upon how the industry's cost structure is affected by these developments; whether or not the overall cost per unit of producing the new level of output will be higher or lower than it was before will depend upon the balance between diminishing returns and economies of scale.

Diminishing returns will tend to operate most strongly in the extractive industries, e.g. agriculture, mining, fishing, etc. Here nature provides an important fixed factor in the combination of factors employed, and while some economies of scale are possible they are unlikely to offset the tendency towards higher costs due to diminishing returns. The long-run supply curve $S_L S_L$ of the industry will therefore slope up from left to right as shown in the diagram, the displacement of the short-run supply curve from $S_1 - S_1$ to $S_2 - S_2$ being insufficient to offset the displacement of the demand curve –

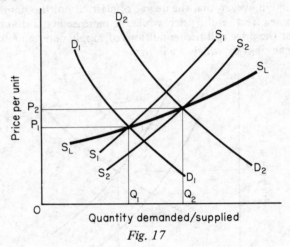

Fig. 17

Conversely, *economies of scale* will cause a considerable displacement of the supply curve in manufacturing industry, and the effect of this will be more than sufficient to outweigh the effect of diminishing returns. As a result the long-run supply curve will slope downwards from left to right, and the price will tend to fall as demand increases –

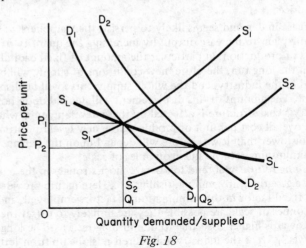

Fig. 18

Whether the long-run supply curve is rising or falling, it will be seen that the second part of the statment made in the question is largely justified; the equilibrium which was disturbed in the short run by an increase in demand has been restored, and rewards to entrepreneurs have reverted after a period of adjustment to a normal level, i.e. one which is sufficient to cover full average cost of production.

Spontaneous changes in supply

The foregoing argument therefore tends to support both parts of the statement contained in the question, but it has been assumed throughout that changes in supply are always initiated by changes in demand. It is quite possible, however, for changes in the conditions of supply to occur for other reasons, the most obvious example being the quantity of a crop which is produced in a particular year. This may turn out to be different from that anticipated because of favourable or unfavourable weather conditions, and the resultant glut or shortage, conditions of demand remaining the same, will raise or lower the short period price accordingly.

SIMILAR QUESTIONS

(i) "The price of a commodity tends to equal its cost of production." Discuss. (CIS Intermediate, June 1965.)
(ii) How do economists distinguish between (*a*) the short period, and (*b*) the long period. Using this distinction, analyse the effects on the price and quantity supplied of a commodity of an increase in the demand for it. (CIS Intermediate, June 1967.)

3.8 *What do you understand by the terms marginal revenue and marginal cost? Explain the rôle of these concepts in the theory of the firm. (U of L Advanced, January 1967.)*

Marginal revenue

This is the amount by which a firm's total revenue increases when it sells one more unit of output. In a perfectly competitive market there are so many firms that individual variations in output do not affect the price, so that marginal revenue and price (average revenue) are equal and constant. In an imperfect market, however, and particularly in the case of a monopoly, price (average revenue) will fall with increasing output, in which case marginal revenue will fall twice as fast, even becoming negative beyond a certain point.

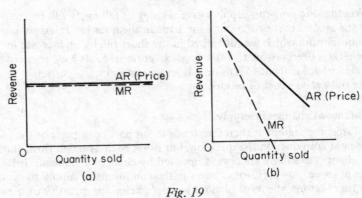

Fig. 19

Marginal cost

This is the amount by which a firm's total cost increases when it raises its output by one unit. The existence of a fixed element in total cost, represented by the firm's capital equipment, means that, starting from zero output, average cost falls quickly at first; at a later stage, when the optimum combination of variable and fixed factors has been reached, average cost is at a minimum; at greater outputs still, the variable factors are being used less and less efficiently, and average cost starts to rise. The arithmetical relationship between marginal cost and average cost is such that marginal cost falls more steeply than average cost at first, then stops falling and begins to rise as the rate of fall in average cost declines (being momentarily equal to average cost at the point where the latter reaches its minimum value), and thereafter continues to rise more steeply than average cost, thus —

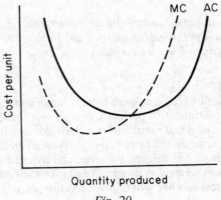

Fig. 20

Profit maximization – general

These two concepts together play an essential part in the theory relating to a firm's most profitable output, whether it is operating in a perfect market or as a monopoly. In the short run, it must pay a firm to increase its output while marginal revenue exceeds marginal cost, but to stop doing so before the reverse happens, i.e. output will always be fixed at the point where the marginal cost curve intersects the marginal revenue curve from below.

Profit maximization – perfect competition

For a single firm in a perfectly competitive market, this might result in subnormal or abnormal profit being earned for the time being, according to whether or not price was sufficient to cover its average cost at that output, but whichever it was the firm would be operating at the best level of output in the circumstances. Fig. 21(*a*) shows the firm earning subnormal profit, and Fig. 21(*b*) abnormal profit, indicated in each case by the shaded area –

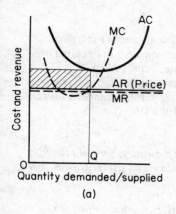
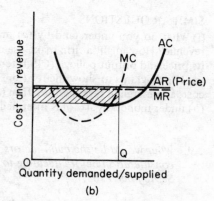

Fig. 21

For a monopoly, equating marginal revenue and marginal cost will normally result in an abnormal profit being earned, as shown in Fig. 22.

As marginal revenue lies everywhere below average revenue, it must be the first of these two curves to be cut by marginal cost; if the output thus obtained is now projected upwards, it will cut the average cost curve at Y and the average revenue curve at X, giving PXYZ as an abnormal profit. This diagram also shows that the monopolist's price will be in excess of his marginal cost, and that his output will be less than that which would minimize average cost, in contrast with the firm in a perfectly competitive market.

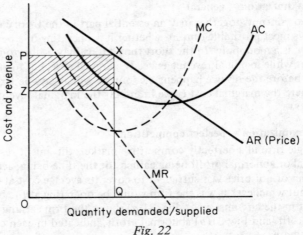

Fig. 22

SIMILAR QUESTIONS
(i) What do you understand by (a) marginal cost and (b) marginal
revenue? How might a firm make use of these concepts in deciding on
its price and output policy? (CIS Intermediate, June 1967.)
(ii) Use diagrams to show the relationship between average cost, marginal
cost, and marginal revenue for a firm (a) under perfect competition and
(b) under monopoly. (C of S Intermediate, June 1966.)

3.9   *What would be the main factors which a business should take into
      consideration before deciding to close down its plant? (I of B Part I,
      September 1967.)*

In the long run, a firm must cover all its costs, including a normal rate of
profit, if it is going to survive; in other words, the average cost per unit of
its output must not be less than the average revenue per unit of its sales.

Theoretical shut-down point
In the short run, however, average cost and average revenue may well
diverge considerably, and one must be prepared to accept the fact that,
taking all costs into consideration, the firm is operating at a loss from
time to time. In this context, it is important to distinguish between fixed
and variable costs; whereas the revenue being obtained from current
sales might not be enough to cover the former, it might exceed the latter,
in which case there would be a net gain for the time being in continuing
production. Consider, for example, the two firms shown in Figs 23(a) and

$23(b)$; in each case, the least unprofitable output is OQ, as determined by the equality of marginal cost and marginal revenue, but whereas in Fig. $23(a)$ the price is greater than average variable cost at that output, in Fig. $23(b)$ it is lower —

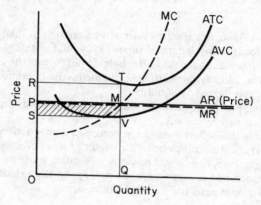

Fig. 23(a)

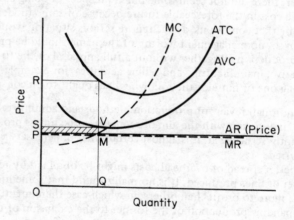

Fig. 23(b)

In Fig. $23(a)$, it is worth while for the firm to continue working in the short run, as that part of total revenue represented by PMVS is available to offset the loss RTVS (i.e. total fixed cost) which would otherwise be incurred in closing down. In Fig. $23(b)$, however, PMVS appears as a loss over and above RTVS, so that the firm is only making matters worse by continuing to produce instead of closing down at once.

Practical considerations (short run)

In practice, the question of whether or not to close a firm down would no doubt involve many other factors, as such a decision, once made, might well prove to be irreversible. The immediate points to be considered would be —

(*a*) Whether the firm's reserves were strong enough to take the strain of working at a loss for any length of time. This would not only be a question of the size of reserves as shown in the balance sheet, but the extent to which they were already committed to financing the operations of the business, i.e. their degree of liquidity.

(*b*) What the prospects were of raising a temporary loan from external sources, e.g. the firm's bankers.

(*c*) How long the deficit involved in continuing production was expected to continue. If the difficulties being experienced were of a seasonal or non-recurring nature, this would obviously be much more of an inducement to all concerned to carry on, even perhaps to the extent of financing a deficit on variable costs for a while if necessary.

Practical considerations (long run)

If, however, there did not seem to be much prospect of being able to cover full average cost in the foreseeable future because of some fundamental change in market conditions, a much more serious situation would present itself. Even so, no management worthy of the name should be prepared to abandon production altogether without a full appraisal of the firm's administrative, manufacturing and selling activities; for example, some action along one or more of the following lines ought to be considered —

(*a*) A thorough review of production methods and administration should be undertaken with the aim of reducing costs; unless procedures are constantly scrutinized, it is almost certain that unnecessary costs are being incurred.

(*b*) A better spread of overhead costs might be obtained by reducing the number of lines produced. It is normally found that some lines contribute more to profit than others, in which case there might be a net gain in expanding production of the former to the exclusion of the latter, especially if greater economies of scale resulted.

(*c*) Conversely, an increase in the number of lines marketed might help both to increase and to stabilize the revenue from sales. The decision to sell a new line need not involve manufacturing it, incidentally; for example a firm manufacturing vacuum cleaners could widen the range of its products by selling imported washing machines under its own brand name.

(*d*) Changes in pricing policy might help to improve profitability. For example, the combination of a fairly elastic demand and the existence of spare productive capacity would suggest the advisability of reducing prices; larger quantity discounts might be offered to distributors; prices might be raised and lowered to counteract seasonal variations in sales, etc.

(*e*) Finally, the whole strategy of marketing might be reconsidered, e.g. the suitability of the firm's products in relation to users' needs, the way the products were advertised, the style of packaging, the channels of distribution, and so on.

SIMILAR QUESTIONS

(i) Does it pay a firm which is losing money to stay in existence? (CIS Final, June 1966.)

(ii) Should a firm cease production if it fails to cover its "average costs"? Give reasons for your answer. (CIS Intermediate, December 1968.)

3.10 *Explain what is meant by the statement that "monopolistic practices are against the public interest". (ICA Final, November 1965.)*

The statement relates to the alleged policy of private monopolies whereby output is restricted in order to maximize profits, and the various devices which are then adopted in order to preserve the abnormal element in those profits which this policy produces.

Revenue and output

While no monopoly is perfect in the sense that there is a completely inelastic demand for its product, the absence of any close substitute for the commodity in question means that the demand curve will fall from left to right, and it might well be inelastic over a considerable part of its length, i.e. marginal revenue would become negative at a relatively low volume of sales. Considered simply from the point of view of maximizing *revenue,* therefore, the firm or group of firms comprising the monopoly is led to restrict its output for a reason which would not apply in a perfectly competitive market, where marginal revenue remains positive at all levels of output.

Cost, revenue and output

When changes in cost consequent upon changes in output are considered as well as changes in revenue, the tendency is to restrict output still further; marginal cost is necessarily positive, and since maximization of *profit* requires that marginal cost must be equal to marginal revenue the latter must also be positive at the chosen output, i.e. the monopoly adjusts its production and sales to the point OQ where it is working on the elastic part of the demand curve, and where marginal cost must be less than price, thus—

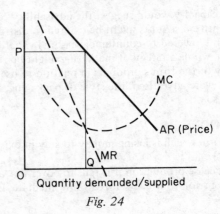

Fig. 24

If we now introduce average cost into the argument, insofar as this falls short of average revenue at output OQ then an abnormal profit of XY per unit, or PXYZ in total, is automatically realized by the monopoly. Moreover, it is now apparent that production stops short of the point where average cost falls to a minimum.

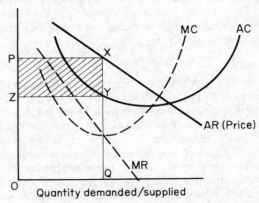

Fig. 25

Theoretical objections to monopoly

Summarizing the argument so far, therefore, the main theoretical grounds for objecting to private monopolies are that, as compared with a state of perfect competition –

  (*a*) they restrict output;

  (*b*) they charge a price in excess of marginal cost, whereas the optimum allocation of resources requires that they shall be equal;

(*c*) they derive a profit from their operations greater than that necessary to provide entrepreneurs with a normal reward for their services;

(*d*) firms are of less than optimum size.

Restrictions on entry and output

If there were no kind of restriction on the entry of new firms into a monopolistic industry, or restraints on the output of individual firms already in it, the major cause of these objectionable features would be removed. In practice, entry may well be restricted by the nature of the industry itself, e.g. it might be necessary to incur very heavy fixed costs as a prerequisite of producing any output at all. In such cases, very little action on the part of the monopoly would be required to maintain its advantageous position, and the only effective remedy would seem to be outright nationalization. In many other industries, however, monopoly profits are under the constant threat of erosion by increased output, originating either from individual firms within the existing group of producers or from would-be new entrants into the industry; it is the various practices adopted by monopolists to restrict these competitive tendencies which evoke the greatest criticism, and which the government has attempted to prevent by legislation.

Cartels

One well-known device is to form a "cartel" among all the existing members of the industry. Although the different firms retain their separate identities, they agree on a common marketing policy whereby the most profitable output and price for the industry as a whole is estimated, and each firm is then allotted its annual "quota" of sales, with a system of fines for firms exceeding their quotas. Variations on this theme include agreements not to have overlapping production of different varieties, grades or sizes of the product, the recognition of exclusive sales areas, common tendering or refusal to tender by all but one of the group, and so on.

Boycotts, etc.

In order to protect themselves from outside competition, members of the "ring" will often resort to the practice known as the "collective boycott" This may either take the form of a threat to withdraw all their orders from a supplier who sells materials to a would-be competitor, or the threat to withhold supplies of all their products from distributors who buy from him. The same weapon can be employed against distributors who cut the recommended retail price of any of the group's products. The legality of such practices was always in doubt, but there is plenty of evidence to show that they were freely resorted to before the Restrictive Trade Practices Act was passed in 1956.

Other ways of eliminating outside competition include the creation of "fighting brands" to undercut a new firm's product until such time as it is bankrupted, harassment by legal actions, binding customers by the promise of a deferred rebate if they refrain from buying outside the group, and so on.

Loss of efficiency

Apart from the effect of all such practices in restricting output and keeping up price, they also operate against the public interest insofar as inefficient firms are protected from the rigours of competition, while efficient firms are prevented from increasing the scale of their operations.

SIMILAR QUESTIONS

(i) "The main disadvantage of monopoly is not that it causes high prices but that it is inefficient." Discuss (CIS Intermediate, December 1965.)

(ii) In what circumstances would a monopolist benefit by selling a smaller amount of his product? Illustrate your answer by a diagram. (ICWA Part I, December 1969.)

3.11 *Under what conditions is "discriminating monopoly" (a) possible, and (b) profitable? Is it always to be condemned?*

Definition and examples

The term "discriminating monopoly" is used to denote a situation where the sole seller of a commodity charges different prices for it in different markets. Such markets may be distinguished from one another by reference to different geographical areas, by different times of the day, week or year, different classes of customer, or different kinds of use; for example, exports may be invoiced at lower prices than home orders, transport undertakings may offer reduced fares at certain times, industrial consumers of gas may get it more cheaply than domestic users, electricity boards may offer current at a lower rate for power than for lighting, and so on.

Separation of markets

All the above examples have one thing in common, namely that there either exists a ready-made division between the different markets, or that it is possible to create one. The essential point is that the monopolist's policy cannot be circumvented by having purchasers of the commodity in the "cheap" market transferring any of it to the "dear" market at a profit to themselves; in the case of home and export markets, for example, the natural insulation between the two provided by return freight costs might be reinforced by the existence of a protective tariff. Sometimes buyers can be left to sort themselves into categories, e.g. first and second class railway passengers, though in such cases it may be necessary to employ inspectors to ensure that people who have paid the lower price do not avail themselves of the more expensive facility.

Different elasticities of demand

Even if it is feasible, the practice of differential charging only confers an advantage on the seller if there are different elasticities of demand in the different parts of his market. If this should be the case, he will maximize his profit by equating the marginal cost of his total output with marginal revenue in each separate market, which will automatically result in prices varying inversely with the degree of elasticity in each market. This may be illustrated by reference to two markets, A and B, in which demand is less elastic in the former than the latter (Fig. 26, see p. 72).

Favourable aspects

It is usual to regard all monpolistic pricing policies as being contrary to the public interest, and a monopoly which discriminated between one customer and another might appear to be especially open to criticism. However, it is possible to defend differential charging in the following circumstances —

(*a*) The pattern of demand so created might enable productive capacity to be utilized more fully. For example, the railways used to claim that the arbitrary division of their freight tariff into 21 classifications enabled them to accept low-grade commodities like building materials which would not otherwise have moved.

(*b*) Where a duopoly existed, the sale of the part of each of the two firms' outputs at a lower price, in all probability under another brand name, might be a tentative form of competition leading eventually to an all-round reduction in prices.

SIMILAR QUESTION

(i) In what circumstances, if any, can price discrimination be justified? (CIS Final, December 1964.)

3.12 *Should the economist's theory of profit-maximizing firms be abandoned because the assumption of profit maximization is unrealistic? Explain your answer. (U of L Advanced, Summer 1965.)*

The nature of economic reasoning

The claim of economics to be regarded as a science is not based on the degree of precision which can be associated with its theories, but on the fact that it adopts scientific methods of investigation. It may well be, as

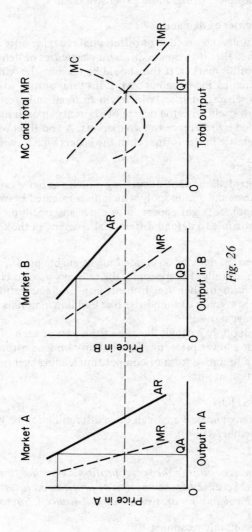

Fig. 26

the question suggests, that entrepreneurs are not invariably thinking and acting in ways calculated to extract the last penny of profit from the businesses they control; on the other hand, one must assume that, given two alternative courses of action, they would choose that which, other things being equal, seemed to offer the greater financial reward, and it would appear possible, therefore, to derive from this some valid generalization about the way in which they behave when confronted with the problems of the market.

Output, price, and profit in theory

Now, the theoretical economist, arguing from first principles, is prepared to state that a firm's profit is maximized when its marginal cost is equal to its marginal revenue, and he goes on to trace the effect of this on output, price and profit under various market conditions. Moreover, according to his reasoning, marginal cost will always be rising at the equilibrium output and development of the argument leads to the proposition that any increase in demand must evoke a greater output at a higher marginal cost, and vice versa.

Output, price, and profit in practice

Having reached this conclusion by a process of purely deductive reasoning, the economist must be prepared to test it by observing the behaviour of entrepreneurs in the real world. He may well find that these individuals (insofar as they can be clearly identified at all in modern large-scale businesses) are in the main far too preoccupied with averting threatened strikes, improvising methods of coping with fluctuations in the volume of work in the factory, investigating breakdowns in the supply of materials and a thousand other practical aspects of management to pay much attention to the niceties of balancing marginal cost and marginal revenue. Indeed, it is unlikely that the problem of output and pricing is considered in these terms at all; being, so to speak, saddled with a particular product (or, more probably, a group of products), a plant of a given size, and a labour force which cannot be varied like the flow of water from a tap, the overriding necessity seems to be to keep working as near to capacity as possible, and try to exact a price from customers which will cover average (as distinct from marginal) cost, including something by way of a conventional percentage of profit per £1 of sales.

Can theory and practice be reconciled?

At first sight, therefore, the economist's theory of profit maximization would not appear to be a very useful guide to the motivation of entrepreneurs in real life, as the profit-maximizing objective is clearly subordinated in varying degrees to the desire to enjoy a quiet life vis-à-vis their employees, the need to steer clear of anti-monopoly laws, the pursuit of power or prestige for its own sake, etc. Nevertheless, until empirical research can provide a better hypothesis than profit-maximization as a general basis for explaining the decisions of businessmen, this would still seem to be the most workable assumption to make. In this respect, the theory of profit-maximization could be compared with the Law of Demand; while consumers have all kinds of motives for buying one product rather than another, they are all influenced to some extent *and in the same direction* by a change in price, so that one is entitled to say that more of a commodity will be sold if its price falls, other things being equal.

In the case of profit-maximization, the issue is further complicated by the time factor, as businessmen may rightly reason that it is better to accept less-than-maximum profits, or even losses, in the short period for the sake of greater gains in the long period. It would therefore require a far more complex model than that of the conventional static Law of Demand to deal with this situation, but the underlying principle that, given similar circumstances, the bulk of entrepreneurs will act in a similar way still holds good.

There is also the possiblity that most entrepreneurs simply do not know what the demand conditions for their products are, nor even the cost conditions with any degree of exactitude, so that they can only aim at an output which they *think* will maximize profit rather than the one which actually *would* do so. All that can be said here is that the ability to estimate MR and MC correctly may be one of the main reasons why some entrepreneurs succeed where other fail; it is surely reasonable to suppose that lack of such ability lies at the root of the bankruptcies which occur over the whole field of business enterprise every year.

Summary

Like all the end products of economic reasoning, the theory of profit-maximizing firms must be hedged about with qualifications, but even though the qualifications may sometimes appear to be more important than the theory itself this is no reason to abandon it unless the premise on which it is based can be shown to be false. In the case we have been discussing, the assumption is that, provided they know the facts, business-men will behave in a rational way, i.e. they will favour the course of action which will increase the firm's profit rather than diminish it, and so far no investigation into entrepreneurial behaviour has demonstrated that this assumption is ill-founded.

SIMILAR QUESTION

(i) Textbooks suggest that businessmen invariably seek to maximize their profits rigorously. Discuss the reasons why this may not always be their policy in practice. (I of B Part I, April 1967.)

4
Rewards to factors

Section 2 examined the part played by the factors of production in the creation of values; this Section deals with the rewards they receive for doing so, often called the Theory of Distribution. As there are four factors; land, labour, capital and enterprise, it is usual to classify their rewards under the headings of rent, wages, interest, and profit respectively, but, in the same way that the factors are difficult to isolate, so these different kinds of payment tend to overlap and merge. For example, the term "rent" was originally applied to land because it was considered unique in having no cost of production, and because its supply was not responsive to changes in price, but now it is recognized that the rewards to all factors may well have a rent element in them. Similarly, in order to distinguish between interest and profit, it is necessary to assume that some investments are entirely free from risk while the return from others arises wholly from riskbearing, whereas in reality almost all investments fall somewhere between these two extremes.

These practical difficulties need not be of great concern to the student, however, as he will find that the majority of questions simply ask him to discuss the theory of rent, to explain why one kind of worker gets paid more than another, to say what determines the rate of interest, or to analyse the nature of profit. In fact, the marginal productivity theory which is usually expounded in connection with wages applies with equal validity to rent and interest as well. The entrepreneurs' demand for land, labour and capital is merely derived from the demand for the goods which they help to make, and while some quantity of all of them may be required in production, the task of organization is to ensure that they are combined in such proportions that their marginal revenue products equal the price paid for them. It follows, therefore, that the general levels of rent, wages and interest will depend on the relative scarcities of land, labour and capital in the economy as a whole, and that all will tend to change in particular industries in sympathy with changes in the market prices of the goods they help to produce.

With this idea at the back of his mind, the student will be on firmer ground in studying theories of rent, wages and interest, and can look forward with some degree of certainty to getting a question on at least one of them.

4.1 *Use Ricardo's theory of rent to explain the statement that "the price of corn is not high because a rent is paid, but a rent is paid because the price of corn is high". (I of B Part I, April 1966.)*

Rent is price determined

Ricardo's theory of rent is based on the fact that the supply of land is fixed for all time, irrespective of changes in the demand for it. This being so, owners of land have no choice but to sell or rent it for any figure it will fetch, even down to zero, in times of slack demand; on the other hand, they can simply charge what the market will bear when demand is high. The same idea is expressed by saying that "land has no supply price", i.e. since there is no cost of production to be considered, demand is the sole determinant of price.

Differences in fertility

Ricardo did not, however, make the assumption that in given conditions of demand all land would command the same price. His theory took account of the fact that the "original and indestructible powers of the soil" varied a great deal, and that at any given time there were likely to be certain relatively sterile areas of land which would not repay the cost of cultivation, others where this cost would be covered exactly by the revenue from the sale of the product, and others again where the abundance of the crop would show a surplus over cost. The first, which would obviously be left uncultivated, he called "sub-marginal" land, the second, which would just be worth cultivating if no charge were made for its use, he called "marginal" land; the third, which would be well worth cultivating, would now be called "intra-marginal" land, and the essence of Ricardo's theory was that competition for the use of such land between would-be cultivators could be relied upon to furnish its owners with an income which he called "rent". In other words, cultivation would be extended into land of declining fertility to a point where the revenue received by tenant farmers from the sale of the product exactly equalled the cost of cultivation (including a normal rate of profit), and any surplus arising from the cultivation of intra-marginal land would accrue to landowners, the size of such surplus being determined by the fertility of their respective plots.

Illustration of Ricardo's theory

This situation is illustrated in Fig. 27(*a*), where the rectangles represent the gross revenue derived from selling corn grown on five pieces of land,

A, B, C, D and E, of equal areas but different degrees of fertility, and the cost of cultivation is shown by the horizontal dotted line. Rent (as indicated by the shaded areas) emerges as the difference between the two in the case of A, B and C (intra-marginal), land D being marginal, or "no-rent" land, and E sub-marginal.

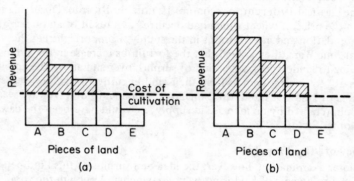

Fig. 27

If now the price of corn should rise (and it was just such a rise at the time of the Napoleonic wars which focussed Ricardo's thoughts on the matter) then the revenue obtainable from cultivating all corn-growing land would rise proportionally, and the situation would change to that shown in Fig. 27(*b*). Now the surplus (shaded area) remaining after paying the cost of cultivation has risen on land A, B and C, with a corresponding increase in the rent which farmers are prepared to pay, land D shows a surplus and will therefore yield a rent, and land E has moved nearer to the margin. Thus, as the quotation in the question indicates, it is the rise in the price obtainable for the product of the land which causes the rent payable for the land to rise, or, as it is sometimes said, "rent is price-determined and not price-determining."

SIMILAR QUESTIONS
(i) Set out the factors that determine a charge for rent. Discuss why rents in the city are higher than in the country? (ACCA Section I, June 1968.)
(ii) What is meant by "economic rent"? Why is it sometimes said that it does not enter into the cost of production? (C of S Intermediate, November 1968.)
(iii) "Rent is price determined and not price determining." If so, what is the point in controlling rents of dwelling units? (C of S Final, May 1969.)

4.2   *Examine the proposition that economic rent is likely to constitute part of the reward of any factor of production. (CIS Intermediate, December 1963.)*

Rent as a reward to landowners

The idea of a rent element in the reward to owners of land was put forward by the classical 19th century economists, notably Ricardo. Observing the rise in the price of wheat which had occurred as a result of an increase in the population and interruptions in the supply of imports during the Napoleonic Wars, they argued that the fortuitous increase in rewards accruing to landowners was a kind of surplus, over and above the amount necessary to induce them to keep their land in cultivation; moreover, since the area of land was fixed, this "unearned increment" in its reward was not counteracted by an increase in supply, as would have been the case with other factors.

Fallacy of "fixed supply"

On closer examination, however, the idea of a surplus of this kind being confined to owners of land is not very convincing. Although the total area of land may be accepted as being permanently fixed, it is seldom true that a given piece of land is completely specific; arable land is often capable of growing a variety of crops, or can be turned into pasture, or be devoted to building, and so on. In other words, when the supply of land *for any particular purpose* is considered, be it for growing wheat or anything else, there is almost always the possiblity of increasing the supply of it at the expense of some other purpose, in much the same way as the supply of one kind of labour could be increased even though the population were static. On the score of supply being fixed, therefore, there is little choose between land and the other factors of production in the ordinary course of events.

Differences in fertility applicable to all factors

Ricardo further argued that the rent element present in the rewards to various landowners would reflect the differences in fertility of their particular pieces of land; whilst all would receive the current price per bushel for their wheat, the lower yields per acre received from less fertile land would drive the revenue obtainable from cultivation down to a point where it barely covered the cost involved. In any given market situation, therefore, there would be this marginal, or "no rent", land, and changes in the price of the product would be reflected by an extension or contraction in the supply of land at the margin, with corresponding changes in rents on better-than-marginal land.

But again, the fact that some units of a factor may be more "fertile", i.e. efficient, than others, is not confined to land. A clear parallel can be seen in the case of workers paid purely on a piecework basis; two men may put in the same number of hours, and exert the same amount of effort, but the more proficient one will earn more money. In any occupation, there are bound to be people who consider it only just worth their while to stay in it, either because the disutility of effort is barely matched by their earnings, or, more likely, because they are on the margin of doubt as to whether they would not do better by transferring to some other kind of job; these marginal workers correspond to Ricardo's "no rent" land, and the by same token their colleagues who are receiving more than enough to retain them in their present employment can be said to enjoy a kind of rent from it. To continue the analogy with land, changes in the wage rate for the occupation in question would be followed be corresponding changes in the employment of marginal workers, and in the amounts of rent enjoyed by others. The same argument could be followed in the case of the other factors, namely capital and enterprise; a particular kind of specific plant will earn abnormally high returns following upon an increase in demand for its products, some entrepreneurs derive extra rewards from their unusual skill in forecasting, and so on. Granted, therefore, that a rent element of some sort occurs in the rewards to all the factors, it only remains to be asked whether there is any difference, in kind or degree, between the rent accruing to the owners of land and that which exists in the payment for the services of other factors.

Most rents are "quasi-rents"

As the theory of rent grew more refined, it became customary to distinguish between rent in the original Ricardian sense and "quasi-rent," the difference between the two turning on whether the supply of factor units in question was absolutely fixed for all time, or whether it could eventually be varied. Once it is allowed that the definition of rent can be extended to include unearned increments in rewards which are only temporary, then it would normally apply to all the factors of production for a certain period of time following upon an increase in demand for their products. It is hardly ever possible to increase the supply of factor units of any kind instantaneously; on the other hand, it is usually possible for supply to be increased provided sufficient time is allowed to elapse for the pull exerted by an abnormally high reward to attract additional factor units of an appropriate kind, no matter whether they come under the heading of land, labour, capital or enterprise. For reasons explained earlier, the supply of land is no more fixed than the supply of any other factor in normal market situations; while there may be exceptional cases of factor units whose nature precludes any possibility of their numbers being augmented, no matter what the reward offering, they are no more likely to be found in practice among the "free gifts of nature" than they are in the other factors.

While it is true that, for example, the total quantity of tin buried somewhere under the earth's surface cannot possibly be affected by changes in the market price of the metal, an increase in the amount currently being offered for sale can be brought about in time by diverting additional units of the other factors of production to mining operations; in the short run, all the units of all the factors contributing to the sale of tin enjoy a quasi-rent, but in the long run their rewards all revert to the normal level at the margin.

Summary

A rent element can thus be said to exist in the rewards to all but the marginal units of all the factors of production at any given moment of time, in that they are receiving more than enough to retain them in their present employment, and in addition all the factors involved in the production of a commodity enjoy the benefit of a quasi-rent during the period of adjustment which follows a rise in price. The proposition contained in the question therefore seems to be entirely justified.

4.3   *What is the "marginal productivity theory of wages"? Assess the validity of the theory in explaining wage levels in a modern industrial society. (CIS Intermediate, December 1966.)*

Statement of the theory

The marginal productivity theory of wages is an application of the general theory of distribution to the particular case of labour. According to this

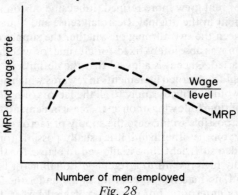

Number of men employed
Fig. 28

theory, the rewards to all factors of production tend to equal the value of their respective marginal products, and since the marginal product of any factor declines as the quantity employed increases relative to other factors it follows that an increase in the supply of labour in any given occupation will tend to lower the level of wages in it. The value of the marginal product of labour will depend not only on the physical size of its contribution to output, but on the price per unit obtained from the sale of that output; in short, we can say that the marginal revenue product and the wage level will tend to be equal (Fig. 28).

The individual entrepreneur buying his labour in a perfect market must of course, take the wage level for each kind of labour as he finds it, and from his point of view the theory operates to determine the number of workers he will employ rather than the wage he will pay them.

Assumptions of the theory

The theory assumes that labour is homogeneous, i.e. that all workers in a certain category are fully interchangeable, so that the wage paid to the marginal worker determines the wage for all of them. It further assumes that employers know what the marginal revenue product of labour is, and that the workers are in a position to know it too, which brings us to the first difficulty in using the theory to explain wage levels as they are found in industrial society today.

Evaluation of marginal revenue product

It is doubtful whether in fact the majority of employers have any clearly defined idea of the marginal revenue product of their labour, partly because of the problem of isolating the contribution made by marginal workers to the value of output from the contribution of co-operating factors. For example, an extra driver is no good without an extra lorry, another turner requires another lathe, and so on. This difficulty can be resolved in theory by deducting the additional cost of the other factors from the total increase in marginal revenue product, but presumably few employers would have costing techniques sufficiently refined to obtain this information. As for the employees' side, it is extremely doubtful whether trade unions make any serious attempt to gauge the marginal revenue product of the labour of the workers they represent; the procedure seems to be to submit a claim for wages a good deal higher than they think the employer can possibly be made to pay, and settle for the best compromise they can get. Moreover, the market for the product is subject to continual change, so that the marginal revenue product is never constant, but is hardly practicable to change wage rates at less than yearly intervals. All one can say is that both sides have at least some intuitive awareness of "what the traffic will bear" in the prevailing conditions, and usually seem prepared to take the rough with the smooth during the periods between bargaining sessions.

"Living wage" and "fair wage"

It appears even more difficult to reconcile the marginal productivity theory with the fact that many wage negotiations do not seem to be related to productivity at all. For example, claims for an increase in pay are frequently made and secured on the basis of a rise in the "cost of living" —

indeed, several important groups, e.g. building workers, have a clause in their standing agreement with employers which guarantees an automatic increase in the wages whenever there is a rise in the retail price index. Again, the trade unions tend to favour the idea of a "fair wage", i.e. one which reflects the degree of skill required to the performance of a task, any danger or discomfort that may attach to it, etc., and this approach to the question of wage payment is often manifested by the existence of traditional "differentials" between crafts which both sides seem willing to accept.

In such cases, however, the divergence between theory and practice may be more apparent than real. While the employer may be obliged to pay a wage which is higher than the marginal revenue product of his labour for the time being, he will be stimulated, indeed obliged, to seek ways and means of bringing the two into equality by somehow making labour more remunerative. Where market conditions permit, this may be achieved by the simple expedient of raising the price of the product, but otherwise his main recourse will be to make more extensive use of machinery, i.e. to substitute capital for labour at the margin.

Summary

While it must be admitted that the marginal productivity theory cannot give a very precise answer to the question of wage determination, it does provide a general framework within which negotiations take place and settlements are made. It is fairly safe to say that an employer who paid his labour more than the value of its marginal revenue product would eventually be forced out of business, while one who persistently offered less would eventually find himself without workers.

SIMILAR QUESTIONS

(i) Does the fixing of wages by collective bargaining, as is common in Great Britain, supersede the market mechanism? (CIS Final, December 1964.)

(ii) "Wages depend on productivity, but productivity does not depend on wages". Consider this statement. (CIS Final, June 1965.)

(iii) Describe and criticize the marginal productivity theory of wages. (ICWA Part I, December 1969.)

4.4   *Why are women's wages sometimes lower than men's for the same work? What would happen if the differences were ended? (C of S Intermediate, November 1966.)*

Marginal productivity theory

If women do indeed get paid less than men for doing work of exactly the same value, there is evidently something wrong with the marginal productivity theory of wages. This is concerned solely with the increase in revenue which will result from the addition of another worker to the labour force, and if there is no difference in this respect between a man and a woman it should be a matter of complete indifference to the employer which he decides to engage.

Non-competing groups

However, when the claims of women for equal pay are subjected to anything more than a superficial examination it is often found first of all that the exact type of work they do differs from that of men in the same occupation. The broad categories might be the same, e.g. "clerk, teacher", etc., but closer investigation may well reveal that men and women are performing complementary tasks rather than identical ones. In an office, for example, it is mainly men who dictate letters and women who type them; in education, the lecturers in universities are mainly men while the teachers in infant and primary schools are mainly women, and so on. There is in fact a tendency in most occupations for men and women to separate themselves into non-competing groups, which is not really surprising as there are inherent differences in physical strength, temperament, etc., which no amount of education or training can eradicate, and both sexes naturally seek the kind of job in which their comparative advantage is greatest.

"Womens jobs" tend to be less productive

It does not follow in principle that women should get paid less for the kind of jobs in which they tend to specialize, since they bring to them qualities which men on the whole do not possess, but once this kind of self-segregation has occurred one important condition of the marginal productivity theory of wage determination has been broken, namely that the workers in a given occupation are fully interchangeable. If, therefore, the marginal productivity of the tasks in which men specialize tends to be higher than those in which women specialize, the basis of the argument for equal pay is destroyed, and more often than not this proves to be the case; because women crowd into the kind of jobs for which they are inherently more suitable than men the marginal revenue product of their labour is forced down, and lower wages are the inevitable result.

Difference in Motivation

There are, nevertheless, many jobs demanding purely intellectual qualities for which men and women would seem to be equally well suited, e.g. the professions, and it is in these that the controversy about equal rewards is keenest. Now the question of women's pay no longer turns on the *type* of work which is being done but on the amount of *time and effort* which is devoted to it, and here one is brought up against the essentially different rôles which men and women play in society. From the time she leaves school a girl's ambition to make a career for herself is tempered by the prospect of becoming a wife and mother, and if this does happen the interests of her employer normally take second place to those of her husband and family. Consequently, the majority of women lack the drive and sense of purpose which men are more inclined to bring to their work, the willingness to sacrifice leisure in order to study or work overtime, etc. The result is that in the present socio-economic environment the more responsible duties tend to be given to men, together with the higher rates of pay that they merit.

Women's reluctance to bargain

Even if the work should be identical, and a woman's productivity equal to that of a man, there is still a tendency for her pay to be less than his. Again, however, the marginal productivity theory of wages is not at fault, as it assumes a desire and ability on the part of workers to exact the *full value of their marginal product* from the employer, and women are usually less militant in this respect than men. Whether this reluctance to drive a hard bargain reflects women's *less aggressive nature,* or whether they are usually under *less economic pressure* to maximize their earnings than men, the fact that women seldom take an active part in trade union affairs bears witness to their relatively *passive attitude* towards wage negotiation.

Effects of enforced "equal pay"

The likely effects of legislation to enforce pay for women would *not appear to be altogether favourable* to their cause. Whereas previously an employer might have been prepared to tolerate somewhat lower productivity from women workers in consideration of their lower wage, any attempt to make him pay them a *man's wage* would tend to make him *employ men instead* if possible. The net result might well be to push still more women into the kind of occupations where they have a relative advantage over men, thus *depressing the marginal revenue product* of their labour and the wages paid in those occupations to even lower levels than before.

SIMILAR QUESTIONS

(i) Why are women's wages usually lower than those of men? (CIS Intermediate, December 1965.)
(ii) Why are women sometimes paid less than men for the same work? What would be the effects of prohibiting this by law? (CIS Intermediate, June 1970.)

Rewards to factors

4.5 *"Railway workers' wages cannot be raised to the level of wages in comparable occupations because of the deficit in British Railways' finances." Discuss this statement. (U of L Advanced, January 1966.)*

Comparability v marginal productivity

One of the basic tenets of trade union philosophy is the right of the worker to receive the "rate for the job". If a job demands a certain kind of skill, then it must be more highly rewarded than unskilled work; if a degree of personal risk is involved, then this must be recognised by the payment of "danger money"; if there is some kind of discomfort or unpleasantness associated with the work, then this qualifies for "dirt money", and so on. This approach to the question of wages is, of course, at complete variance with the economist's Theory of Marginal Productivity, which says in effect that the wage rate can be no more than the value of the marginal worker's contribution to his employer's total receipts, i.e. it is determined by the physical size of his output and the market price obtained for it.

Which principle for railway wages?

The difference between these two principles is clearly seen when considering the question of railway workers' wages. On the face of it, it is impossible to reconcile the unions' insistence on comparability in pay with "outside" employment with the fact that the railways have been losing money ever since they were nationalized in 1947. Repeated attempts have been made to eliminate this loss, but without success: charges have been raised time and again, but total receipts have failed to respond to the desired extent; economies in working have been introduced, but these have not kept pace with rising costs, not least the cost of wage increases themselves.

Even the official pronouncements on the subject of railwaymen's pay in relation to overall finances lack coherence. On the one hand, the original Transport Act, in common with all other statutes relating to nationalization, laid down the principle that the railways should "pay their way, taking one year with another" — a fairly clear mandate for the Railway Board to apply the marginal productivity principle in determining wage rates. On the other hand, the Guilleband Committee, set up by the Government in the 1950's to examine the whole question of railway wages, gave its unqualified support to comparability when it stated that "the nation has willed the end, the nation must will the means" — in other words, if we wanted a viable railway system, we must be prepared to pay current wage rates for the kind of work involved, even if this means subsidization.

Attempts at a solution

Both the major political parties and many different Transport Ministers subsequently wrestled with the problem, and, as might be expected, the result was an uneasy compromise between the two opposing principles;

policy vacillated between an all-out attempt to cut losses under the Beeching Plan by eliminating unprofitable lines and services, and an almost unquestioning acceptance of the need for an annual subsidy to keep the railways going as they were. In 1968, however, the Transport Act broke new ground by allowing the railways to account separately for uneconomic but socially desirable services, and to claim a subsidy as of right to cover the specific losses involved in operating them; at the same time, a substantial proportion of their fixed assets was written off so as to reduce the burden of annual interest charges. It might be argued that this was a mere exercise in bookkeeping which did nothing to change the realities of the situation, but it is on this basis that the railways, in common with all other nationalized industries, are now supposed to earn a given percentage return on their assets in operating "commercial" services.

Future prospect

Whether this latest attempt to solve the problem of British Rail's finances will eventually enable them to pay their workers at rates comparable with those in "outside" employment and still make the required margin of profit remains to be seen, but for the time being wages continue to be a sore source of grievance with the railway unions.

4.6 *Is there any limit to the increase in real wages which a trade union may secure for its members in a particular industry? (ICWA Part I, June 1967.)*

Short v long run

It is difficult to say whether there would be any limit in the long run to what a trade union could do to increase the real wages of its members. While the scope for improvement at any given time might be quite large, it would certainly be subject to a number of limiting factors; on the other hand, given sufficient time and the right conditions, there seems to be no reason why the real incomes of the workers should not go up as far and as fast as improvements in production techniques allowed.

Short-term possibilities (1)

Leaving aside the long-term possibilities for the moment, the position would depend mainly on the bargaining strength of the union concerned. First, it would help if the principle of the "closed shop" could be enforced; in this way, the union would be able to take full advantage of monopoly power in its negotiations with the employers. Second, the union's position would be greatly strengthened if both sides knew that a strike would have serious consequences, either for the public or for the employers. Workers in certain key industries, e.g. transport, electricity supply, etc., where a withdrawal of labour would have immediate and damaging repercussions on large sections of the population, are in a position to drive a very hard bargain indeed, whereas a strike by teachers would only have indefinable and long-term effects. Similarly, employers in highly capitalized industries, e.g. chemical products, oil refining, etc., would be loath to see millions of pounds' worth of plant lying idle for the sake of making a possible saving in their relatively small wages bill.

Short-term possibilities (2)

Given these powerful aids to bargaining, a union should have no difficulty in exacting the full value of the workers' marginal revenue product from the employer — the next question is, could he be compelled to part with more? In fact, it is quite possible that he could, in one or more of three ways, depending on the circumstances —

(a) Profit margins might be squeezed below normal, at least for a time, as part of the price for industrial peace and continuity of production.

(b) If the market were imperfect, or if there was an undercurrent of demand inflation in the economy as a whole, the employer could attempt to pass on his excessive wage costs to consumers in the form of higher prices.

(c) If it were a nationalized industry, or any other which could get a subsidy, the higher costs might be shifted to taxpayers.

All these methods would mean that the trade union had succeeded in raising the living standard of its members at the expense of other people in the community, but there would presumably be opposition on their part to an indefinite prolongation of these tactics, and therefore a limit, however ill-defined, to the increase in wages which could be obtained by such means.

In other words, the marginal revenue product of the labour concerned will ultimately determine the maximum reward it can secure by the exercise of bargaining power alone; any prolonged attempt to obtain more than this, even by strike action, would be defeated by bankruptcy of the employer, consumer resistance, or a taxpayers' veto.

Long-term possibilities

There remains the long-term possibility of the trade union securing an increase in real wages through an increase in productivity per head of its members. This would involve a radical change of attitude in its dealings with employers; instead of concentrating on getting as large a slice as possible from a cake of given size, the union officials would have to think in terms of increasing the size of the cake by —

(a) putting their main effort into devising ways of helping the employer to improve efficiency, and (*b*) educating their members into agreeing to the installation of labour saving machinery and the adoption of schemes of all kinds to increase productivity.

Given the necessary degree of co-operation, the rate at which real wages might be increased would then depend solely on the success of the industry in solving the purely technical problem of incorporating new scientific developments into their production processes as and when these came along.

SIMILAR QUESTIONS

(i) Can trade unions raise wages? Explain your answer. (U of L Advanced, Summer 1968.)

(ii) To what extent has a trade union power to affect the level of real wages in an industry? (ICWA Part I, June 1967.)

4.7 *How is the rate of interest determined? (U of L Advanced, Summer 1967.)*

There are two alternative answers to this question which are equally acceptable and not incompatible with one another. The first, which originated with the classical economists, regards interest as the price which equates the supply of and demand for loans, and is called the "Loanable Funds Theory"; the second, which is associated with Keynes' Theory of Employment, states that the rate of interest depends on the demand for money in relation to the existing stock of it, and is called the "Liquidity Preference Theory".

Loanable funds theory

It is characteristic of human nature to prefer present to future satisfaction. This being so, potential lenders require some compensation, i.e. payment of interest, before they will voluntarily refrain from spending the whole of their incomes on consumption; moreover, since each increment in the amount lent involves proportionately more sacrifice, according to the Law of Diminishing Marginal Significance, the inducement necessary to evoke large loans will have to be at a higher rate, pound for pound, than small loans. Hence, risk factors apart, there will be a supply curve for loans of money which lenders are willing to offer.

Although some people borrow so as to be able to enjoy present satis-faction at the expense of future income (for example, when a young married couple decide to buy a house), the majority do so in order to invest in revenue-earning assets. Thus investors' demands for loans will reflect their estimate of the rate of return to be derived from such assets in relation to their cost, i.e. the marginal efficiency of capital. Moreover, the rate of return will be governed by the Law of Diminishing Returns, since the larger the amount of capital invested, the smaller the marginal product tends to be. Hence from the borrowers' point of view there is a demand curve for loans, showing an inverse relationship between the rate of interest and the amount of money they wish to take.

By combining the two curves, therefore, a rate of interest emerges which equates the supply of and the demand for loans, thus —

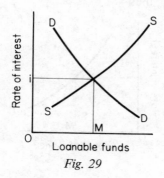

Fig. 29

Liquidity preference theory

Money as such has no utility; the only reason people want to have money is that it is capable of being exchanged for any other kind of asset at a moment's notice. Keynes analysed the demand for "money to hold" under three headings —

(*a*) *The transactions motive.* A certain amount of money is needed in everyday living to satisfy a stream of relatively small and predictable demands for goods and services. It would be extremely inconvenient to cater for these except by making immediate money payments.

(*b*) *The precautionary motive.* Here the emphasis shifts to meeting wholly unforeseen contingencies; a person may be willing to incur a certain amount of "opportunity cost" for the satisfaction of knowing that he has a fund of liquid resources to draw upon in case of emergency, or if the chance of making some exceptionally favourable purchase should present itself.

(*c*) *The speculative motive.* Values of commodities are constantly changing in terms of money, and in particular the value of securities. There is a customary range over which the rate of interest varies (e.g. Bank Rate has never been below 2 per cent, and could hardly be expected to rise above 8 per cent), so that when it is near the bottom end of the scale the market value of fixed-interest bonds is unlikely to go much higher, and vice-versa. When such extreme positions are approached, therefore, there is a general tendency to anticipate a reversal in the trend of security prices, i.e. when the rate of interest is low, people prefer money to bonds, but when the rate is high they prefer bonds to money.

The combined effect of these three motives is to produce a demand schedule for money to hold, which Keynes called "liquidity preference", at any moment of time; the rate of interest at that time is then determined by the state of liquidity preference in relation to the total amount of money in the economy, thus —

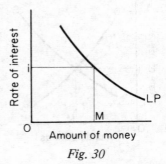

Fig. 30

SIMILAR QUESTIONS
(i) "The rate of interest is the reward for parting with liquidity for a specified period". Assess the adequacy of this definition of the rate of interest. (CIS Intermediate, December 1964.)
(ii) Define interest and say what factors determine the rate of interest. (ICWA Part I, December 1964.)

4.8 *How, and to what extent, do changes in the rate of interest influence the level of economic activity in an economy? (CIS Intermediate, December 1967.)*

Upward and downward movements in the rate of interest will, of course, have reverse effects on the economy. In order to simplify the wording of the answer, upward movements only have been discussed, so that the opposite results would follow from a downwards movement.

Investment
In general, investment in all kinds of capital goods tends to be discouraged by a rise in the rate of interest, because of the higher cost of borrowed money; even when self-finance is possible, the opportunity cost is greater. It has been found by empirical research, however, that a one or two per cent rise in the rate of interest has a negligible effect on decisions relating

to the average run of investment projects; this is because the margin of error in calculating the return on most kinds of new plant is so great that business men do not normally decide to invest in it unless the cost can be written off in a period of three to five years, in which case the difference in the amount of interest payable becomes quite insignificant in relation to the other sums involved.

There are, however, two kinds of investment to which a rise in interest rate would act as a considerable deterrent —

(*a*) Constructions of a very durable nature, not exposed to the risk of obsolescence, e.g. buildings, bridges, tunnels, etc. In such cases, even a one per cent rise in rate would result in a marked increase in the amount required to amortize a loan repayable over, say, a fifty-year period.

(*b*) Any investment in stocks of goods or materials, e.g. those held by wholesalers. In such businesses, the interest on money borrowed to finance stocks is a major part of total cost, and steps will immediately be·taken to reduce them.

Savings

Since interest is the reward for postponing consumption, the overall tendency is for savings to be encouraged by a rise in the rate of interest. Again, however, the typical small saver is relatively insensitive to minor changes in the rate; much saving is done automatically because of what Keynes called the "precautionary motive" rather than for the sake of financial gain. It is possible that a really spectacular increase in the rate, say to 10 per cent or 15 per cent per annum, might arouse a good deal more attention, always provided that the security for the loan was not in question, but the fact that the Post Office can continue to attract deposits at 2½ per cent when other short term rates are about double speaks for itself.

There is in fact one kind of saving which tends to be reduced when interest rates rise, namely that undertaken by people who have in mind the provision of a fixed income on retirement. In such case, a given amount can be secured at a smaller current sacrifice; as insurance companies can invest their funds to better advantage, annuity premiums will be reduced.

Budget

An annual sum must be found by the Chancellor to meet interest charges on the National Debt. The amount required to service the floating part of the debt will increase at once in line with the increase in short-term rates; should the higher structure of rates persist, larger sums will also have to be found to pay the interest on the funded part of the debt as various long-term loans are converted into new issues. In short, therefore, higher interest rates will result in higher taxation.

Balance of payments

Provided foreigners had no lack of confidence in the value of sterling, a higher rate of interest would attract money on short-term deposits to London away from other financial centres. This influx of so-called "hot money" would improve the UK's balance of payments on capital account for the time being, but the resultant increase in our gold reserve would obviously be subject to an equally sudden reverse movement, and the increase in the amount of interest payable to foreign holders of sterling would put some additional strain on the current account balance.

A more fundamental improvement in the balance of payments would almost certainly result at a later stage if the rise in interest rates formed part of a sustained "credit squeeze" policy leading to a reduction in domestic demand; this would have the effect of reducing imports and increasing exports, albeit at the expense of new investment and the general level of employment.

4.9   *"Profit is the price paid by society for the services of the entrepreneur".*
       Discuss this statement. (ICWA Part I, June 1967.)

Rôle of the entrepreneur

The statement is a very fair summary of the part played by profit in a free enterprise economy. In the absence of a centrally-determined plan for production and consumption, the allocation of resources must be decided by certain individuals in the community: the task falls to those who think they can foresee the way in which consumers' demands, and the methods of satisfying them, are evolving, and who are prepared to risk financial loss by contracting for the supplies of land, labour and capital necessary to put their ideas into practice. It is *uncertainty* about the future which makes the rôle of the entrepreneur necessary; if conditions of demand and methods of production were competely static, the economy would soon settle down after a brief period of trial-and-error to a routine pattern of production and distribution, and revenues arising from the sale of products would simply be divided between rent, wages and interest.

Normal profit

The entrepreneur's reward therefore consists of the residue from the earnings of the business after these contractual payments to the other factors of production have been made, and unless this residue is considered sufficient to compensate him for the risk of loss which he alone must bear he will withdraw his services. As to what is sufficient, this will depend on how much risk is involved in the industry concerned; obviously, the greater the risk, the higher will be the rate of profit considered "normal" to induce the entrepreneurs to stay in it. It should theoretically be possible to specify actual percentage rates as being normal for various industries, but the crucial point is whether entrepreneurs are on balance inclined to go into an industry or to leave it; hence the best criterion of normal profit is an equilibrium number of entrepreneurs.

Abnormal profit

It does not follow, however, that all entrepreneurs will be making normal profit even when the industry is in equilibrium. Some are bound to be more skilled than others in forecasting the trend of events, or more successful at improvising solutions to unexpected problems as they crop up, and the extra profit which they are able to earn is called a "rent of ability". This is a normal and inevitable outcome of the inherent differences between one individual and another, and society should not complain about these higher rewards as they are in effect paid for a superior service. On the other hand, where abnormal profits are due to some kind of restriction on entry into the industry or output from it, i.e. "monopoly rent", then the community is justified in seeking ways and means of breaking down that restriction.

Normal profit as part of cost

Reverting to the statement in the question, it is now clear that normal profit should indeed be regarded as part of the price which society must pay as a condition of getting goods produced under free enterprise, and it is for this reason that a normal rate of profit is always included in economic analysis when dealing with the question of cost. It is important to remember, however, that the expression "the services of the entrepreneur" relates only to his unique and specific function of risk-bearing; insofar as part of his reward is earned by giving labour services, e.g. as manager of the business for which he is providing the risk capital, then that should be assessed separately and classified as wages.

SIMILAR QUESTIONS

(i) "Profit is residual income." Assess the adequacy of this description of profit. (CIS Intermediate, June 1966.)
(ii) "Profit is the reward for risk and uncertainty." Explain this definition and consider its relevance in the present-day economic structure. (ICA Final, November 1966.)

4.10 *"A tax on profits is a tax on enterprise." Explain and discuss.*
(U of L Advanced, January 1966.)

Rôle of profit

The "free enterprise" system relies on profits as the main form of incentive for entrepreneurs to supply the kind of goods consumers require at the

lowest practicable prices. Always provided that competition can be kept
fully effective throughout the system, i.e. in respect of the factors of
production as well as the end products themselves, any changes in the
pattern of demand or techniques of production will be reflected by a
change in the relative profits obtainable from the innumerable ways in
which the public's wants can be satisfied, and hence by a change in the
allocation of resources.

In general, the constant endeavours of businessmen to maximize
their profits will cause a continuous movement of resources out of lines of
production where profit is relatively low into others where it is relatively
high, and whether the increased profit in the new lines is attributable to
increased demand or reduced cost, their activities will lead to a marginal
improvement in the value obtained by the community from the total
volume of resources.

Uninsurable risks

Entrepreneurs' decisions to change the pattern of resource allocation are
invariably fraught with risk, however; contractual arrangements with the
owners of land, labour and capital must be entered into before any new
line of production can be started, but there is no way in which an individual
entrepreneur can make certain that the proceeds arising from his venture
will eventually be sufficient to cover his costs. He can, of course, pool the
risk of incurring certain kinds of random cost, e.g. fire damage, with other
entrepreneurs, and he can minimize the degree of error in estimating his
revenue by engaging in market research, but there is bound to be a residue
of uninsurable risk which he alone must bear. In deciding whether or not
to embark on a new enterprise, he must therefore estimate as best he can
the chance of making a profit against the chance of incurring a loss, and
he will only proceed if the former outweighs the latter.

Perhaps the most unfortunate aspect of a tax on profits is that it operates
most strongly against the riskier kinds of enterprise. Economic progress
depends in large measure on the rate at which innovations can be introduced into production, but pioneers in any field of human activity are
exposed to an exceptionally high degree of risk, and to take away a
large part of their prospective reward is to discourage enterprise in
precisely those areas where society stands to reap the greatest benefits in
the long run.

Summary

It is now apparent that there is ample justification for the statement contained in the question. A tax on profits acts as a constant deterrent to a
would-be entrepreneur, as it does nothing to reduce the penalty he must
pay if his estimates turn out to be wrong, but it takes away part of his
reward if he proves to be right. His situation could be compared with that

of a gambler who is invited to go into a game knowing beforehand that the dice are loaded against him, and who is thereby discouraged from putting his stake on the table.

This is not to say, of course, that business enterprises should escape taxation altogether. On grounds of equity alone, those who derive their income from providing finance for business should make some suitable contribution to the national exchequer, and the large amount of revenue now gathered from this source would indeed be difficult to replace. It is a matter for debate, however, whether the incidence of the tax on profits as such should be so heavy; the advent of an employment tax suggests the possibility that businesses might be made to pay an equally large amount of tax in a way which encouraged them to economize in the use of resources rather than one which penalized them for success in doing so.

5
Money and banking

Many students welcome this part of the course as it seems to hold out a promise of a closer affinity with life as they know it than, say, the Law of Diminishing Returns. It is true that certain events occur exactly as described in the textbooks, e.g. Bank Rate is decided upon and announced every week, and the Index of Retail Prices is published every month with unfailing regularity, but it must always be remembered that economics is chiefly concerned with *why* things happen rather than *how* they happen, and there is a very little scope for purely descriptive answers.

Nor are we free from the difficulties associated with definitions and the use of words. "Money" sounds simple enough for a start, but the student soon realizes that it is impossible to draw a hard-and-fast distinction between what is money and what is not; the word "deposit" assumes different meanings in different contexts; "banks" are of many different kinds, and the exclusion of some is often implied rather than stated. In short, the student will encounter the same need for disciplined thought and argument that is demanded of him in the other sections, and there is in addition the need to keep reasonably up-to-date with the factual background.

Perhaps the commonest type of question is the one which asks how the banks are able to create money, and/or what limits their ability to do so. The student should therefore make quite certain that he knows the main items in a typical commercial bank's balance sheet, and how these are affected by the Bank of England's attempts to control credit by the use of open market policy; questions involving Bank Rate require in addition an outline knowledge of how the London money market works. Anyone who really understands a bank balance sheet and the function of a Bill of Exchange should be able to produce a satisfactory answer to any question likely to be set on banking; anyone who does not will almost certainly fail to do so.

Questions on the price index are often asked, and it is well worth learning the method by which it is calculated, but those which enquire into the causes and affects of rising prices are more difficult, and cannot be answered satisfactorily without introducing matters dealt with in Sections 6, 7, and 8.

5.1 *What is Gresham's Law, and what are the attributes of a "good" currency? (ACCA Intermediate, December 1963.)*

Statement of Gresham's law

According to Gresham any attempt to maintain two kinds of money in circulation was almost certain to fail. Sooner or later, he argued, one kind was bound to be more highly esteemed than the other, so that it would be hoarded while the inferior variety was used to make exchanges, or, as he put it, the bad money would drive the good money out of circulation. His theory was well illustrated by what happened during the period of "bi-metallism", when a legal ratio was established between the values of gold and silver coins; if, as a result of a change in the relative bullion prices, gold coins appeared to be undervalued, only silver coins would circulate, and vice-versa.

Token coinage

Our coins today have only a "token" value, that is to say their face value far exceeds their value as metal, but even so Gresham's Law would tend to operate if coins made of the same metal were not "weight related", i.e. the weight/value ratio were not constant. In this connection, an interesting situation developed with the decimal coinage; the 5p, 10p, and 50p coins are all made of the same cupro-nickel alloy, but whereas a 1:2 weight ratio is maintained between the 5p and 10p coins, the 50p one now weighs much less *pro rata*. It still remains to be seen whether the authorities have been justified in saying that forgers would not be able to melt down 5p and 10p coins to make 50p ones at considerable profit to themselves.

Acceptability of money

The only essential attribute of a good currency is that it shall be accepted without question whenever it is offered for payment. There are, however, a number of qualities which can make an important contribution to acceptability, and the more of these a money material possessed the more chance it would have of doing its job successfully. These are as follows—

(a) *Intrinsic value.* It might help, especially in a primitive society, if the material chosen had some value in its own right, e.g. cattle, salt. The underlying thought is, of course, that failing all else the material could be put to some direct use; gold and silver have traditionally been favoured as money materials partly because of the alternative possiblity of using them for ornamental purposes.

(b) *Scarcity.* Whatever material is chosen should be restricted in supply, either naturally or artificially, otherwise a unit of money would not hold its value. Precious metals again emerge well from this test — if they were not scarce, they would not be precious, and no violent fluctuations in value are to be anticipated either as a result of losses or new discoveries.

(*c*) *Portability*. The money material should not be too heavy or bulky to carry about, nor on the other hand should it consist of such small pieces that they are difficult to pick up or easily lost. It follows that in order to cover a wide range of values conveniently, it is necessary to have at least two denominations of money, e.g. pounds and new pence, using two or three different materials.

(*d*) *Durability*. The money material should not deteriorate with constant use or the passage of time. This is why the precious metals were always alloyed with base metals when used as coinage in order to increase their resistance to wear.

(*e*) *Divisibility/homogeneity*. The money material should be such that it can be divided easily into pieces of equal weight, appearance, quality, etc., so that coins can be easily minted from it and shall be indistinguishable from one another. Otherwise, Gresham's Law will operate, and only the "inferior" pieces will circulate.

(*f*) *Cognizability*. Units of money should be instantly recognizable for what they are, and proof against forgery. The minting of coins of a standard size and value, with raised and/or milled edges, and the printing of notes of a highly complex design on specially watermarked paper, are examples of the steps taken by the state to assist ready identification of its money.

Conclusion

As stated above, however, the only essential attribute of good money is that all members of the community are willing to accept it. The islanders of Yap seem to manage quite well with the famous "stone money", which breaks nearly all the rules, while our modern notes only last a few weeks and are not particularly stable in value. The fact that some kinds of money are declared to be legal tender is an aid to acceptability, but is far from being decisive; marks were legal tender in Germany in the late 1940's, but cigarettes were far more acceptable as a means of payment, whereas cheques, which are not legal tender, usually change hands without any trouble. In short, the situation defies logical analysis; one can only echo the words of Cannan, who remarked "Money is as money does".

5.2   *What are the function of money? How are these affected by the existence of inflation? (U of L Advanced, January 1967.)*

It is possible to distinguish four functions of money —

(*a*) It serves as a *medium of exchange*. If it were not for the existence of money, the complex system of specialization and exchange on which a modern economy is based would be completely impossible, and we should be reduced to barter as the only means of providing for all the wants we could not satisfy from out own resources.

(*b*) It is a common *measure of value*. Since it is the one commodity against which all others are exchangeable, money is the only common denominator by which we can compare the values of unlike things. If we say a chair is worth £5 and a table £20, it means that four chairs rate equal to one table on the community's scale of preferences; if wages are £15 a week, and a machine will replace ten men, an employer will want to replace labour by capital at the margin if he calculates that the "all-in" cost of a machine is less than £150 a week.

(*c*) It sets a *standard for deferred payments*. Contracts frequently involve a period of waiting before all the conditions are fulfilled. The rights and obligations arising from such contracts, e.g. hire-purchase agreements, are expressed in terms of money, so that both creditor and debtor know clearly what their future position is to be. In the absence of money as a standard for defining contractual obligations, many business transactions would be quite impracticable.

(*d*) It acts as a *store of value*. Money enters to some degree into the compostion of every individual's assets, i.e. we are free within certain limits to decide what proportion of our wealth we will hold in goods and what proportion we will hold in claims to goods. At a time when our income tends to be high relative to our needs, we may well decide to accumulate a stock of money so that we can augment our purchasing power when the position is reversed, e.g. most people save during the working part of their lives so as to provide for their needs when they have retired.

Inflation clearly undermines the efficiency with which money performs the last of these functions. A persistent rise in prices means an equivalent fall in the value of money; it may well be that on balance savers are penalized for their abstinence from consumption instead of being rewarded, insofar as the interest which they receive is insufficient to compensate for the loss of purchasing power of their money capital. Hence any degree of inflation has serious implications, both for savers themselves and for the community as a whole; in extreme cases, virtually no rate of interest will induce people to refrain from consumption.

This leads to a situation where even the first and third functions are affected. If everyone becomes acutely conscious that money is losing its value day by day, no one will want to hold it for a moment longer than necessary, and no one will agree to the least delay before being paid for the supply of goods or services. The ultimate consequence of this would be the abandonment of the existing kind of money in favour of another, whether official or unofficial, with all the dislocation and individual hardship which this would entail.

SIMILAR QUESTION
(i) What are the chief functions of money? To what extent are these functions impaired by changes in the general price level? (CIS Intermediate, June 1965).

5.3   *How would you measure the average level of retail prices? What difficulties are likely to arise in doing so? (U of L Advanced, January 1965.)*

The official price index

It is by no means easy to measure changes in the average level of prices, but as a result of their experience going back over half a century the Government have evolved a system in compiling their Index of Retail Prices upon which it would no doubt be difficult to improve.

In general, their procedure is to collect information about the pattern of consumption by means of a sample survey of household expenditure, but to exclude from the results households where (*a*) the main income accrues to an old-age pensioner, and (*b*) where the head of the household has an income exceeding £40 per week, as in both cases the pattern differs so much from that of the majority. Having thus discovered how much the "average family" spends on different kinds of goods, weights are assigned to each so that due importance can be given to price changes in them when calculating the overall percentage change which has taken place since the "base year" selected for the index, i.e. a rise in the price of an item taking a big share in the family budget is reflected by a bigger movement in the index than a similar increase in an item on which the family spends comparatively little. In the current Index, the average level of prices as at 16th January, 1962, is taken as 100; by January 1971, this had risen to 147, i.e. retail prices had increased during the intervening nine-year period by an average of 47 per cent.

Difficulties arising

The main difficulties which arise in the calculation of such an index are as follows —

(*a*) The *pattern of consumption* changes as the community's income and habits change. This difficulty is met by changing the weights every year, e.g. the weight assigned to the "food" group of items fell from 319 in 1962 to 250 in 1971 out of a total of 1000.

(*b*) The *quality* or *specification* of goods changes from time to time. In such cases, the Ministry consults the trade concerned and makes the fairest allowance it can for changes in value, but the result is at best arbitrary.

(*c*) Certain payments are for *services* of a *variable and non-measureable nature*, e.g. insurance premiums, subscriptions to trade unions, betting stakes, etc. These are simply excluded from the Index.

(*d*) The prices recorded are the prices actually paid by consumers to retailers, i.e. the Index takes no account of the fact that *many goods are taxed* and some are *subsidised*. If, therefore, there should be any change in the Government's budget policy, e.g. a change from direct to indirect

taxation, this will be reflected by a rise in the Index, but no corresponding rise will really have taken place in the "cost of living", which the Index is popularly supposed to measure.

(*e*) Obviously, the Index can take no account of *changes in the value of money itself.* While this is no way invalidates the accuracy of the results obtained in relation to the purpose for which the Index is designed, a fall in the value of money automatically raises the "cost of living", and workers are inclined to argue that their *standard* of living has gone down, i.e. they tend to disregard parallel increases in the Wages Index which may very well have occurred. The publicity given to the Index of Retail Prices would therefore appear to be a factor aggravating the "wages/prices spiral" during a period of inflation.

SIMILAR QUESTIONS

(i) Describe the practical use of index numbers. How are they constructed? (I of B Part I, September 1965.)

(ii) How is it possible for the standard of living to rise at the same time as the cost of living is rising? (ICWA Part I, December 1965.)

5.4   *Describe a typical commercial bank's balance sheet. What are the chief factors determining the composition of its assets? (U of L Advanced, January 1965.)*

Balance sheets

The main items in the balance sheet of a commercial bank are as follows —

Liabilities	*Assets*
Deposits.	Cash in hand and at Bank of England.
Capital.	Money at Call and Short Notice.
Reserve.	Bills Discounted.
	Investments.
	Loans and Advances

Deposits is an omnibus word used to denote all the potential demands for cash which could be made on the bank, either on demand by customers with current accounts, or within 7/14 days by those with deposit accounts. The bank's solvency depends upon no more than a small and steady proportion of these claims being presented from one day to another, as in total they far exceed its liquid assets at any given time.

Like all other limited companies, a commercial bank has among its liabilities the amount of *Capital* subscribed by its shareholders; similarly, its *Reserve* represents profits earned in previous years which have been re-invested in the business instead of being paid out in dividends.

Turning to the assets, *Cash in hand and at Bank of England* means precisely what it says; part of the total amount shown against this item, usually about half, consists of actual notes and coin held ready to meet customers' demands for cash, while the remainder is in the form of a credit balance at the Bank of England which can be drawn upon in cash at a moment's notice.

Money at call and short notice represents loans made for periods varying from a few hours to a week or so to Bill Brokers and Discount Houses so that they in turn may invest the money in Treasury Bills and commercial bills of exchange.

Bills discounted is the value of the bank's own holding of bills; it is their common practice, especially in the case of Treasury Bills, to acquire parcels of bills from brokers and discount houses with maturity dates which correspond to their anticipated needs for cash.

Investments consist almost entirely of gilt-edged securities, which are, of course, easily marketable, and which usually have no more than five to ten years to run before maturity.

Loans and advances represent the finance given to individual firms and private customers of the bank; overdrafts are in theory repayable on demand, but repayment of sums advanced for specific purposes may extend over two or three years.

Composition of assets

Cash is, or course, the bank's most liquid asset, but it contributes nothing towards revenue. The remaining assets are listed in descending order of liquidity, but ascending order of revenue-earning ability, so that their respective amounts are a compromise between (*a*) the need to maintain a sufficient degree of liquidity and meet all conceivable demands for cash, and (*b*) the desire to maximize profit. It has become the accepted convention for banks to maintain a ratio of 8 per cent between cash and deposits, so that they have virtually no discretion as regards the amount of this item; moreover, they have an understanding with the Bank of England that their "liquid assets", i.e. cash, money at call and bills discounted taken together, will constitute not less than 28 per cent of deposits, so that there is comparatively little room for manoeuvre here either. They are thus left with about 70 per cent of their assets to distribute between investments and loans; while it is not possible to speak of a normal relationship between these two, the present position where investments are somewhat below 20 per cent of deposits and loans are above 50 per cent probably approximates to the proportions which the banks find suit them best.

Special deposits

At times when the banks' liquid assets are abnormally large, the Bank of England may compel them to make "Special Deposits" in excess of their normal cash balances, such deposits to be shown separately in their balance sheets as illiquid assets and to remain "frozen" until such time as the Bank of England sees fit to release them. By this means the banks' "liquidity ratio" can be summarily reduced by up to 3 per cent, and their ability to make loans thereby curtailed.

SIMILAR QUESTIONS

(i) What is meant by (*a*) the cash ratio and (*b*) the liquid assets ratio of commercial banks? Why do banks maintain these ratios? (C of S Intermediate, November 1966.)

(ii) Describe in detail the items you would find on the assets side of the balance sheet of a typical commercial bank. Explain the significance of the proportion in which these items are held. (ICWA Part I, December 1967.)

5.5 *"Banks do not create money; they only lend money which has been deposited with them." Discuss. (CIS Intermediate, December 1964.)*

Money is purchasing power

The statement contained in the question is hardly a true reflection of the part played by the commercial banks in the operation of the monetary system. The banks are in fact responsible for creating the greater part of the country's supply of money according to the economist's definition of the word, i.e. any generally acceptable form of purchasing power.

Evolution of "bank money"

The nature of "bank money" can perhaps best be illustrated by considering how the banking system evolved in the late 17th century. Until that time the money supply system consisted mainly of gold coins, but the risk and inconvenience of carrying these about led to the practice of depositing them for safe keeping with a reputable goldsmith. He would issue the requisite number of "deposit receipts" as evidence of his liability to repay the coinage on demand, and a number of goldsmiths in the City of London acquired such a high reputation for prompt and unfailing payment against presentation of these receipts that it became customary to settle debts by transferring them from hand to hand rather than the gold which they represented.

Creation of money (1)

This made it possible for the goldsmith to contemplate using his comparatively idle stock of gold for the purpose of making loans; so long as he took care to maintain a sufficient reserve of coinage, or "cash" as we shall now call it, to cover the day-to-day fluctuations between withdrawals and new deposits, he could both maintain his reputation for prompt payment and add to his income by charging interest to borrowers. But the significant point to appreciate is that borrowers were accommodated not by the handing over of cash but by the issue of further "deposit receipts", indistinguishable from the original receipts given to those who had actually deposited cash with him, and of course giving holders the same right to claim cash whenever they were presented for payment. By thus trading on the reputation he had acquired for invariably meeting his obligations on demand, the goldsmith was able to maintain a circulation of deposit receipts whose total value far exceeded the cash entrusted to his care; all such deposit receipts, or "bank notes" as they came to be called, were a "generally acceptable form of purchasing power", and the ones issued by way of loans were therefore a net addition to the total money supply.

Creation of money (2)

Following the Bank Charter Act of 1844 the issue of these "private" bank notes gradually came to an end, but this did not stop the banks from making loans, and their ability to create money in so doing remained unchanged. What they now did was to set up one account in their books wherein the borrower appeared as a creditor of the bank for the sum agreed, and another in which he appeared as a debtor for the same amount; in respect of the former, he was given a book of cheques by means of which he could instruct the bank to make sundry payments on his behalf up to the total amount permitted by his credit balance, while in respect of the latter he undertook to repay the amount lent at the expiry of an agreed period of time. Again, the fact that cheques soon became a generally acceptable method of payment meant that they, or more strictly speaking the credit balances which they served to transfer from one ownership to another, became part of the total money supply.

In effect, a bank's debts, whether they are expressed in terms of a "deposit receipt" or of a credit balance on a customer's current account, *are* money so long as people have complete confidence in its ability to meet its obligations in full and on demand; while this confidence exists, the public is willing to accept the transfer of such debts in payment for goods and services, i.e. they possess the one essential characteristic of money.

Summary

The statement contained in the question is therefore true only in the limited sense that *one* bank alone is unable to create money, as any attempt to do so would lead at once to a crippling loss of cash to the other banks. To go on to argue that the banking system as a whole cannot create money is a fallacy of composition, however; in fact, about 90 per cent of the total value of all transactions is settled by means of cheques, so that cash (now mainly in the form of Bank of England notes, which are legal tender) satisfies only a comparatively small proportion of the community's need for money.

SIMILAR QUESTIONS

(i) The Banks, through the creation of credit balances, have the ability to increase spending power. How is this increase brought about and what limits exist to such an increase? (ACCA Section I, June 1967.)

(ii) How can banks create money? How can the central bank limit this process? (C of S Intermediate, May 1969.)

(iii) "The art of banking is to reconcile liquidity with profitability". Discuss. (CIS Intermediate, December 1966.)

(iv) (a) How can banks create credit?

(b) What limits the amount of credit they can create?

(ACCA Section I, December 1969.)

5.6 *How does a central bank control the quantity of money in an economy?* (*U of L Advanced, Summer 1965.*)

Definition of money

In a modern economy, "money" includes any generally acceptable form of purchasing power. While cash, i.e. bank notes and coin, is used to settle the majority of retail transactions, the value of these is far outweighed by payments of other kinds, and these are usually made by cheques which are simply debited to one bank account and credited to another. The quantity of cash in the system is in fact usually about 1/5th or 1/6th of the total amount of bank depositis, so any action by the central bank to control the quantity of money must concentrate mainly on the latter.

"Open market" policy

The major weapon which the central bank uses to control the size of bank deposits is "open market" policy. Relying on the fact that (a) the banks adhere fairly rigidly to an 8 per cent ratio between the cash figure shown in their balance sheets and their total deposit liabilities, and (b) that about half of this so-called "cash" consists in fact of a deposit which each bank holds with the central bank itself, the latter can increase or reduce bank deposits by buying or selling Government securities in the "open market", i.e. the Stock Exchange. When the central bank buys securities, payment is made by cheques drawn on itself in favour of the sellers, who in turn pay them into their banks for collection so that at the subsequent clearing bankers' deposits at the central bank are increased; conversely, when the central bank sells securities, buyers pay by cheques drawn on their respective banks in favour of the central bank, which at the clearing has the effect of reducing bankers' deposits. The increase or decrease in the volume of bank credit resulting from the operation of open market policy is restricted to some 3 or 4 times the initial change in the banks' holding of cash, however, since the greater part of the cash injected into the banking system by a purchase of securities will be drained away by the public's demand for it, whereas the opposite will happen in the case of a sale of securities.

Unfortunately for the authorities, there are certain things which may frustrate their intentions if they rely on open market policy alone to control the quantity of money. Buying securities will undoubtedly increase the banks' cash holdings, and hence their ability to increase deposits, but their willingness to make loans may not be matched by their customers' willingness to borrow, so that deposits do not necessarily increase *pro rata*. On the other hand, the banks can counteract the loss of cash following a sale of securities by drawing down their other liquid assets, namely money at call and bills discounted, provided that in total these three items remain in excess of 28 per cent of deposit liabilities, in which case the latter need not be reduced.

Bank Rate

It is therefore necessary for the central bank to reinforce open market policy in various ways. First, the traditional weapon of Bank Rate may be used; by raising the rate when securities are sold, credit is made more expensive as well as being more difficult to obtain, and vice versa. Speaking in terms of credit restriction, the effectiveness of Bank Rate depends upon the operation of open market policy. When the central bank sells securities, the commercial banks' first reaction to the resultant loss of cash is to call in their short-term loans to bill brokers and discount houses, who in turn are "driven into the Bank" to rediscount part of their holding of bills of exchange at Bank Rate. An increase in Bank Rate without recourse to open market policy would therefore be a pointless gesture — it is only because bill brokers know they will have to pay a higher rate the next time they are driven into the Bank that they raise their own discount rate for bills, thus causing the commercial banks to increase the rate on their "day-to-day" loans, and so on all through the structure of interest rates.

Special deposits

Second, the central bank can overcome the problem of excess liquidity by compelling the commercial banks to make "Special Deposits". This means that, over and above the normal working balances which the banks have with the Bank of England, they must deposit with the Bank a further amount of cash equivalent to up to 3 per cent of their own total deposit liabilities; such deposits must be made by drawing only upon liquid assets, so that the banks' liquidity ratios are reduced to something approaching the bare minimum of 28 per cent. As a result, the banks are unable to frustrate open market policy by relying on money at call and bills to counteract loss of cash in the manner described above.

Directives

Last, the central bank relies to a considerable extent on "directives" to control the activities of the commercial banks. While they do not have the force of law, the banks do in fact pay a great deal of attention to the wishes of the Bank of England as expressed in these directives; moreover, they enable the Bank to influence the direction as well as the amount of credit creation, so that, for example, exporters may get the benefit of any loans that it is possible to make during a period of credit restriction.

SIMILAR QUESTIONS

(i) How and why does the central bank buy and sell government securities? (C of S Intermediate, June 1967.)

(ii) How does the Bank of England influence the total volume of bank deposits? (ICWA Part I, June 1967.)

(iii) How does the Bank of England control the operation of commercial banks in the United Kingdom? (C of S Intermediate, November 1968.)

(iv) Define the "money supply" and consider whether and how it can be controlled. (C of S Final, May 1969.)

(v) How does the Central Bank control the credit policy of the commercial banks? (U of L Advanced, Summer 1970.)

(vi) What methods of control over commercial banks should a central bank have if it wishes to control the quantity of money? (CIS Intermediate, December 1969.)

5.7 *Outline the functions of the Bank of England, commenting on their relative importance. (ICWA Part I, June 1965.)*

The Bank of England was established as an ordinary joint-stock bank in 1694, but it gradually assumed a privileged position in the conduct of the nation's economic affairs, and ceased to compete in the normal commercial banking field after the Bank Charter Act of 1844. It was formally nationalized in 1946, but this made little difference to its functions, which are as follows —

Note issue

It supervises the issue and replacement of bank notes, which are the principal form of legal tender in the UK.

Government's bank

It is the Government's bank, keeping the accounts of the Exchequer and many other Government departments. It receives money (e.g. the proceeds of taxation) and makes payments on their behalf. It manages the National Debt, arranging new bond issues and repaying or converting old ones, keeps the register of bondholders, and makes the regular interest payments due to them. It also makes short-term loans direct to the Government by "Ways and Means" advances.

Bankers' bank

It is the bankers' bank, acting for the commercial banks in much the same capacity as they act for their customers. About half the so-called "cash" in the balance sheets of the commercial banks consists in fact of their credit balances at the Bank of England, on which they can draw at any time in the form of notes or coin. This balance is also used to settle inter-bank indebtedness at the daily "clearing".

Monetary policy

It carries out the domestic monetary policy of the Government, mainly through its "open market" operations, i.e. the purchase and sale of Government securities, and its power to fix Bank Rate, i.e. the rate at which it will agree to rediscount first-class bills of exchange. It also issues "directives" to the commercial banks from time to time, emphasizing the main objectives of current monetary policy, and requesting their co-opera-tion, though in fact it has compulsory powers if it should ever need to use them.

"Lender of last resort"

It acts as the "lender of last resort" to members of the London money market when they are being pressed by the commercial banks for repay-ment of day-to-day loans, either by discounting bills of exchange or advancing money against them.

International functions

It manages the international aspect of the Government's monetary affairs, supervising the operation of Exchange Control and the Exchange Equalization Account. It also maintains close co-operation with central Banks in other countries, and participates in the work of international financial institutions of which the UK is a member, e.g. the International Monetary Fund.

Gold reserve

It is the custodian of the country's reserve of gold and foreign currency.

Commenting on these functions, the *first* is the exclusive responsibility of the Issue Department. Since there is no longer any obligation on the part of the Bank to give gold in exchange for its notes, the size of the note issue is governed solely by the public's demand for cash, and any impending shortage is readily met by obtaining Government permission to increase the "fiduciary issue".

The *second* function involves an immense amount of detailed work, and the sheer volume of maturing debt may embarrass the Bank in its attempts to control monetary policy.

The *third, fourth,* and *fifth* functions overlap and impinge upon one another, and together represent a task of major importance. The volume and price of credit are, of course, key issues in the Government's monetary policy, and the Bank is responsible for giving advice to politicians and Government departments on the formation of this policy as well as for seeing that it is implemented.

The *sixth* function, which incidentally involves the *seventh,* has also become of major importance since the abandonment of the gold standard. Whereas in the 19th century any loss of gold could easily be counteracted by raising bank rate, and the foreign exchange rate could then be allowed to look after itself, the Bank is now deeply involved in the problem of maintaining equilibrium in Britain's balance of payments. Again, it is not merely a matter of carrying out Government instructions, but of initiating and advising on the policies to be adopted.

SIMILAR QUESTIONS

(i) Distinguish between the characteristics of the Bank of England and those of the joint-stock banks. (ICWA Part I, June 1966.)
(ii) What are the chief functions of a "central bank"? What is the nature of its relationship to the banking system as a whole? (CIS Intermediate, June 1967.)
(iii) How does the central bank discharge its functions as the bankers bank? What other responsibilities has it? (C of S Intermediate, June 1968.)
(iv) Using the Bank of England as an illustration, say what are the major functions of a central bank. (ACCA Section I, December 1968.)

5.8   *What is the "Quantity Theory of Money"? Examine the validity of the theory. (CIS Intermediate, June 1966.)*

The elementary theory

The Quantity Theory in its original form merely looked upon money as a commodity, which was assumed to be subject to the law of supply like any other commodity. Hence it postulated that any increase in the supply of money (M) had the direct effect of reducing its unit value, i.e. of bringing about an increase in the general level of prices (P).

While this simple kind of reasoning was, and still is, sufficient to explain broad long-term changes in the price level resulting from a period of marked inflation (e.g. the three-fold increase in post-war as compared with pre-war prices in the United Kingdom), it threw no light on the cause of short term changes, e.g. why P fell in a slump, when M remained the same.

The "Fisher equation"

This led to an elaboration of the theory by Professor Irving Fisher, who pointed out that a unit of money, unlike units of other commodities, was

used over and over again in the circle of exchange, so that the effective
supply of money was a product of the number of units in existence (still
called M) and the number of times they were used to make purchases
in a given period (which he called V, the velocity of circulation). Moreover,
the demand for money also affected its value; if as the result of an increase
in the number of transactions to be performed (T) there was more work
for a given quantity of money to do, this would tend to drive its value up,
i.e. P would fall. All this he summarized in the form of an equation,

$MV = PT$; alternatively, this could be written $P = \dfrac{MV}{T}$.

Analysis of meaning

There is no denying that this covers all the possible elements in the
situation, but in a sense the tidy logic of Professor Fisher's version of the
theory robs it of any value. Once M has been defined in such a way as to
exclude any kind of money which is not available for circulation, then MV
is necessarily the amount of money being *surrendered* for goods; equally
the number of transactions taking place over the same period multiplied
by their average value must denote the amount of money being *received*
for goods. But the "equation" then really amounts to no more than a
statement of the obvious — MV and PT are not merely equal, they are in
fact one and the same thing looked at from opposite points of view,
and the so-called "theory" might be dismissed as nothing more than a
tautology, i.e. it is simply true by definition.

Definition of terms

Even so, it could be argued that, by focussing attention on the essential
factors which determine prices, it should serve as a guide to policymakers
in their endeavours to keep them stable. Unfortunately, this is not the
case: as soon as one tries to arrive at any precise definitions of the terms
used in the equation, they cease to have much practical value —

M. Is this simply cash, i.e. legal tender, or does it include bank money
and other claims to cash of varying degrees of liquidity?

V. This can only be a purely theoretical concept, though some idea of
changes in V might be obtained by observing changes in the amounts
passing through the Bankers' Clearing House.

P. The theory does not explain why the prices of different kinds of
goods change to different extents, e.g. capital goods and consumer goods.
If the argument is restricted to consumer goods, and the value of P is
related to changes in the Index of Retail Prices, then the definition of M
ought to be restricted to money spent on consumer goods.

T. Again, this is a highly theoretical concept which would defy any
attempt at evaluation. Even in theory, is one supposed to include all

the intermediate transactions between producers, or does T only relate to the sale of finished goods?

Other difficulties

Furthermore, expressing the theory in the form of an equation suggests that the relationship between the terms is purely mathematical, e.g. that an increase in M might equally well be offset by an increase in T as by an increase in P. In fact, an increase in T is hardly conceivable without a corresponding increase in V so that these two terms always tend to balance out, and one is left with nothing more in essence than the theory in its original form.

Finally, while in retrospect the theory enables us to explain low prices in a slump by saying that V must have fallen rather than M, it does not help very much if we do not know why this happened, and how to prevent it from happening again.

Summary

While the Quantity Theory is perfectly valid as far as it goes, it amounts in practice to nothing more than a piece of abstract reasoning which arrives at the same conclusion that common sense would lead us to expect, namely that prices are likely to go up if the amount of money increases relative to the amount of goods available for purchase.

SIMILAR QUESTIONS

(i) What do you understand by the supply of, and the demand for, money. (ICWA Part I, June 1966 *and* December 1969.)
(ii) What is the "Quantity Theory of Money"? How, if at all, should it influence the actions of the Bank of England when acting as a central bank? (CIS Intermediate, December 1968.)
(iii) Explain what is meant by the formula MV = PT. What is it meant to show and how satisfactorily does it fulfil its purpose? (I of B Part I, April 1969.)
(iv) If "MV = PT" does a change in M always affect P? (CIS Intermediate, June 1969.)
(v) Discuss the likelihood that a 10% increase in the quantity of money would lead to a 10% increase in prices (AEB Advanced, June 1970.)

5.9 *Why is it that economists fear large changes in the value of money? (Associated Examining Board Advanced, Summer 1968.)*

It is convenient to discuss changes in the value of money in relation to their effects on *individuals* in the community, on *business units*, and on the *national economy* as a whole. For the sake of brevity, such changes

Money and banking

are assumed to be downwards only, i.e. the average level of prices is assumed to be rising, as this has been the general tendency for many years past.

Individuals

Rising prices affect different kinds of individuals in different ways –

(*a*) People with fixed incomes are hard hit, and can usually do nothing about it.

(*b*) Wage and salary earners are somewhat better off, depending on how strongly they are unionized and how much bargaining power unions are in a position to exert. Some may be safeguarded by "cost of living" clauses in their wage agreements.

(*c*) Those deriving their incomes from profits will receive a disproportionate increase in money incomes from the tendency for revenues to rise faster than costs.

(*d*) Creditors will suffer a loss of real income and capital value, whereas debtors will gain.

Economists are concerned not so much with the unfairness of these developments as with their arbitrary and unpredictable nature. At the worst, they could damage public confidence in money altogether, thus undermining the principle of division of labour on which a modern economy operates.

Business units

Changes in the value of money also have an adverse effect on the conduct of business affairs. The increase in profit referred to above is in part illusory, since in the long run all assets must be replaced, but current depreciation allowances are based on historical costs. Consequently, it becomes a matter of judgement as to what proportion of book profit should be set aside to make good the erosion of capital, and directors and shareholders are apt to take different views about this. If directors yield to pressure to distribute profit to the full extent permitted by Company Law, then the company fails to maintain its real capital intact, thus incidentally defeating the object of the law, which takes no account of inflation; if, on the other hand, they succeed in withholding sufficient book profit to maintain or even increase the value of the company's real capital, the paradoxical result may well be to depress the market valuation of its shares, thus opening the way for a take-over bid and imperilling their own positions.

The Commissioners for Inland Revenue are similarly unable to distinguish between genuine profit and windfall gains due to inflation, so that the effect of levying Corporation Tax on profit calculated by the conventional bookkeeping methods is to increase the difficulty of maintaining the real value of capital intact.

A prolonged period of inflation will also complicate and distort the pattern of finance for business enterprise. Since the value of debentures and the interest on them suffers a constant fall in real terms, investors will demand more and more "equity" capital, to a point where the terms attaching to the issue of debentures will have to be extremely generous, or be coupled with the option to convert into shares at a later date. The anomalous situation is thus created whereby the yield on what is normally regarded as the riskier kind of investment is lower than that on the "safe" one.

The national economy

A substantial rise in the price level will have the two-fold effect of reducing the volume of exports and increasing the volume of imports. In the case of exports, demand is normally elastic, so that the reduction in volume will be more than enough to offset the rise in unit price, thus leading to a reduction in foreign currency earnings; as regards imports, an increase in volume at constant prices will necessitate an increase in the amount of foreign currency required to pay for them. The inevitable outcome is therefore a deterioration in the country's balance of payments on current account, and if nothing is done to restore prices to their former level relative to the rest of the world, serious consequences of one kind or another are bound to follow.

In the short run, the country's reserves of gold and foreign currency might be allowed to run down, but there is an obvious limit to which such a policy, or lack of it, might be allowed to go. Attempts might also be made to attract money on capital account by raising interest rates, or to restrict the export of capital by imposing some kind of control over it, but such tactics would only re-inforce doubts about the ability of the country to pay its way, and would moreover tend to make the current account balance worse. The ultimate result would therefore be devaluation of the currency so as to bring its external value once more into line with its internal value, but even this could not be relied upon to restore equilibrium in the balance of payments; not only would there be the risk of other countries devaluing in their turn, but the increased cost of imports might well initiate another major rise in the price level, thus starting the whole cycle over again.

6
Macro-economics

This part of economic theory is of great and growing importance, as reflected by the increasing number of questions being asked on it even at intermediate level. Whereas the "classical" economists of the 19th century were mainly concerned with "micro-economics", i.e. the responses of *individual* consumers and producers to particular changes in the supply/ demand situation, and applied marginal analysis to the solution of all problems, economists of the post-Keynesian era have tended to concentrate their attention on *aggregate* quantities, and to construct theories about the cause-and-effect relationships between them.

The first essential is to understand the concept of "circular flow" as applied to the measurement of the national income, the national expenditure and the national product, and to see how the size of this flow is increased by "injections" and diminished by "withdrawals". In particular, the relationship between the major injection and the major withdrawal, namely investment and savings respectively, and how equality between the two is brought about by changes in the size of the national income, must be understood. This implies a grasp of the savings/consumption functions and the multiplier on the one hand, and the forces, namely the quantity of money, liquidity preference and the marginal efficiency of capital, determining the level of investment on the other. With this as a background, it is possible to appreciate why and how the Government intervenes in the working of the system in order to achieve certain economic aims, e.g. full employment, and how monetary and fiscal policies may be used to complement one another, although this encroaches into the field of Section 7.

While questions relating to the measurement of the national income should not give too much trouble the inherent level of difficulty in the remainder of this section is higher than that in, say, the elementary theory of value, and the average student will find that he needs to concentrate very closely indeed on the analysis and terminology involved in order to produce worthwhile answers.

114

6.1 *Discuss the difficulties of defining and measuring the real national income of a country.* (*CIS Final, June 1965.*)

Allowance for changes in the price level

The measurement of a country's national income is necessary in order to provide the planning authorities with information about how much wealth is being produced annually, and in what forms and from what sources, so that steps can be taken to improve the country's economic performance from year to year. Since the only way to compare and add the values of unlike things is to use money as a common measure, statements about the national income are bound to be expressed in money terms, so that changes in the general level of prices must be allowed for when attempting to compare the real national income of one year with another; currently, the practice is to adjust all prices to the level of those of 1963 for comparative purposes.

The circular flow of money

The task of measuring the national income is approached by government statisticians in three ways; not only do these different ways act as a check on one another, but the different constituents of each total give valuable guidance in formulating economic policy. The method as indicated in the diagram below, is to measure the circular flow of money three times as it changes hands from "firms" to "households" and back again by reference to —

(*a*) The total factor cost of the goods and services produced by firms, i.e. the "National Output";

(*b*) The money received by factors of production for their part in generating the National Output, i.e. the "National Income" and

(*c*) The money spent by consumers and entrepreneurs on purchasing the goods and services produced by firms, i.e. "National Expenditure".

Taking these aspects in turn, the procedure is —

(*a*) *The National Output.* The value of goods and services produced by all the various industries in the country, e.g. agriculture, manufacturing, services, etc., is arrived at, mainly by reference to the Census of Production. Care is taken to avoid "double counting", i.e. the inclusion of the total value of firm A's product plus the value of firm B's product, where A buys its materials from B. Changes in the value of stocks are taken into account after allowing for "stock appreciation" due to rising prices, e.g. an increase in the quantity of finished steel would augment the total, but not a rise in its price per ton. (N.B. "Firms" refers to productive units of all kinds, including those owned by Central and Local Government).

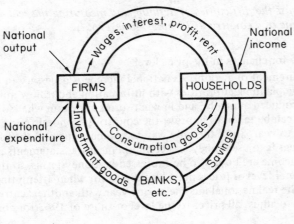

National output

National income

Wages, interest, profit, rent

FIRMS

HOUSEHOLDS

National expenditure

Investment goods

Consumption goods

Savings

BANKS, etc.

Fig. 31

(*b*) *The National Income.* The starting point for this method is the total amount of rent, wages, interest and profit accruing to "households", i.e. members of the public, as evidenced by their returns to the Department of Inland Revenue. The total figure thus obtained is subject to a number of corrections, however, namely —

(i) it is necessary to *add* the undistributed profits of companies in the private sector, plus the surpluses earned by nationalized industries and other publicly-owned undertakings, plus estimates of the market value of agricultural products consumed by the farmers who grow them and the annual rentable value of owner-occupied houses.

(ii) It is necessary to *subtract* various kinds of "transfer incomes", i.e. those like pensions, interest on the national debt, etc., which do not reflect any contribution to the value of the national output, also stock appreciation as above.

(*c*) *National Expenditure.* This third method begins by aggregating the expenditure of consumers and public authorities on consumption goods, expenditure of all kinds on fixed investment and the value of the physical increase in stocks, giving total domestic expenditure at market prices. It is then necessary to allow for the fact that —

(i) some prices are artificially raised by *indirect taxes* while others are reduced by *subsidies,* therefore in order to arrive at factor prices the former must be subtracted from the total and the latter added;

(ii) Some of the money spent by households is used to purchase *imported goods,* while some of the money received by firms is from the sale of *exported goods.* Therefore in order to arrive at the value of the domestic product, the former must be subtracted from the total and the latter added.

Net National Product

Theoretically, the answers obtained by these three methods should be the same, but where there are discrepancies which cannot be reconciled the National Expenditure figure is usually adopted. Even so, the result is only a measure of the *Gross Domestic Product;* if the *Net National Product* is required (which would give a better indication of the real national income) the following further corrections are necessary —

(i) Income received from property owned abroad must be added, and income paid to foreign owners of property in this country must be subtracted, thus giving the *Gross National Product.*

(ii) A deduction must be made to allow for depreciation of the country's fixed assets during the course of the year. Such an allowance is difficult to estimate, and is at best arbitrary, which is why the Gross National Product figure is more commonly quoted than the *Net National Product.*

Conceptual difficulties

The somewhat involved procedure which has now been described gives the statistical measure of a country's real national income, but it leaves at least one important conceptual difficulty unresolved, namely the existence of "cost" elements in income. For example, the money paid to traffic wardens helps to swell the national income in just the same way as the value of the motor cars we produce, but if it were not for the latter we should not need the former. Similarly, if an increase in output is achieved by working longer hours, there is obviously some loss to be set against the gain, but this is not revealed by the statistics.

As matters stand, however, Gross National Product per head is the best way of assessing a country's real national income until some refinement in technique can be devised to measure welfare rather than wealth.

SIMILAR QUESTIONS

(i) What do you understand by the "Gross National Product"? What problems are encountered in attempting to measure the Gross National Product of a country? (CIS Intermediate, June 1968.)

(ii) Explain the three ways of measuring the Gross National Product. What difficulties are produced in this measurement by indirect taxes and subsidies? (C of S Intermediate, May 1969.)

(iii) What is meant by real national income? How is it measured? (U of L Advanced, Summer 1969.)

(iv) How and why do economists measure the real national product of a country? (AEB Advanced, June 1970.)

6.2　*Define the Gross National Product. What difficulties arise in using GNP per head to compare international standards of living? (C of S Intermediate, November 1967.)*

The Gross National Product of a country is the annual income from the production of goods and services accruing to its citizens, without allowing for any depreciation in the value of its fixed assets, and when expressed as GNP per head provides the most convenient and widely-accepted measure of the living standard of its population. There are, nevertheless, a number of reasons why a simple comparison of different countries' GNP's per head may create a misleading impression as to their respective standards of living; these are as follows —

Exchange rates

Any comparison involves converting one country's currency into another's, or perhaps both into a third currency, e.g. US dollars, but exchange rates are subject to various controls, and are bound to be somewhat arbitrary. For example, on a particular day in November, 1967. Britains' GNP would have been converted into dollars at the rate of $2.80 to the £, whereas the following day the rate would have been $2.40; obviously both answers could not have been right. Indeed, controls over the foreign exchange rate of currencies of the so-called "iron curtain" countries are so complete as to make any comparisons of this kind quite unrealistic.

Nature of goods produced

The kinds of goods and services produced in different countries can vary a great deal one from another. In large part this is the outcome of their different geographical environments — people's requirements and production capabilities will both differ widely as between, for example, a country in the equatorial region and one in the temperate zone. Traditions and social customs are also responsible to some extent for the assortment of goods produced, but whatever may be the reasons for differences in the composition of different countries' outputs one is in effect attempting the impossible task of comparing unlike things.

Defence

The rewards to factors of production engaged in the manufacture of armaments, the pay of the armed forces and the cost of maintaining military installations all help to increase the total GNP, but there is no corresponding contribution to raising the standard of living. It follows, therefore, that the GNP per head of a country which devotes a high proportion of its resources to military purposes gives an over-optimistic impression of its standard of living.

Capital formation

Exactly the same argument applies in any given year to a country which is keeping its output of consumer goods down so as to release resources for the creation of new capital. In this case there is, of course, the future rise in the volume of production to compensate for the present sacrifice of consumption, but in the short run the GNP per head overestimates the standard of living.

Distribution of the National Income

If one is trying to get an idea of the standard of living of the typical inhabitant of a country, i.e. what statisticians would call the "mode", the arithmetical average income per head can give quite a misleading impression of conditions in countries where the total national income is very unequally distributed.

Products not marketed

The statistics tend to flatter advanced countries with highly developed exchange economies, as with certain exceptions they only measure the value of incomes earned by selling goods and services through the market. It is true that for example, some estimate is made of the value of major items like food consumed by the farmers who produce it and the satisfaction enjoyed by people occupying their own houses, but there can be little doubt that the real national income per head in underdeveloped countries is understated by their GNP figures.

Overcoming disutility

A simple addition of the amounts paid to factors as a reward for services rendered conceals the fact that many are employed solely to counteract various kinds of disutility rather than to create utility. Some kinds of disutility are an inevitable consequence of environmental conditions (e.g. countries which experience a severe winter must devote resources to keeping streets clear and houses warm), while others are of man's own creation (e.g. the urban congestion which makes people decide to live a long way from their work, thus creating additional demands for travelling facilities), but in a country were such adverse conditions exist the GNP tends to overstate the standard of living as compared with other countries where they do not.

SIMILAR QUESTIONS

(i) Why do some countries have a large, and other countries have a small, national income per head of their population? (CIS Intermediate, December 1960.)

(ii) The gross domestic product in 1965 in the less-developed countries of the world averaged $133 a head, but in the advanced countries $1,300 a head. Suggest explanations of the difference in these figures. (CIS Final, June 1967.)

6.3   *What are the main factors which determine the national income of a country? (ICWA Part I, June 1965.)*

The main determinants of the size of national income are as follows —

Natural resources

Fertile land, an abundance of easily-worked mineral resources, a temperate climate, and so on are the kind of things which first suggest themselves as having a beneficial influence on a country's productive capacity, and hence on the size of its national income. While countries thus favoured by nature were the first to make economic progress, the part played by the "land" factor in the creation of values diminishes as man's mastery over nature increases, so that today it is possible for a country to have minimal natural resources and yet to enjoy a high standard of living.

Population density

At one time great stress was laid, especially by Malthus, on the harmful consequences of unrestricted population growth, and it is indeed possible to argue that much of the poverty in countries like India can be traced to their high population density. Again, however, there are now many countries with more people relative to their size than India which nevertheless have high incomes per head, so evidently it is not purely a question of numbers. In fact, the main influences on a country's national income per head as far as population is concerned are the age structure, i.e. what proportion of the whole consists of non-producers, and whether the people are well educated and in a good state.of health; it is in these respects that countries like India show up so badly.

Type of economy

There are enormous potential gains in output to be secured from a high degree of specialization which can only be realized if a country has a well-developed "exchange economy". This presupposes an efficient monetary system, adequate facilities for transport, banking, warehousing, finance and insurance, a good system of communications, and so on. Production in countries which lack these essential aids to marketing is necessarily confined to the small-scale manufacture of goods for local needs made from local materials, and can never benefit from the economies of mass production..

Capital and technology

This brings us to the major influence on a country's national income. As the pace of industrial progress quickens, so the countries which can maintain ample supplies of up-to-date capital equipment will keep to the fore. In technologically advanced industries every worker is backed by thousands of pounds' worth of plant, and productivity per man is such that the employer can well afford to pay high wages. The countries which have such industries may well have to import their raw materials, and export a fairly high proportion of their output to pay for them, but this is no real disadvantage provided international trade remains reasonably free. The significance of this factor is such that there is a high degree of correlation between living standards and installed horse-power per worker.

Position

A favourable geographical position in relation to the world's major trading powers is of some importance. Holland undoubtedly benefits from her nodal position in Europe, whereas New Zealand suffers by being so remote from the major economic powers.

Terms of trade

While trade freely entered into must necessarily benefit all countries who engage in it, the degree of benefit enjoyed by any particular country will vary according to changes in the price levels at which it sells its exports and buys its imports. Provided no balance of payments difficulties are experienced, favourable terms of trade will increase a country's national income.

Foreign investment

Of two countries having equal gross domestic products, the one with the more favourable net return from international investment will have the higher national income.

SIMILAR QUESTIONS

(i) Is an increasing national income the best measure of increasing prosperity? (C of S Intermediate, June 1966.)
(ii) What are the limitations to using the National Income as an indicator of economic progress? (C of S Intermediate, November 1968.)
(iii) What is the National Income, and on what factors does its size depend? (ICWA Part I, June 1967.)
(iv) What determines the extent of the differences between the standards of living in two countries? (U of L Advanced, Summer 1970.)

6.4   *How would you define the level of unemployment in a country? What factors cause unemployment? (U of L Advanced, January 1966.)*

Definition

The level of unemployment can either be defined in *absolute* terms, i.e. by simply stating the total number of unemployed, or in *relative* terms, i.e. by expressing this figure as a percentage of the total number of employees insurable in the National Insurance Scheme. The "number unemployed" is defined as the number of people registering week by week at Employment Exchanges as available for and willing to work; the "employees" consists of all people over the age of 15 in paid civilian employment, plus the unemployed as above, part-time workers each counting as one unit.

Structural unemployment

One inevitable cause of unemployment is the ever-changing structure of the economy. As new techniques replace old ones, some firms expand and others contract, one region prospers and another declines, so there will be a never-ending stream of men and women being thrown on to the labour market, and seeking re-absorption elsewhere. How much unemployment results from structural changes depends primarily upon the scale and rate at which they occur; though it would be undesirable to create artificial restraints on changes in the pattern of production, much can be done to reduce the incidence of structural unemployment by measures designed to improve mobility of labour, e.g. industrial retraining schemes.

Transitional unemployment

A certain amount of unemployment of a more transitional nature is also bound to occur because of the ebb and flow of demand and supply in the labour market over relatively short periods of time. There may be a regular season of peak demand for labour, as in the holiday trade, or a sudden influx of workers, as when large numbers of young people leave school at the end of the summer term, or perhaps there are random fluctuations in the amount of work available as in the loading and unloading of ships. While it is in the interests of both employers and workers to "dovetail" jobs wherever possible, a high proportion of unemployment over a twelve-months period can be ascribed to transitional factors, as witness the normal difference of about 150,000 between winter and summer levels.

Deficiency of demand

The combined effort of structural and transitional unemployment can be far exceeded by that which arises through deficiency of effective demand, however. The classical economists used to think that any general and permanent tendency for the number of unemployed to exceed the number of jobs on offer was impossible, as it would correct itself by a fall in wages. Having seen the fallacy of this reasoning demonstrated to the full during the long-drawn out slump of the early 1930's, Keynes argued that there could be persistent unemployment at almost any level if too little investment was being undertaken in relation to money savings. The effect of this would be to reduce the size of the national income, and hence the demand for goods, to a level where there were simply no jobs available for some proportion of the labour force. Now that the solution to this problem is known, the possibility of widespread mass unemployment seems to have receded somewhat; indeed, the cures for it are normally so easy, and moreover so popular with the majority of the electorate (e.g. reducing taxation), that the danger is mainly one of creating "overfull employment", with all the difficulties which such a state of affairs brings in its train.

SIMILAR QUESTION

(i) What are the various types of unemployment? Briefly explain the cause of each type and give examples to illustrate your answer. (ACCA Section I, December 1969.)

6.5 *If savings must always equal investment, how can we talk of an excess or deficiency of savings in relation to investment? (CIS Intermediate, December 1968.)*

Definitions

Logically, if investment and savings must indeed always be equal, one can only speak of an excess or deficiency of savings in relation to investment if one of the words is being used in two different senses. It is therefore necessary to define first of all what the two terms mean.

(*a*) *Investment.* Having discarded the popular meaning associated with this word, which denotes the purchase of income-bearing securities on the Stock Exchange, one is left with the economist's concept of investment, i.e. the decision to commit productive resources to capital formation, which is fairly unambiguous. It is possible to argue about the precise distinction between capital goods and durable consumer goods, but what the economist has principally in mind when he speaks of investment, and what is relevant for the purpose of this question, is the diversion of factors of production currently available into projects which are not an end in themselves, but which are designed to increase the output of consumer goods and services in the future.

(*b*) *Savings.* It is in the meaning attaching to the term "savings" that the ambiguity referred to above arises. In one sense, it is possible to define savings simply as "not spending", i.e. it is that part of individuals' money incomes which might have been used to purchase consumption goods, but which for one reason or another they decided to keep in money form for the time being. From the point of view of the community as a whole, however, saving can only be said to have taken place if, over a given period, there has been a net increase in the real value of its assets; as such an increase can only come about at a result of refraining from consuming some part of what has been produced, saving in this sense is the same thing as investment, and is necessarily equal to it.

Decisions to Invest and to Save

In a free enterprise system, there is no reason whatever to suppose that investment and money savings will coincide in any way, since for the most part the two sets of decisions involved are taken at different times by different people who are actuated by different motives. In the final analysis however, investment and real savings must be equal, as stated above; what the question really amounts to is, therefore, how are money savings brought into line with real savings?

The key to the answer lies in the nature of what Keynes called the "savings function". With a given distribution of the national income, the main determinant of the community's aggregate money savings is the size of the community's aggregate money income; as money income rises, there is a progressive increase in the propensity to save, as shown in Fig. 32.

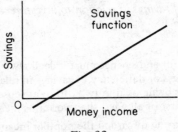

Fig. 32

On the other hand, Keynes postulated that the main determinants of investment were the rate of interest and the marginal efficiency of capital, i.e. that investment decisions were *not* governed by the size of the community's money income. Linking this assumption with the savings function, as shown in Fig. 33, it follows that there can only be one level of community income, OE_1, which will equate the level of investment and money savings.

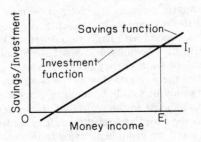

Fig. 33

Maintenance of equality between I and S

Now the effect of a tendency for investment and savings (i.e. money savings) to diverge can be examined. Since the savings function is fairly stable, it is mainly changes in investment plans which upset the state of equilibrium, in which case the two possibilities are —

(*a*) *Planned investment greater than planned savings.* In this eventuality, the increased investment will generate higher incomes, first in the capital goods industries and subsequently in the rest, to a level OE_2 where savings are *pulled up* into equality with investment, as in Fig. 34.

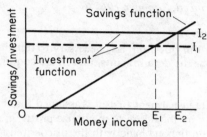

Fig. 34

(*b*) *Planned investment less than planned savings.* Now, conversely, reduced investment leads to a reduction in incomes to a level OE_3, where savings are *pulled down* into equality with investment, as in Fig. 35.

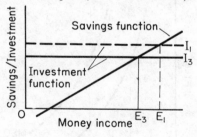

Fig. 35

In other words, while *plans* to invest and *plans* to save have an inherent tendency to diverge, because they have different origins, *realized* investment and *realized* savings are forced into equality by changes in the size of the national income.

SIMILAR QUESTIONS

(i) "Saving always equals investment. It is because saving gets out of line with investment that variations in the level of national income occur." Discuss. (CIS Intermediate, December 1964.)

(ii) Distinguish between "actual" and "planned" saving and investment. Explain the importance of this distinction in the study of macro-economics. (I of B Part I, April 1969.)

(iii) Explain and comment on the statement that Savings are always equal to investment in a given period. (ACCA Section I, June 1970.)

(iv) Does Investment always equal savings? (U of L Advanced, Summer 1970.)

6.6 *Describe and discuss the main determinants of the level of investment. (U of L Advanced, Summer 1967.)*

Kinds of investment

In order to answer this question, it is necessary to dinstinguish private from public investment as the determinants of each are completely different.

Private investment

Dealing with private investment first, it is assumed that businessmen will be motivated solely by the desire to maximize profit, in which case they will be concerned on the one hand with the discounted return to be expected from any given act of investment, and on the other with the cost of raising the capital necessary to finance it. Of these two, the anticipated return is both the more significant and the more difficult to

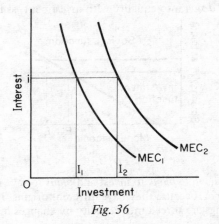

Fig. 36

estimate; in theory, it should be possible to apply the Law of Diminishing Returns to the problem, in that a marginal addition to the existing stock of investment goods in a given state of business activity should lead to a corresponding reduction in the return obtainable, but it would be extremely difficult to collect all the relevant data for such a calculation.

Moreover, the state of business activity is always changing, or expected to change, and businessmen are apt to base their decisions on broad generalizations made almost intuitively from observing the pattern of past and present events, so that the degree of error is likely to be fairly high. Nevertheless, it is possible to speak of the "marginal efficiency of capital" as denoting the collective demand on the part of businessmen for investment goods, the "price" being the current rate of interest on borrowed money, and to show the relationships involved by means of a diagram (Fig. 36).

With a given rate of interest, Oi, an increase in entrepreneurs' expectations of revenue will shift the marginal efficiency of capital from MEC_1 to MEC_2, and the level of investment from OI_1 to OI_2. It is clear, however, that a fall in the rate of interest would have a similar effect, and this could be brought about either by a Government decision to increase the quantity of money, or by a fall in liquidity preference. The main determinants of private investment can therefore be displayed in a combined diagram, where OM equals the quantity of money, LP denotes liquidity preference, and MEC the marginal efficiency of capital; a change in any one of these would change OI, the level of private investment.

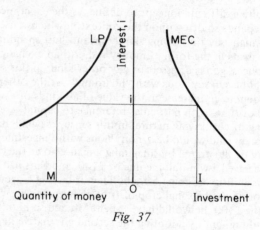

Fig. 37

Public investment

The Government is under no such constraints in making its investment decisions, however. Its overriding concern is the public interest, and this might well be served by deciding to ignore commercial considerations altogether; indeed, the tendency now is for Government to undertake investment projects, either directly or through the nationalized industries, at such times and in such quantity as to offset variations in the level of private investment. Failure to do this to any significant extent resulted in an unnecessary prolongation of the slump in the 1930's, but acceptance by all political parties of the 1944 White Paper on full employment implies that the Government's capital expenditure will always be adjusted so as to maintain total investment at a steady level.

SIMILAR QUESTIONS

(i) What do economists mean by "investment"? What considerations determine the level of investment in a country? (CIS Intermediate, December 1965.)

(ii) Outline the major factors which determine the demand for funds available for investment. How far is this demand influenced by the rate of interest? (I of B September 1967.)

6.7   *What do economists mean by "saving"? What are the chief determinants of the volume of saving in an economy? (CIS Intermediate, December 1966.)*

Nature of saving

"Saving" is quite a difficult concept to define, as the exact meaning of the word depends so often upon the context in which it used. At one extreme, one might say that saving simply meant "not spending", i.e. accumulating assets in the form of money rather than exchanging money for services, goods or assets of any other kind; in this sense, "saving" would be synonymous with "hoarding". At the other extreme, saving would denote an increase in the value of all kinds of assets over a given period of time, with particular reference to capital assets of a revenue-earning or cost-saving nature; in this sense, "saving" has nothing to do with money, and would be synonymous with "investment". The difference may be illustrated by imagining a man who at the beginning of the summer received a windfall income of £100, and thus had the alternative possibilities of going for a holiday or buying a deep-freeze cabinet for storing the seasonal crop of fruit and vegetables; whichever way he used the £100, he would have "spent" it, and so in one sense would have saved nothing, but by adopting the second alternative he would still possess £100 more wealth in the autumn than he had in the spring, and could moreover anticipate a reduction in his cost of living for many years to come.

The desire to save

Whether or not people save depends partly on their desire to make provision for the future and partly on their ability to do so. Most people's desire to save arises from the need to feel *secure* rather than the promise of reward in the shape of interest — indeed, the fact that money earning only 2½ per cent continues to be held in the Post Office savings accounts when prices are rising by more than 2½ per cent per annum must mean that some are content with a negative rate of interest. It is possible for the public's underlying attitude towards personal thrift to change markedly over the years, however; there can be little doubt, for example, that Victorian ideas about the virtues of saving no longer hold good today, perhaps because of the provisions which the State now makes to safeguard people in adversity and old age. Moreover, there is a growing realization that the value of savings held in money form is being seriously eroded by rising prices, and this has had the effect of causing people to turn their money into various kinds of physical assets, e.g. precious stones, purely as a "hedge" against inflation.

The desire to save is also influenced in quite a fundamental way by the degree of *confidence* which prevails about the individual's rights over property. Obviously, there is not much incentive to save in a society where the State is unable to guarantee the safety of private property, or indeed where the State itself may decide to confiscate it.

One further influence on the desire to save is *propaganda*. On the one hand we have the government which is constantly exhorting us to put our money into Savings Certificates or the like, while on the other the combined efforts of the advertisers are persuading us to spend it on their products. Perhaps if it were not for the latter, the government would not have to re-inforce its pleas for voluntary saving by such a high level of taxation.

The ability to save

Turning now to the ability to save, the oustanding factor is the *level of income*. Very poor people are obliged to live from hand to mouth and so can save nothing, but the very rich accumulate wealth more or less automatically. In between these two extremes, the proportion of income saved rises as the income itself rises, so for the population as a whole a more equal distribution of a given national income will result in less saving being done. In this connection, the terms "poverty" and "wealth" are to a large extent relative and subjective; once an individual has become accustomed to a certain standard of living at any level he cannot easily make adjustments either upwards or downwards, and it is therefore the short-run effects of changes in income which are of most significance in determining the amount of saving done.

The only other factor influencing the ability to save is of marginal importance, namely the kind and number of *methods which exist* for making deposits. To have a variety of institutions like banks, building societies, post offices and so on obviously makes saving easier, but these facilities only develop to the extent that there is a demand for them.

SIMILAR QUESTION

(i) Define saving, and say why people save. (ICWA Part I, May 1968.)

6.8   *Analyse the effects on the price level and aggregate employment of an increase in households' propensity to consume. Distinguish in your answer between conditions of full employment and unemployment. (U of L Advanced, Summer 1964.)*

Definition of propensity to consume

In the short run, there is a fairly stable connection between the size of households' incomes and the amount they spend on consumption, and Keynes coined the expression "propensity to consume" to denote the functional relationship which exists between the two. In algebraic terms, if we call consumption "C" and incomes "Y", then $C = f(Y)$, and it is "f" which indicates the propensity to consume.

Income, saving, and spending

The proportion of income spent is not constant, however; at very low levels of income people will endeavour to maintain their living standards by drawing on past savings, so that spending on consumption will actually exceed income, but as income rises so the proportion saved out of every additional £1 increases and the proportion spent decreases. The relationship between the size of the national income, the amount saved and the amount spent (consumption) can be illustrated as follows*—

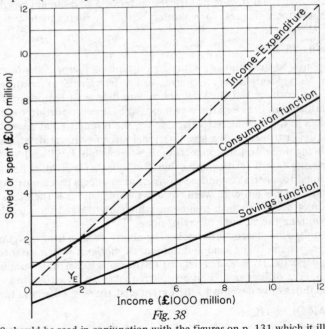

Fig. 38

*Fig. 38 should be read in conjunction with the figures on p. 131 which it illustrates.

| Income | £000,000 | | Income | £000,000 | |
	Saved	Spent		Saved	Spent
0	−800	800	7,000	2,000	5,000
1,000	−400	1,400	8,000	2,400	5,600
2,000	0	2,000	9,000	2,800	6,200
3,000	400	2,600	10,000	3,200	6,800
4,000	800	3,200	11,000	3,600	7,400
5,000	1,200	3,800	12,000	4,000	8,000
6,000	1,600	4,400			

Equilibrium level of National Income (1)

Since all incomes received by households, i.e. wages, rent, interest and profit, are derived from expenditure, it follows that national income and national expenditure must be equal; if the latter consisted solely of households' expenditure on consumption, national income (Y_e) in this example would therefore be limited to £2,000 m. (N.B. This corresponds with the point at which a line drawn at 45° from the origin of the diagram cuts the consumption function.) In fact, however, the "withdrawal" of savings from the circular flow of incomes is offset to a greater or lesser extent by the "injection" of expenditure on investment, which for our present purpose will be assumed to be determined by factors other than the size of the national income. We can now redraw the diagram, omitting the savings function but adding, say, £2,000 m. of investment expenditure, which will have the effect of raising the level of the national income to £7,000 m., thus —

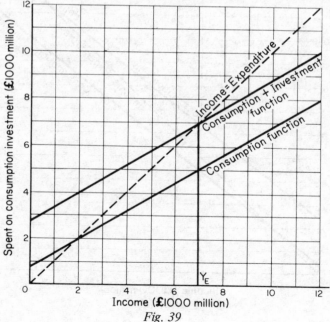

Fig. 39

Equilibrium level of National income (2)

We can now begin to trace the effect of a change in the propensity to consume on the size of the national income, and hence on employment and prices. Reverting to Fig. 38, the slopes of the savings and consumption functions will be seen to depend upon the propensity to consume; if we assume, for example, that only £200 m. out of every additional £1,000 m. of income is saved instead of £400 m., denoting an increase in the propensity to consume as postulated in the question, the savings and consumption schedules change to the following —

£000,000			£000,000		
Income	Saved	Spent	Income	Saved	Spent
0	−400	400	7,000	1,000	6,000
1,000	−200	1,200	8,000	1,200	6,800
2,000	0	2,000	9,000	1,400	7,600
3,000	200	2,800	10,000	1,600	8,400
4,000	400	3,600	11,000	1,800	9,200
5,000	600	4,400	12,000	2,000	10,000
6,000	800	5,200	13,000	2,200	10,800

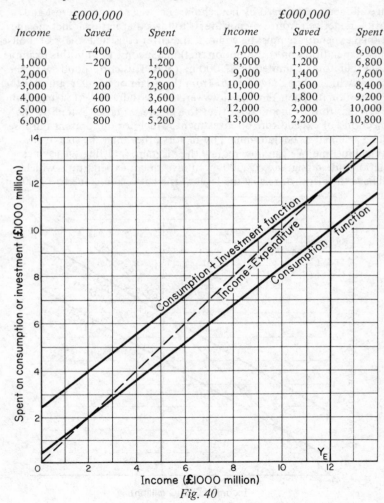

Fig. 40

Adding £2,000 m. of investment expenditure to consumption expenditure as before, a new equilibrium level of £12,000 m. is established for the national income, as shown in Fig. 40.

Under and overfull employment

An increase in national income from £7,000 m. to £12,000 m. would, of course, give rise to an increase in demand for most kinds of goods, but if we assume that an income of, say, £10,000 m. would be sufficient to produce full employment then the effects on employment and prices would be as follows —

(*a*) From £7,000 m. to £10,000 m. there would be a roughly proportional increase in the number employed at first, with little or no increase in the general level of prices. How great the increase in employment was in particular industries would depend on which goods were most affected by the increase in demand, and on their respective labour contents, but as the general level of full employment was approached the additional numbers pulled into employment of all kinds would get less.

(*b*) From £10,000 m. to £12,000 m. the effect would be mainly to raise the general level of prices, as industries would be working at or somewhere near full capacity. The increased money demand would therefore result not so much in increased output as in employers bidding against one another for scarce labour, all relying on the fact that their increased costs could be covered by charging higher prices. In short, once the point of full employment had been reached, further increases in money national income would merely generate inflationary pressure, with the emphasis shifting more and more from a rise in employment to a rise in prices.

SIMILAR QUESTIONS

(i) What are the likely consequences for an economy if a substantial proportion of its inhabitants decide to save larger fractions of their incomes? (CIS Intermediate, June 1965.)

(ii) What would be the effects in an economy if a large percentage of the population decide to save a greater proportion of their income? (ACCA Section I, December 1967.)

6.9 *What do you understand by the "multiplier"? What factors influence the size of the multiplier in a country? (CIS Intermediate, June 1966.)*

Definition

The use of the term "multiplier" dates from the early 1930's, when it was first used by Kahn to indicate the increase in employment which would result from a given increase in investment. The idea of a "multiplier effect" was later incorporated by Keynes into his "General Theory of Employment,

Interest & Money" to denote the increase in the national income which would result, directly or indirectly, from a given increase in investment. In the circumstances prevailing at the time, there was not much point in distinguishing between the two, but now it is necessary to mention that as the state of full employment is approached and passed so the size of the employment multiplier falls, tending towards zero.

Marginal propensity to consume

Speaking, then, in terms of the effect of increased investment on the national income, and assuming for the moment that there is no international trade, the size of the multiplier depends upon what proportion of an increase in their incomes people will decide to spend (called the "propensity to consume") and what proportion will be saved (the "propensity to save"). Since all income is either spent or saved, it follows that the total of these two must always equal one, e.g. if the propensity to consume is ¾, then the propensity to save will be ¼, and so on; in practice, it is found that these proportions change as income changes, so that in considering the effect of any change in the investment on the level of national income one is always concerned with the *marginal* propensity to consume (MPC), which falls as income increases, and the *marginal* propensity to save (MPS), which rises as income increases.

The "multiplier effect"

We can now trace the effect of a given "injection" of investment, e.g. by government expenditure on public works, on the size of the national income, (see also Fig. 39, p. 131). If we assume that £1 m. is spent on building a new road, this money will emerge as wages in the pockets of the contractor's employees, dividends and interest to those who have supplied the firm with capital, payments to sub-contractors and so on — in short, £1 m. of new incomes will have been created. Now, if the MPC is ¾ and the MPS is ¼, £750,000 of this will be spent and £250,000 will be saved, and the former will re-appear as incomes in the hands of shopkeepers, wholesalers, etc., right back through the chain of supply involved in producing the goods which the £750,000 is used to buy. Applying a MPC of ¾ once more to this income, £562,500 will be spent, and so on through an endless number of "rounds" until finally £4 m. of spending power has been created. This figure is arrived at by applying the formula for the sum of a geometrical progression, namely $A \times \dfrac{1}{1-r}$, where A is the initial term in the series (£1 m.) and r is the ratio between each term and the one before it (¾), i.e.

$$£1 \text{ m.} \times \frac{1}{1-¾} = £1 \text{ m.} \times \frac{1}{¼} = £1 \text{ m.} \times 4 = £4 \text{ m.}$$

The multiplier in this example is therefore 4, a conclusion which can be arrived at even more simply by turning the MPS fraction upside down, i.e. the multiplier is always the reciprocal of the MPS.

Marginal propensity to import

If we now drop the assumption that there is no international trade, the size of the multiplier will decrease, as not only will ¼ of any increase in income be lost to the circular flow by reason of savings, but some part of the money spent will be used to buy imported goods, thus producing incomes only for factors of production abroad. If we assume a marginal propensity to import of $1/6$, this therefore creates another "leak" in the circular flow of incomes precisely analogous to savings, and the multiplier becomes

$$\frac{1}{1/4 + 1/6} = \frac{1}{5/12} = {}^{12}/_5 = 2{}^2/_5$$

Marginal rate of taxation

Taxation will constitute a similar "leakage" by forcibly raising the MPS, and if we assume a rate of taxation on marginal income of $1/3$ the multiplier is further reduced to

$$\frac{1}{1/4 + 1/6 + 1/3} = \frac{1}{9/12} = {}^{12}/_9 = 1{}^1/_3$$

While the effect of these "leakages" (i.e. savings, imports and taxation) on the circular flow of income will be offset by the effect of corresponding "injections" into it (namely investment, exports and government expenditure respectively), the former are all governed by the size of the national income, whereas the latter are presumed to be independent of it. Only the "leakages" will therefore affect the *slope* of the combined "consumption + investment" function, and hence the size of the multiplier (see also Fig. 40, p. 132); changes in the volume of "injections" will be manifested by a shift in the whole function upwards or downwards, its slope remaining the same.

SIMILAR QUESTIONS

(i) Define the multiplier. How is it related to the marginal propensity to consume? (U of L Advanced, Summer 1969.)
(ii) What is the multiplier and how is it affected by imports and exports? (CIS Intermediate, December 1969.)

6.10   *Explain how the Government may use tax and expenditure policy to remove unemployment. What difficulties are likely to emerge? (U of L Advanced, Summer 1967.)*

Deficit finance

The government can attack unemployment on a broad front by allowing expenditure to exceed taxation, thus providing the community as a whole with more purchasing power. The deficit thus created can be covered by

borrowing, and the fact that such a policy involved an increase in the
National Debt would be of negligible importance if it were a question of
curing unemployment on the massive scale which existed in the early
1930's. A Budget deficit, is, however, apt to be rather a blunt instrument
for dealing with the kind of unemployment more normally experienced
nowadays, e.g. when it is a question of reducing it from 2½ to
2 per cent, or when it is concentrated in certain industries or regions.

Amount and timing

First, it becomes a matter of considerable difficulty to judge the amount
and timing of the necessary deficit. Any initial injection of purchasing
power will be increased by the "multiplier effect", and in circumstances
where the propensity to consume is fairly high, a slight overestimate of
the amount required can easily lead to a situation where there are more
jobs on offer than there are unemployed to fill them. It is even more
difficult to get the timing right — whatever form the Budgetary changes
took, it could be weeks, months or even years before their effects perme-
ated right through the economy, and by the time they had done so other
influences might have supervened to make them unnecessary or even
undesirable.

Elements contributing to deficit

Next, there is the question of the way in which the deficit is to be created.
Obviously, this can be done either by reducing taxation or increasing
expenditure, and, within these two alternatives, there is a wide range of
choice between different kinds of taxes and different kinds of spending.
Other things being equal, a Government would no doubt prefer to increase
its expenditure on productive capital equipment, since this would not
only have a favourable effect on employment, but lay the foundations for
increased prosperity; if it wanted to get quick results, however, it might
very well opt for raising family allowances or State pensions. The other
main alternative, namely reduced taxation, would have the effect of
increasing incentive, especially if it were concentrated on income tax;
on the other hand, selective reductions in outlay taxes could be used to
reduce unemployment in particular industries. Other selective measures
could involve assessing the claims of various regions when allowing investment grants, employment premiums, or other forms of financial assistance
to industry.

Dangers of deficit finance

Apart from the complex questions arising in the detailed application of
deficit financing, however, the overriding danger is that it will be carried
too far. No Government is going to lay itself open to the accusation of
tolerating unemployment when the methods of counteracting it are so

easy to apply, and the tendency is therefore for policy to err on the side of overfull employment. As a consequence, there is persistent upwards pressure on costs and prices, with recurrent crises in the balance of international payments, and no lasting solution to this problem has yet emerged from the political arena since the end of World War II.

SIMILAR QUESTIONS

(i) Discuss the policies available to the government for reducing the present level of unemployment. (ICA Final, November 1967.)
(ii) Discuss the use of fiscal policy as a means of reducing aggregate unemployment. (U of L Advanced, Summer 1969.)

7
Government policies

This section is concerned with the various ways in which the Government intervenes in the working of the economy to correct the shortcomings of the "laissez-faire" system. Sometimes it operates by taking things out of the price mechanism altogether, e.g. education and health, but very often it works *through* the price mechanism, i.e. by taxes and subsidies, and simple supply-and-demand theory therefore remains a valid way of analysing some problems. More and more questions involve the application of macro-economic principles, however, and the student who has mastered the subject matter of Section 6 will be much better equipped to answer these.

The most obvious way in which the Government can influence the economy is through its budgetary, or "fiscal", policy. The student should familiarize himself with the broad outline of a modern budget, and notice the various ways in which it seeks to modify the circumstances or behaviour of consumers or entrepreneurs by discriminatory taxation and expenditure. Particular attention should be paid to measures designed to encourage investment or savings, to policies in aid of development areas, and to the way in which the size of the budget surplus is calculated to hold the balance between inflation and unemployment.

Since World War II the Government has also taken an increasing interest in the structure of industry, as evidenced by the various measures which have been taken to restrict the power of privately-owned monopolies to exploit consumers. Questions are frequently set on these, but it should not be forgotten that the Government has also been active in promoting mergers as part of its policy to encourage economic growth, and to enable British firms to compete successfully against their foreign rivals.

This takes us into the last major area of Government economic policy, namely measures to improve the balance of payments. Apart from the general effect of a deflationary budget in restraining domestic demand, protective customs duties and/or quotas can be used to restrict imports, and, within the limits set by international agreements, some encouragement can be given to exporters by way of rebates and long-term credits at favourable interest rates. The Government is also involved through the

138

Bank of England in controlling the foreign exchange value of the £, but questions on this subject are reserved for Section 8.

Even so, the present section covers a great deal of ground, and is highly productive of questions, many of them being of a topical mature. It will certainly pay the student to keep an eye on the news while he is studying; even if there is no question based specifically on some recent event, answers gain considerably if they contain appropriate examples drawn from current affairs.

7.1 *"The original purpose of the Budget was to raise revenue to meet Government expenditure. Nowadays, it is the major instrument for regulating the economy." Explain this statement, illustrating your answer by reference to recent budgetary policy. (ICA Final, May 1967.)*

Changed rôle of the budget

It is true that in its inception the only consideration dictating budgetary policy was the need to raise enough money to cover essential government activities, foremost among which were the maintenance of law and order and "defence against the King's enemies". Even in Victorian times any encroachment of the authorities into other aspects of the country's affairs was regarded with suspicion, and the widely-accepted view was summed up in the saying "money is best left to fructify in the pockets of the taxpayer". Over the years, however, and especially since the 1930's, this simple attitude towards public finance has changed almost beyond recognition, and the annual budget has indeed become a "major instrument for regulating the economy".

Expansion in government activity

First among the reasons for this change is the great expansion which has occurred in the government's sphere of activity. In conformity with the general shift of opinion against "laissez faire", the state assumed responsibility for elementary education in 1870, started the provision for welfare payments in the early 1900's, introduced subsidies for agriculture during the 1920's, committed itself to assist the "depressed areas" in the 1930's, undertook to maintain full employment in 1944, instituted the national health service in 1946, and so on down to the present time with subsidies to support nationalized industries, to finance research, to promote the arts and even to encourage sport. Taken in conjunction with a 500-fold rise in the National Debt (with a corresponding obligation to meet interest payments on it) since 1900, these developments have resulted in a huge increase in taxation, which now, including rates and social security contributions, takes about 37½ per cent of the national income, as compared with about 10 per cent before World War I. From the point of view of sheer size, therefore, the budget is bound to have an important influence on the country's economy — presumably the government is going to spend the tax money in some way different from that in which taxpayers would have spent it, otherwise there would be no point in raising it!

Discriminatory measures

Not only is the budget much larger than it used to be, but taxation and expenditure are often designed to discriminate in various ways between different people, products, areas, etc. This is true of all the principal *taxes*, e.g. —

(*a*) Income tax and surtax (as between people with different levels of income, different family circumstances, different sources of income, etc.);

(*b*) Corporation Tax (as between distributed and undistributed profits);

(*c*) Estate Duty (as between different ranges of value);

(*d*) Import duties (as between different kinds of goods, with lower rates for certain Commonwealth and EFTA goods);

(*e*) Purchase Tax (as between goods of various degrees of luxury);

(*f*) Selective Employment Tax (as between one kind of worker and another).

These are the major examples, but discrimination even extends to different kinds of advertising media, different forms of gambling, different kinds of sport and entertainment, and different kinds of borrowing.

The *expenditure* side of the budget also provides many examples of discrimination, e.g.—

(*a*) Subsidies for certain kinds of producers (e.g. farmers, shipbuilders);

(*b*) Subsidies for certain kinds of investment (maufacturing as opposed to distribution).

(*c*) Subsidies for development areas and "intermediate" areas on two different levels (e.g. investment and building grants, regional employment premium, lower rating assessments, training grants, interest-free loans);

(*d*) Allowances for people with children (but only if there is more than one in the family, and at a rate which depends on the number of children;

(*e*) Subsidies for tenants of council houses;

(*f*) Rates relief for poorer classes of householders.

There are also many other kinds of payment, ranging from university grants to national assistance, which are geared to individual circumstances.

In short, both sides of the budget are contrived so as to bring about a substantial redistribution of the national income, and in a way calculated to encourage certain kinds of economic activity and to discourage others.

Balancing the economy

Finally, the budget has been used since World War II as a means of balancing supply and demand in the economy. The White Paper on Employment, 1944, stated that there was "no merit in a rigid policy of balancing the budget each year, regardless of the state of trade", and since then the aim of the Chancellor has been to counteract any tendency towards inflation or deflation by budgeting for a surplus or a deficit respectively. For example, the 1968/69 budget aimed at a surplus of about £900 m. in a full year to deflate home market demand following the devaluation of the £ in 1967.

SIMILAR QUESTIONS

(i) In what ways may the budget be used as an instrument of economic policy? (ICWA Part I, December 1965.)

(ii) In what ways can the budget be used as an instrument of economic policy? (I of B Part I, April 1966.)

(iii) For what purposes may the tax system be used other than to raise revenue for the government? (I of B Part I, September 1967.)

(iv) Taxation can serve many functions in addition to raising revenue. Discuss these additional functions in relation to the system of taxation in your country. (C of S Intermediate, June 1968.)

(v) Explain the means by which a budget may be used as an instrument of control. (ACCA Section I, June 1969.)

7.2 *Distinguish between direct and indirect taxation. Set out the advantages and disadvantages of each. (AEB Advanced, June 1965.)*

Definition

The classification of taxes into "direct" and "indirect" is based on the assumption that whereas people paying taxes of the first kind to the Government also bear the financial burden of them, payers of the second kind can and do pass on the burden to someone else, i.e. they merely act as intermediaries between taxpayers and the Government. The distinction is therefore based purely on a matter of administrative convenience; by contrast, a classification into taxes on income and taxes on expenditure has more economic significance, in that the latter can legitimately be avoided, whereas the former cannot. However, apart from taxes coming into the general category of licences, the two kinds of classification amount to much the same thing, and for our present purpose the distinction between them will be ignored.

Direct taxes are fair

The most important thing to be said in favour of direct taxes is that they can be adjusted with some degree of fairness to the individual's capacity to pay. Naturally, opinions as to what is fair are bound to differ considerably, but most would no doubt agree that the principle of fairness is best served by a "progressive" tax, i.e. one which exacts a contribution from rich people more than proportionate to their higher incomes. This can, of course, be done with a good deal of precision with a direct tax, e.g. income tax, but hardly at all with indirect taxes, e.g. tobacco tax.

Indirect taxes better for incentive

On the other hand, the great advantage which indirect taxes are said to have is that they are much less of a disincentive to effort. It is difficult to justify this statement on purely economic grounds, but there is little doubt that in practice the wage earner would rather get £20 in his pay packet and then spend it on goods bearing £5 tax than receive £15 and use it to purchase untaxed goods. Perhaps the reason is that, in much the same way as the benefits arising from taxation tend to be taken for granted, so a tax on goods comes to be accepted in time as part of their price, in contrast to the undisguised impact of a direct tax. When, moreover, the direct tax is progressive, like surtax, the disincentive effect is even more marked, as marginal earnings are taxed at the highest rate for which the individual is liable — they may indeed have the effect of moving him from his present maximum rate to the next higher one.

Consumers' and producers' surplus

Apart from questions of fairness and incentive, there is something to be said on purely theoretical grounds for raising a given amount of revenue by direct rather than indirect taxation. The effect of the latter on the demand/supply/price situation can be shown thus —

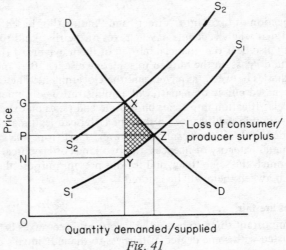

Fig. 41

If D—D and S_1—S_1 are the demand and supply curves before the tax is applied, and OP the price, the effect of imposing the tax is to raise the supply curve by a vertical distance equal to the amount per unit of tax (XY) to a new position S_2-S_2, and to increase the price to OG (gross price including tax), of which the Government gets GN (= XY) per unit and sellers ON (net supply price). Consider now what has happened to the combined amount of consumers' and producers' surplus; whereas previously this was denoted by the area lying below D—D and above PZ plus the area lying above S_1-S_1 and below PZ, it has now shrunk by an amount equal to the area GXZYN. Of this, GXYN, which represents the total revenue from the tax, presumably comes back in various forms to the community via Government spending, but this leaves the triangle XYZ unaccounted for. It looks as if some satisfaction has got lost somewhere; this conclusion is supported by the commonsense argument that if, prior to the imposition of a tax on a particular commodity, the community had succeeded in maximizing total satisfaction by equating the marginal utilities of all products, any arbitrary change in the price structure leading to a new pattern of resource allocation must be inferior to the original pattern. Incidentally, another point which emerges from the diagram is that the seller cannot normally pass on the whole of an indirect tax — he absorbs NP per unit, an amount which will vary according to the relative elasticities of supply and demand.

The pattern of consumption

Despite the theoretical loss of consumers' and producers' surplus, the fact that the Government can influence the pattern of consumption through its policy of indirect taxation might in certain circumstances be deemed an advantage. A high rate of tax on tobacco, for example, not only serves to help the balance of payments by cutting down dollar expenditure, but also may do something to prevent lung cancer. It is also argued by the Government that purchase tax on cars forces manufacturers to export a higher proportion of their output, though manufacturers themselves have other ideas on the subject. Whether one takes the view that discriminatory outlay taxes are a legitimate and useful instrument of Government policy really depends upon whether one thinks the "gentlemen in Whitehall" invariably know best; if is purely a question of raising revenue, many economists favour some kind of flat rate sales tax, e.g. the French "value added" tax.

Are indirect taxes inflationary?

Some people argue against indirect taxes on the grounds that, since they raise prices, they are inflationary. If one defines inflation simply as a state of affairs where prices are rising, regardless of the reason, then of course this statement is necessarily true, but if it is defined as a rise in prices caused by excess purchasing power, then direct and indirect taxes are in themselves equally disinflationary, as both have the effect of reducing purchasing power. It must be conceded, however, that when the underlying inflationary forces are sufficiently strong, any rise in the retail price index is seized upon by organized labour as justification for claiming wage increases (indeed, the wages of some 2,000,000 workers are adjusted automatically with changes in the index), so that the ultimate effect of a rise in indirect taxation might indeed be inflationary.

Two types complement one another

To conclude, it has been shown that both direct and indirect taxes have their advantages and disadvantages, and it is not therefore surprising to find that the present-day UK budget relies to an almost equal extent on taxes of each kind for raising revenue. The exact point at which the balance is struck will depend upon non-economic considerations to some extent, but no pronounced departure from the present position is likely in the foreseeable future.

SIMILAR QUESTIONS

(i) Set out what you understand by direct taxation and discuss the advantages and disadvantages of this form of taxation. (ACCA Section I, December 1967.)

(ii) Examine the case for raising a larger proportion of total tax revenues from indirect taxation. (ICA Final, May 1968.)

(iii) Should an economy rely heavily upon indirect taxation when budgeting for a surplus? (CIS Final, December 1968.)

(iv) Do you agree with the view that any further increase in taxation would have to be an increase in indirect taxation? Give your reasons. (C of S Final, November 1968.)

(v) Are indirect taxes inflationary or deflationary? (U of L Advanced, Summer 1970.)

(vi) Discuss the advantages and disadvantages of direct as opposed to indirect taxation, explaining and illustrating the various terms in your answer. (ACCA Section I, December 1969.)

7.3 *Outline the main headings of central government expenditure, and explain briefly the economic effects of each. (AEB, Summer 1968.)*

The main kinds of government expenditure are as follows —

Defence

From an economic point of view, the cost of defence is almost entirely a waste of resources. In effect, about 6 per cent of the gross national product is absorbed by the manufacture of military equipment and upkeep of the armed services, with only two possible economic gains to show for it —

(*a*) It allows productive activity to be carried on in a somewhat more secure environment, and

(*b*) Research undertaken for military purposes sometimes throws up useful "by-products" for civil production.

On the other hand, the harmful effect to the economy may be even more serious than the figure of 6 per cent implies, as —

(*a*) A disproportionately large amount of research effort is devoted to military ends, to the detriment of progress in industrial technology, and

(*b*) A high proportion of the expenditure is incurred in foreign currency, thus imposing a heavy burden on the balance of payments.

Education

By contrast, expenditure on education, also about 6 per cent of the GNP, represents a highly desirable form of investment. The children and young people in schools and universities today are the working population of tomorrow, and their success in meeting the ever-increasing demands of advanced technological industries for skilled employees will largely determine Britain's living standards in the years that lie ahead.

Like all forms of investment, increased expenditure on education, e.g. to raise the school leaving age to 16, imposes a sacrifice upon the community in the short term, but it is one which should be handsomely repaid by increased productivity in the future.

Health and welfare

This expenditure, now running at about 5 per cent of the GNP, is also partly in the nature of an investment, for healthy people, like well-educated people, should be more productive. This argument only applies to children and people in the working population, however; beyond that, expenditure on improving the lot of sick and disabled people, together with assistance for growing numbers of old-age pensioners, is justifiable only in terms of humanitarianism and social justice. Without calling into question the desirability of spending money in this way, its economic effect is undoubtedly inflationary, as the payments are financed out of the rewards for productive effort.

Social security

This now comprises the largest item of public expenditure, amounting to some 8 per cent of the GNP. Its growth reflects both the increased rate of benefits and the growing number of beneficiaries, which again includes a high proportion of elderly people. There can be little doubt that the effect of these increasing provisions in strictly economic terms is inflationary, for the reason given above, and there are some who argue that the level of certain payments, e.g. unemployment benefit/family allowance, is a disincentive to effort. However that may be, there is little possibility in terms of practical politics of the level of such expenditure being reduced. Indeed, the upward trend seems likely to continue as the number of pensioners increases and the scale of payments becomes more generous.

Housing

Expenditure on slum clearance and to meet the continuing shortage of rented housing is now running at about 3 per cent of the GNP. This is part of a broad policy of maintaining social capital intact, and must therefore be regarded as an investment of a kind, but to what extent it can be justified in terms of yield is problematical. Its primary purpose is undoubtedly social, the main economic effect being to add still further to inflationary pressure by putting an additional strain on scarce resources.

Roads

This is another aspect of maintaining and even improving social capital, with expenditure now running at over 1 per cent of GNP. In this case, however, the investment is amply rewarded by improvements in the efficiency of road transport which it makes possible, and yields of up to 10 per cent have been estimated on the money spent on new motorways.

Investment in nationalized industries

More than half the capital investment in nationalized industries, not to mention the operating deficit of some, is financed by the government. Capital expenditure has been rising rapidly in recent years (e.g. modernization of the railways and coal mines, new generating plant for electricity, expansions to GPO telecommunications services, reorganization of the steel industry and distribution of North Sea gas), and criteria have been laid down by the government to ensure that a satisfactory return is obtained either on a strict commercial basis or in terms of various social benefits.

In view of the inflationary effect of most public expenditure, now running at almost half the GNP, it was announced in November, 1967, that both central and local government spending plans were to be reduced as part of post-devaluation strategy. Further measures were announced early in 1968 to restrict subsequent increases to an annual rate of under 3 per cent roughly in line with the anticipated rise in the GNP, and this principle is likely to be followed in the future.

SIMILAR QUESTION
(i) Given that Government expenditure is to be cut, how should it be cut? (C of S Final, June 1968.)

7.4 *What arguments might be advanced for subsidizing services such as health or education from public funds? (U of L Advanced, Summer 1967.)*

Although children were not obliged to attend State schools at all before 1870, and the National Health Service was not inaugurated until 1946, very few people would now seriously contend that the provision of education and health services should be left entirely to private enterprise.

Lack of effective demand

The benefits of good health and a good education, both to the individual and the community, are difficult to overestimate, even in strictly economic terms, yet there can be little doubt that the population as a whole would not be prepared to meet the full cost of adequate provision of either if they had complete freedom of choice in the spending of their incomes. Consequently, it is desirable for the State to intervene in the public interest by making health and education services available to all, either free of charge or substantially below cost, and raise the bulk of the necessary finance through taxation.

Equal provision for all (1)

Another reason for not leaving the provision of health and education services to free enterprise is that what demand there was would be concentrated in the upper income groups of the population. The inherent physical and mental qualities of infants are in no way related to the wealth of their parents, however, so that any discrimination against poorer families in the distribution of resources devoted to health and education would result in a net loss of potential skill and energy. The logic of this argument therefore demands that all health and education services should be financed from the public purse; in no circumstances should the community allow them to be treated as goods which can be sold to the highest bidder.

Equal provision for all (2)

Similar reasoning can be applied to the differences in the standards of provision which would be bound to develop between different areas of the country under a system of private enterprise. The tendency would be to cater most effectively for people in the more heavily populated areas, but again there is no reason to suppose that individuals in such areas are of greater potential benefit to the community than those in sparsely populated districts. This is not to say that the State should aim to make identical provision for town and country dwellers; its object should rather be to give the kind of service best suited to the needs of each locality within the overall limits allowed by finance.

Standards and costs

Finally, whatever resources were devoted to health and education, a centrally-administered system should be capable of ensuring that the best use was made of them —

(a) by laying down minimum standards for these services and securing their enforcement through their control over capital spending and staff recruitment, and

(b) by taking all possible advantages rising from economies of scale, e.g. in the design and construction of buildings, purchase of supplies, etc.

7.5 *What do you understand by the term "inflation"? Discuss the main factors contributing to the current inflationary pressure in the United Kingdom, and indicate the various measures adopted by the government to control it. (ICA Final, November 1965.)*

General rise in prices

In common parlance, inflation simply means a state of affairs where the general level of prices is persistently rising, i.e. the value of money is continually falling. Apart from a few years in the 1930's the inhabitants of all the so-called "western countries" have been accustomed to some degree of inflation as a normal part of economic life during the 20th century; it is only when it develops into a "runaway" inflation like the one which occurred in Germany in 1923 that it becomes at all remarkable. Nevertheless, even the effects of a steady erosion of the value of money can be extremely harmful, and Governments are constantly proclaiming their intention to halt inflation, even though they do not seem to enjoy much success in doing so.

Demand and cost inflation

In order to understand the measures which might be effective in combatting inflation, it is first necessary to enquire into what causes it, and we come at once to the analytical distinction between demand inflation and cost inflation. Demand inflation causes prices to rise through an excess of purchasing power, as summed up in the familiar phrase "too much money chasing too few goods"; prices are, so to speak, drawn up by the willingness and ability of one buyer to outbid another. Cost inflation, on the other hand, causes prices to rises because of a rise in the cost of factors of production; in this case, the price of goods is being pushed up because the materials or labour required to make them are becoming more expensive, and entrepreneurs are forced to pass on their higher costs to consumers.

Control of demand inflation

The appropriate measures to check demand inflation are those which reduce spending in some way, and the two broad alternatives open to the Government would be to operate through (*a*) *monetary*, and (*b*) *fiscal* policies. The former would involve a general restriction of credit by the sale of securities in the open market (thus reducing commercial banks' cash, and hence their ability to make loans), coupled with an increase in Bank Rate (thus raising the cost, and hence the profitability, of obtaining loans). Such general restraints on the creation of credit might be supplemented by directions to the banks as to the nature and extent of the loans which it was desirable for them to make, a lowering of the ceiling figure for new issues to be approved by the Capital Issues Committee, and a tightening of the restrictions governing hire-purchase agreements.

Fiscal policies are those which operate through the Budget. The major problem which the Government has to consider in this connection is how much purchasing power needs to be removed from the economy by means of a surplus of taxation over current expenditure, and in making this decision they can tip the scales against inflation to any extent they consider practicable and/or desirable. The balances between different kinds of taxation will also have a bearing on the question, e.g. taxes on income are likely to be more effective in keeping prices down than taxes on goods.

Control of cost inflation

Turning to cost inflation, the possible methods of controlling it are both more difficult to define and more difficult to apply. If rising prices originate in rising costs of imports, there is, indeed, very little of a practical nature than can be done; to impose rigid price controls, for example, would simply mean that the supply of goods would dry up. By far the most serious cause of cost inflation, however, is rising money wages without any corresponding increase in productivity, and the extent to which the Government can control this tendency is conditioned by its willingness and ability to interfere in the process of wage bargaining between employers and the trade unions. Short of assuming dictatorial powers, the Government can only endeavour to create a climate of opinion opposed to unjustified increases in both prices and wages, supported by the creation of a quasi-judicial body to investigate major examples of rising prices or incomes as they occur, and the sanction of Parliament for limited periods to exercise an absolute veto over such increases at times of particular difficulty.

SIMILAR QUESTIONS

(i) What is meant by inflation? What measures might a Government use to combat it? (U of L Advanced, January 1964.)

(ii) Distinguish between cost-push and demand-pull inflation. Has the distinction any value in practice? (C of S Intermediate, June 1967.)

(iii) What is inflation? (U of L Advanced, Summer 1970.)

7.6   *Should the Government seek to influence the location of industry?*
         (*C of S Intermediate, November 1967.*)

Non-economic factors

The justification for Government interference in industrialists' location
decisions must be that it results in the greatest good for the greatest
number, but it must be admitted at the outset that social as well as
economic factors are involved in this question, and that even the latter
are extemely difficult to evaluate.

Policy instruments

The means which the Government has at its disposal to influence location
decisions are —

(*a*) The use of various kinds of *subsidy* to induce firms to move into
Development Areas, e.g. investment grants on new buildings and plant, loans
on favourable terms, provision of ready-made factories on new "trading
estates" at low rentals, reduced rating assessments, training grants, regional
employment premiums, etc.

(*b*) The provision or improvement of general *amenities and services* in
Development Areas, e.g. the construction of new trunk roads, the building
of new houses for key personnel, improvements in local transport, power
and health services, schemes for new harbour and dock installations, and
so on.

(*c*) The refusal to grant *Industrial Development Permits* to firms wishing
to expand in other areas, thus presenting them with the choice of going
into Development Areas or abandoning their plans altogether.

Cost to the Government

The direct cost of these measures since World War II has been about
£800 million, but it is impossible to say what additional expense should be
charged to general Development Area policy, e.g. to what extent the
pattern of the motorways network has been influenced by the desire to
improve communications between Development Areas and the south-east.
One recent survey of Development Area policy in Northern Ireland put the
overall cost to the taxpayer of creating new jobs at £1,000 per worker, to
which must be added the subsequent cost of Regional Employment
Premium at £1.50 per man per week for a minimum of seven years from
1967, plus the continuing subsidy element in rental and interest charges.

Cost to firms

In addition to the charge on the public purse, there is the possible loss
suffered by firms themselves as a result of going to a Development Area,
notwithstanding the reduction in their costs due to subsidies. Here it is
only possible to speak in the most general terms; some managements

maintain that they are worse off on balance by being so far removed from their major markets and sources of supply, the lack of skilled labour, an indefinable sense of being "out of the swim", and so on, while others say that they have suffered little or no hardship once they have had time to acclimatize to the new conditions. It is noteworthy that a high proportion of American investment has been made in Scotland since World War II, with and without financial inducements, and on the whole these firms seem well satisfied with their locations.

Economic benefits

The gains to the economic health of the country are even more difficult to assess than the costs, partly because it is impossible to say what conditions would have been like in the absence of such a policy and partly because the full benefits may not yet have been reaped. It is regrettably true that, although schemes to assist these areas in one way or another have been in existence for over 35 years, the level of unemployment in them remains at some two or three times the national average, and a steady movement of population towards the more prosperous areas of the country persists. While conditions are nothing like as bad as they were in the worst days of the slump, this is primarily due to the high level of employment which has been maintained in the country as a whole since World War II, plus the payment of unemployment benefit and national assistance on a much more generous scale.

Some diversification of industry has certainly been achieved, firms engaged in electronics and light engineering being prominent among those which have established themselves successfully in these areas. While this may have the desired effect of giving more stability than the original capital goods industries, it has tended to create more jobs for married women and juveniles than for the older men who form the "hard core" of the unemployed; a factory making radio receivers has not a lot to offer men who have worked for the best part of their lives down a coal mine or in a steel foundry. There has also been a natural tendency on the part of the authorities to favour labour-intensive industries at the expense of capital-intensive ones, which, looking still further into the future, may not be altogether desirable.

Summary

Judged from a purely economic standpoint, therefore, it seems doubtful whether the gain from Development Area policies justifies the considerable amount of money and effort that has been expended on them. As stated in the opening paragraph, however, there are important social issues to be considered as well; even if the relief of unemployment in these areas involved some net loss to the rest of the community, this might still be a price worth paying for the prevention of a great deal of human suffering.

SIMILAR QUESTIONS

(i) What are the advantages and disadvantages of the various remedies for local unemployment? (C of S Intermediate, November 1966.)

(ii) On what economic grounds, if any, is there a case for the government control of the location of industry? (C of S Final, November 1966.)

(iii) "Taking work to the workers is a better cure for localized unemployment than taking workers to the work." Discuss. (CIS Intermediate, June 1968.)

7.7 *Describe and assess recent British policy on monopolies. (U of L Advanced, Summer 1967.)*

Position before World War II

Britain's increasing tendency to resort to protection between the two world wars gave rise to fears in many quarters about creating conditions favourable to the abuse of monopoly power by domestic producers, but such enquiries as were undertaken by the Government of the day did not provide grounds for anti-monopoly legislation. Indeed, many aspects of official policy before and during World War II could even be said to have encouraged monopolistic tendencies in coalmining, steel, and manufacturing industry generally, but the postwar Labour Government lost no time in proceeding with its declared intention of curbing the power of private monopolies.

The immediate postwar period

First, all the important basic industries like coal, steel, electricity, gas and transport were nationalized, thus removing these from the area of debate concerning exploitation of the consumer for private profit. Second, the Monopolies Commission was set up by Act of Parliament in 1948 with power to investigate the affairs of any large private firm or group suspected of acting in such a way as to prevent or restrict competition, e.g. by price fixing, exclusive dealing, discriminatory rebates, sales quotas, limitation of raw material supplies, impeding entry of new firms, etc.

Laws to combat restrictive practices

The Commission proved to be very slow in issuing reports, but its enquiries showed time and again that the kind of restrictive practices just mentioned were normally devised and enforced by Trade Associations in their respective industries. Consequently, a new Act was passed in 1956 compelling Trade Associations to lodge all members' agreements of a restrictive nature with a newly-appointed Registrar, and then to justify them as being in the public interest by giving evidence to that effect in a newly-created Restrictive Practices Court. In order to succeed, it became necessary to prove to the satisfaction of the Court that removal of an agreement would, for example, expose the public to physical danger, or the loss of some "specific and substantial benefit"; that the agreement was necessary to ensure fair competition between producers, e.g. to counterbalance the effect of an agreement already approved between another group of manufacturers; that abandonment of the agreement would result in a significant increase in unemployment in an area; that condemnation of the agreement would lead to a subsequent reduction in the industry's exports, etc. Even so, justification on one of these grounds alone would not serve to justify the agreement as a whole; approval would only be granted by the Court if it considered that the general effect was beneficial to the public interest. Individual price maintenance, i.e. the power of a particular manufacturer to insist on a minimum retail price for his product, was specifically allowed by the 1956 Act, but this practice too was made illegal in the Resale Prices Act, 1964, subject again to certain grounds for exemption similar to those in the 1956 Act.

Aftermath of 1948, 1956, and 1964 Acts

The combined effect of these three Acts has been to give an appreciable stimulus to competition in British industry. Relatively few of the agreements coming before the Court have been approved, and in view of the general trend of their decisions many more have been voluntarily abandoned. It was found, however, that the virtual elimination of restrictive agreements between firms was tending to promote outright mergers, thus making it necessary in 1965 to empower the Board of Trade to hold up such moves pending an investigation into their possible anti-social effects by the Monopolies Commission. On the other hand, the manifest advantages arising from mergers in some industries, e.g. from rationalization of production and economies of scale, are of such potential benefit to the efficiency of the economy that the Industrial Reorganization Corporation was formed in 1966 to encourage them, if necessary by the promise of financial assistance.

Present position

In view of the difficulty in laying down clear-cut principles governing the desirability or otherwise of large-scale enterprises, one can only define the Government's present policy in the most general terms. They certainly have all the power they need to promote or to discourage mergers; how this power is used remains a matter of judgement as to where the public interest lies in any particular case.

SIMILAR QUESTIONS

(i) "It is inconsistent for a government to have anti-monopoly legislation and to promote mergers." (U of L Advanced, Summer 1968.)

(ii) What evidence is there to support the view that the Government's policies on (*a*) mergers, and (*b*) monopoly, are inconsistent and incompatible? (ICA Final, May 1969.)

7.8 *"Price stability, continuous economic growth and balance of payments equilibrium are incompatible in conditions of full employment." Explain and discuss this statement. (ICA Final, May 1967.)*

Conflict of economic aims

Although stable prices and economic growth are both in the general interest, and equilibrium in the balance of payment is obligatory in the long run, none of these policy objectives seem capable of achievement in conditions where the demand for labour is maintained above a certain level. One could, indeed, go on to name other possible economic aims, e.g. lower taxation, increased leisure, etc., each of which, taken separately, would be both desirable and feasible, but experience seems to show that success in any one direction tends to be at the expense of failure in others.

Full employment and price stability

For example, stability in the general level of prices can only be expected if there is a state of balance between demand and supply, i.e. if people as a whole do not attempt to take more out of the pool of goods and services than they put into it. In a primitive kind of society where each family had to be self-supporting, such a possibility would of course be ruled out from the start, but when a vast and complex system of division of labour has been built up, relying wholly on money and the price mechanism to co-ordinate people's efforts, there is naturally no longer the same compulsion on individuals to accept the overall limitation which production imposes on consumption. There is a tendency common to most of us to want to exert the minimum effort for the maximum reward, and while some are more successful than others in bargaining for shorter hours and higher pay no one is averse to seizing whatever advantage he can, even though it may only be temporary. Administered controls over prices are both clumsy and ineffective, so that one is perhaps inclined to agree with Professor Paish when he says that with unemployment below 2 per cent a prices and incomes policy is unworkable, while if it was above 2¼ per cent it would be unnecessary; in other words, some degree of unemployment may be the only practicable way of curbing the excessive bargaining power of organized labour in conditions of very full employment.

Growth and price stability

Economic growth has now become mandatory as an objective of government policy, and various rates have been declared to be attainable from time to time, e.g. 4 per cent per annum under the 1961–66 economic plan. Again, however, it is basically a question of what individuals are prepared to do or to endure to make such an objective possible; growth rates of more than 4 per cent would be quite practicable without rising prices if people were willing to sacrifice consumption to the extent necessary to free resources for the appropriate amount of capital creation, and to accept the personal inconveniences and risks arising from the need to reorganize production at fairly frequent intervals. Sacrifice can in fact be forced on an unwilling community by a government which is prepared to finance the creation of capital by inflation, but of course this would only be at the expense of stability in the price level.

Balance of payments and price stability

Price stability is also clearly bound up with the question of maintaining equilibrium in the balance of payments. Failure to prevent a rise in the domestic price level as compared with world prices inevitably leads to the loss of exports, and while it may be possible to control the flow of imports, to do so not only retards economic progress but tends to make prices rise still faster. It may therefore be necessary to accept a certain amount of unemployment and to limit the rate of economic growth in order to maintain equilibrium in the balance of payments; while it is possible to finance a deficit on current account by borrowing abroad, e.g. from the IMF, or by encouraging investment by foreign firms, both these expedients have an adverse effect on the balance in later years. Devaluation may also give a brief respite from the adverse trade balance caused by rising domestic prices, but it represents no lasting solution to the problem.

Inevitability of compromise

It would appear, therefore, that in considering the desirability of maintaining stable prices, promoting economic growth, ensuring full employment and avoiding a balance of payments deficit we have a problem which illustrates the principle of opportunity cost, except that equilibrium in the balance of payments must ultimately be an overriding imperative. Although one may hope for improvements in the techniques of government planning, more awareness on the part of responsible trade unionists of the need for restraint in wage bargaining in conditions of full employment, and an increased willingness on the part of people in general to accept current sacrifices as the price of future prosperity, some kind of compromise solution to the problem of conflicting economic aims will always have to be accepted.

SIMILAR QUESTIONS

(i) Write a short essay on what you think should be the aims of economic policy. (I of B Part I, September 1965.)

(ii) "The triple objective of economic policy is a strong currency, a steadily-growing industrial strength and full employment." (Chancellor of the Exchequer, Budget Speech, 1966.) Discuss this statement. (CIS Final, June 1967.)

(iii) Should the rate of growth of national income per head be the central aim of economic policy? (CIS Final, June 1969.)

7.9   *What is meant by economic growth? How can it be fostered in Britain?*
     (I of B Part I, September 1965.)

Economic growth and the standard of living

Economic growth denotes an increase in the value of the annual output of goods and services achieved by a country. Apart from the possibility of changes in the terms of trade and fluctuations in the balance of overseas payments, the rate of economic growth determines the rate at which living standards can increase, so that policies designed to produce or accelerate growth have become part of the philosophy of all political parties. It is clear, however, that there is no simple or generally acceptable way of fostering economic growth, as witness the fact that no government in post-war Britain has been able to maintain any given rate of growth for any sustained period.

Growth depends on investment/savings

There is no difficulty in prescribing the main requirement for a high and steady rate of growth, namely a high level of investment coupled with a correspondingly high level of money savings. The latter are necessary so that productive resources can be switched from the manufacture of consumer goods to capital goods without inflationary pressure, but all too often we have allowed capital and consumer goods to compete for productive resources in an economy that was already fully employed. The inevitable result has been a rise in prices, a fall in exports and a rise in imports, so that a slow-down in the rate of growth has been necessary to protect our gold reserves.

Investment in the public sector

Much of the investment required for long-term growth is of a kind that Government itself can best undertake, e.g. education, transport and communications, basic research, etc., but it is scarcely within the bounds of practical politics to finance any large increase in Government expenditure on these objectives out of the budget; any party which openly advocated increased taxation in the UK today could scarcely hope to win the support of electors. The only alternative, namely Government borrowing, would be inflationary unless matched by voluntary savings, and these have not been forthcoming in sufficient volume to meet the needs of the situation.

Investment in the private sector (1)

As for investment in the private sector of the economy, many business men might say that the most helpful contribution the Government could make would be to do as little as possible to discourage it. The tax on business profits is sufficiently high to act as a constant deterrent to private investment; while there may be a great deal to say on other grounds in favour of a heavy tax on profits, it is hardly calculated to encourage investment, and particularly investment in the newer industries, where a potentially high reward is necessary to offset the greater prospects of possible losses. It is also a considerable discouragement to investment when industrialists feel that they are exposed to incalculable risks in the shape of changes in purchase tax on their commodity, or, more generally, by periodical restrictions on general purchasing power.

Investment in the private sector (2)

Some positive policies to encourage private investment are possible, however, one being a differential rate of taxation as between *distributed and undistributed profits,* which has been fixed at times in the ratio of 10:1 in favour of the latter. This constitutes a clear inducement to directors to recommend the "ploughing back" of profits, which permits an increase in the firm's investment in productive assets, but such policies do not necessarily commend themselves to shareholders. There is a tendency for shares paying a low rate of dividend to be sold and their market price unduly depressed, thus opening the door to "take-over bids" and the possible removal from office of the directors themselves; to the extent that directors fear or can foresee these consequences, the intentions of the Government are likely to be frustrated. In any event, there is considerable doubt whether it is invariably in the country's best interest to favour investment in established firms to the detriment of new ones.

Investment in the private sector (3)

Investment in the private sector can also be encouraged by *subsidies.* These can take the form of "investment allowances", which entitle firms to write off a given percentage of the value of newly-purchased assets at once, so that their liability for profits tax is reduced at the end of the year. Alternatively, "investment grants" may be given in the form of a straight cash refund of part of the price of new assets, with the minimum of delay and without reference to subsequent profit, if any. Both forms of subsidy can be varied according to the type or location of the plant, and can therefore be used with particular effect to attract industry to development areas, where pockets of unemployment represent a potential means of increasing the national average output per man.

Investment in the private sector (4)

The only other positive encouragement the Government can offer to private investment is to maintain a *low rate of interest,* which is normally accompanied by easy credit conditions. The obvious danger is that consumption is encouraged, too; while there is nothing wrong with this when resources are under-employed, all the familiar symptoms of inflation begin to appear once the point of full employment has been reached. Unfortunately, it is no good waiting until the evidence of inflation is unmistakable before tightening up the controls over credit, as there is a considerable time-lag between changes in monetary policy and their effect on the employment/wages/prices situation. One useful contribution to the efficiency of Government action in this field would therefore be an improvement in the speed, range and quality of statistical information reaching policymakers.

Planning for growth

Britain's desire to foster economic growth was symbolized by the creation of the National Economic Development Council by a Conservative Government in 1961, and a plan was drawn up in that year in which the implications of a 4 per cent rate of growth for five years were worked out in terms of increased imports and exports, manpower requirements, etc., though nothing very conclusive emerged from it. Another plan was put forward by the Labour Government in 1965 for a 25 per cent increase in output by 1970, but again performance soon began to fall short of targets, and the plan had to be abandoned. The idea of a "national plan" has still not been finally shelved, apparently, but when all has been said no government in a democratic country like the UK can guarantee any sustained rate of economic growth if the people themselves are not disposed to accept the conditions which make it possible. As we have seen, these amount to a willingness to make present sacrifices for the sake of future advantage, and the acceptance of change as part of the normal course of business life; without this foundation, no plans or policies, however ingeniously devised, can hope to succeed.

SIMILAR QUESTION

(i) How can economic growth be assisted? (CIS Final, June 1965.)

7.10   *Do you consider that the national debt is a serious burden upon the UK economy, and should be reduced as rapidly as possible? (I of B Part I, April 1967.)*

Size and composition of the debt

At the end of the 1960's the UK national debt stood at about £33,500 m., a sum rather less than the value of one year's output of goods and services.

Of this total, £27,000 m. was "internal" debt, i.e. money owed by the British Government to its own citizens, as evidenced by their holdings of various Government securities, e.g. Consols, War loan, National Development Bonds, Treasury Stock, Treasury Bills, etc., balances in National Savings Bank accounts, postwar credits, premium bonds, and so on. The remaining, or "external", part of the debt, namely about £6,500 m., represented –

(*a*) Foreign currency obligations of the monetary authorities to overseas creditors, notably the USA and Canada in respect of the loans granted by them in 1946, "swap" arrangements with foreign central banks, drawings from the International Monetary Fund, etc.;

(*b*) "Sterling balances", i.e. British bank deposits, Treasury Bills and other Government securities held by Sterling Area countries, either as currency reserves or as working balances to finance current trading operations.

Burden of the internal debt

It is a matter for debate whether the internal part of the debt constitutes a burden at all. While most people are called upon in their capacity as taxpayers to help to meet the annual interest payments, most of the same people appear again as recipients of that interest, either directly as bondholders, etc., or indirectly through their participation in insurance and superannuation schemes, i.e. the interest is merely a transfer payment which does not affect the size of the national income. There are some who believe that the indirect effects of this transfer are harmful to productivity, but it is unlikely that these are very serious. The grounds for this belief are –

(*a*) That the budget is made larger than it otherwise would be, which brings us nearer to the limit of taxable capacity, whatever that might be;

(*b*) That in so far as bondholders are to found among the older, retired members of the community, and taxpayers among the younger and more productive elements, then there is a loss of incentive.

Burden of the external debt

As to the external part of the debt, the foreign currency obligations are indeed a burden, in that both the interest charge and the eventual repayment of capital can be met only from surpluses on the balance of payments, i.e. by producing more than we consume. Fortunately, even the total amount is not large compared with the annual national income, and the interest represents an insignificant fraction of the turnover in the balance of payments.

The sterling balances are another matter, however; they are a revolving debt which, in the normal course of events, does not fluctuate very much, and which may never need to be repaid. It is true that holders are usually

allowed to convert their claims into foreign currency if they so desire, but
on the other hand they are normally satisfied to receive a sterling credit
in exchange for foreign currency earnings which they contribute to the
Sterling Area pool.

Repayment of the internal debt

There is not the remotest possibility of the internal debt ever being repaid,
although of course any excess of taxation over expenditure in the Budget
will serve to reduce it somewhat. One or two attempts were made in
Victorian times to set up a sinking fund with the object of repaying the
debt completely, but now the level of taxation required to achieve this in
any measureable space of time would be so high as to make the idea quite
impracticable. More recently, proposals have been made to pay off some of
the debt by giving bondholders the right to convert their claims into termin-
able annuities, or to apply the proceeds of a capital levy to reduce the
amount outstanding from time to time, but the latter would be tantamount
to repudiation as the bulk of the repayment would be made to the same
people from whom the levy had been raised.

Over and above the *means* whereby the internal debt might be repaid,
however, is the question of whether any useful *purpose* would be served by
so doing. Holders of gilt-edged securities look upon them as a never-failing
source of income, and if this were taken away they would only try to find
another affording the same freedom from risk. In so far as the Government
can offer better security than any other kind of borrower, the repayment
of its debts would therefore do bondholders a disservice; it is not too much
to say that if the national debt had not developed in the ordinary course
of events, it would have had to be invented.

Repayment of the external debt

We are, of course, clearly committed to meeting our foreign currency
obligations, but the terms of repayment of our various loans are laid down
by contract, and there is no particular reason why we should strive to
accelerate the process. Indeed, the balance of payments difficulties which
we experienced in the 1950's and 1960's made it necessary to take advantage several times of the "waiver" clause in the American loan agreement
whereby only the annual interest charge was met, and our short-term
liabilities to the IMF were "rephased" after the crises of 1965 and 1967
so as to allow further time for the long-awaited balance of payments
surplus to develop. Although this sounds as if this part of the external
debt is a fairly serious burden, the adjustment to our living standard which
is necessary in order to repay it is really slight when viewed against the
size of the national product and the annual increase which might reasonably be expected in it.

7.11 *It is just as important to reduce the volume of imports as it is to increase exports if the country's external accounts are to be brought into equilibrium. Discuss this view, and outline the measures available to the government to limit imports.* (*ICA Final, November 1966.*)

Reduced imports v. increased exports

The view expressed in the first part of the question may be arithmetically correct, but, other things being equal, it would be preferable to increase the volume of exports rather than to reduce imports as a way of correcting an adverse balance of trade. There are a number of reasons for making this statement, as follows —

(*a*) Any artificial restraint on international trade would conflict with the principle of comparative costs, and would react adversely on the standard of living to some extent.

(*b*) It would restrict the field of consumer choice, and reduce the amount of competition on the home market.

(*c*) It might well result in similar action being taken by other countries against one's own exports, either in a spirit of retaliation, or, more simply, because the damage done to their export trade would reduce the amount of foreign currency they could earn to finance their imports.

(*d*) It would contravene the spirit, if not the letter, of agreements with international trading bodies, e.g. GATT, IMF.

(*e*) It would require a certain amount of manpower and other resources to operate the controls.

Measures to limit imports

If, nevertheless, some urgent action to prevent a loss of gold was imperative, the only certain way to do this would be to reduce the demand for imports by one or more of the following methods —

(*a*) *Import duties.* The erection of a tariff barrier is a simple and fairly flexible way of reducing the amount of foreign currency being spent on imports. Import duties will tend to raise the domestic price of imported goods, and even though demand may be inelastic the quantity demanded will contract to some extent; hence, assuming that prices in terms of their own currencies do not rise, the amount of foreign exchange required to finance the purchase of imports will be reduced. Indeed, it is quite possible that foreign suppliers will reduce their prices in an attempt to maintain sales, thus affording the protected country the added benefit of an improvement in its terms of trade. A tariff can be made selective to any desired extent, and the maximum saving of foreign currency could be achieved by discriminating against those products for which elasticity of demand was greatest.

(*b*) *Quotas.* A more direct method which is at the same time even more flexible than import duties is the setting of quotas, i.e. a quantitative restriction on the volume of imports during a given period, normally one year. Quotas have a more predictable effect on annual foreign exchange costs, but foreign and domestic suppliers alike may take advantage of the reduced supply of goods to raise their prices, i.e. in this case there is a tendency for the terms of trade to deteriorate. Moreover, if the quota is a "global" one, there may be a sharp increase in imports during the early part of the year due to the anxiety of competing foreign suppliers to get their shipments delivered before the quota is exhausted.

(c) *General deflation.* Another method of reducing the money spent on imports is for the Government to restrict the volume of credit in the economy, thus reducing general purchasing power. This policy will not produce quick results, and since it does not discriminate between imported and home-produced goods it is bound to create unemployment, but sooner or later the foreign exchange cost of imports is certain to come down. The effect of reduced purchasing power will be most manifest in products which have the greatest income-elasticity of demand.

(d) *Devaluation.* The effect of devaluation is to raise the domestic price level for all imported goods to a similar degree, so contracting the demand for them, and thus ensuring an immediate reduction in total foreign exchange costs; as in the case of import duties above, if one assumes that prices in terms of exporting countries' currencies do not rise, some saving of foreign exchange is certain in the immediate post-devaluation period. After a time, however, rising domestic prices may lead to a rise in money incomes, so that the former level of demand for imports is restored; to the extent that this is allowed to happen, devaluation will be abortive in reducing the demand for foreign currency.

(e) *Exchange control.* This is perhaps the most effective and widely-adopted method of reducing the foreign exchange cost of imports. It can be applied with any degree of severity as current circumstances may dictate against imports from any or all countries, and needs no more than the passing of a single law (in Britain, the Exchange Control Act of 1947) to give the authorities all the power they need for an indefinite period. Like any other device designed to keep out imports, it tends to have an inflationary effect, but its extreme flexibility and administrative convenience make it an obvious choice in any policy directed towards reducing the foreign exchange cost of imports, either alone or in conjunction with one or more of the other methods mentioned above.

SIMILAR QUESTIONS
(i) In what ways can a government correct a balance of payments deficit? (I of B Part I, April 1966.)
(ii) Outline the various policies which might be adopted by a country suffering from a deficit in its Balance of Payments. State the disadvantages of each of these policies. (I of B Part I, September 1967.)

(iii) Consider the view that the government should impose limitation of imports into Great Britain. (CIS Final, June 1967.)

(iv) In what circumstances, if any, should a rise in imports be checked? What means of control do you suggest? (C of S Advanced, May 1969.)

8

International trade and payments

The traditional importance of this aspect of economics has been enhanced by Britain's persistent difficulties in the field of international trade and payments since World War II, and it is rarely that an examination paper is set without some question touching on this topic.

This may simply ask for an explanation of the gains to be derived from international trade, which of course calls for an exposition of the Theory of Comparative Costs. There need be nothing here to worry the student if he remembers that international trade is merely a world-wide application of the principle of specialization, or "division of labour writ large" as one writer has expressed it, but it should be borne in mind that the "costs" which are being "compared" are the opportunity costs of producing one commodity as against another *in each particular country*, not the money costs of producing one particular commodity in different countries.

Despite the manifest advantages of free trade in theory, many countries, not least Britain, rely heavily on protection, and the student should be able to weigh the arguments for and against this policy. International attempts to lower trade barriers, e.g. the General Agreement on Tariffs and Trade, the European Economic Community, the European Free Trade Association, are also liable to produce questions, so again it pays to be fairly conversant with recent developments in these fields.

Considerable importance attaches to the terms of trade, especially in the case of small countries which rely heavily on imports and exports. The student should therefore be quite sure that he understands this concept, and how changes in the *terms* of trade are related to the *balance* of trade — there is a regrettable tendency to confuse the two, or at least to assume that a favourable movement in the former necessarily has a favourable effect on the latter.

All problems in the field of international payments arise simply from the fact that exporters normally demand payment in their own money. Although trade between England and Scotland may show a surplus in favour of one side or the other, no "balance of payments" problem as such occurs as they have a common currency and banking system; obviously, it would be highly desirable for the whole world to have the same currency, but as matters stand countries with a deficit on their current transactions with the rest of the world must find some way of obtaining the necessary foreign currency to meet their obligations.

Gold is and always has been internationally acceptable as a means of payment, but almost certainly no one has enough of it to support the present volume and value of international transactions, so in the circumstances the best we can do is to devise schemes like the International Monetary Fund to economize in the use of gold as much as possible, while continuing with attempts to keep international trade as free as possible, as mentioned above.

Finally, there is the vexed question of foreign exchange rates. No system has yet been developed which reconciles the desire for stable exchange rates with the fact that the internal purchasing powers of different countries' currencies are always changing relative to one another. Since 1944, the IMF has attempted to impose regulations fixing all rates within very narrow limits for as long a period as possible, but from time to time the pressure on foreign exchange markets has necessitated fairly drastic adjustments. As a consequence, some relaxation in the rigidity of the structure is now being considered whereby a series of gradual changes will replace these periodical crises, but apart from an agreement to create "special drawing rights", thereby increasing all countries' liquid resources, little progress has been made in reforming the IMF system.

This Section covers a lively and interesting part of economics, and the kind of question which is usually set should not present any undue difficulty once the basic principles of comparative cost and international payments have been understood.

8.1 *"The reasons for specialization between individuals are essentially the same as the reasons for international trade." Discuss. (U of L Advanced, January 1964.)*

Principle of comparative advantage

The statement contained in the question is entirely correct; the basic principle which makes specialization advantageous for individuals, namely that of comparative advantage, is just as valid when applied to countries, and is moreover subject to the same kind of limitations.

Opportunity cost and specialization (1)

No matter how strong or clever he is, there will be some tasks in which an *individual* will be particularly outstanding; conversely, however low the general level of an individual's performance may be, his inferiority in some kinds of work will be less marked than in others. In either case, the individual will be most highly rewarded if he concentrates on the job in which his relative advantage is greatest, or his relative disadvantage is least; to occupy himself in any other kind of task would represent an unnecessary sacrifice of potential earning power. In other words, the cost to the individual of using his time and effort in one way is the opportunity which he forgoes of using them in some other way; it is therefore in his best interest to discover the highest point at which his abilities match the rewards offered by the labour market for different kinds of services, and then to exploit his value fully by specializing in what is for him the most rewarding field.

Opportunity cost and specialization (2)

Precisely the same kind of reasoning can be applied to the way in which *countries* use their productive facilities. No two countries have the same assortment of natural resources, the same combination of skills in their labour forces, or the same kinds of capital equipment; it is therefore desirable for the factors of production in each country to be employed in such a way as to obtain the highest reward, having regard to the prices offering on world markets for the various alternative goods and services which it is possible for them to offer. Like individuals, countries will have to accept the necessity for abandoning one kind of specialization in favour of another if the relative prices of products change; neither may find this easy to do, but unwillingness to adapt to changing circumstances will inevitably result in failure to maximize income.

Limits to specialization

Practical considerations which may prevent complete specialization as between individuals are also closely analogous to those which tend to limit the degree of international specialization. Foremost among these is the fact that the market simply may not be large enough to absorb the whole of the specialist's potential output; a small village would not require the full-time services of a barber, nor would the total world demand for toast-racks provide full employment for any one country. Furthermore, there are obvious dangers in having all one's eggs in one basket; the general handyman is likely to find steadier employment than the narrow specialist, and countries, too, may benefit from a certain amount of versatility in coping with the vicissitudes of world trade.

Specialization and money

Finally, whatever form specialization takes, it is wholly dependent on the existence of an efficient monetary system to make it workable. We rather take this for granted in our individual rôles as sellers of specialized services to the rest of our own community, but lack of a

really satisfactory form of international money threatens to inhibit
the continued development of specialization among countries.

SIMILAR QUESTIONS

(i) Explain with examples the view that international trade is essentially
a special application of the principle of division of labour. Outline the
factors that may hinder the free application of the principle. (I of B,
September 1966.)

(ii) Is international trade anything more than an arrangement for world-
wide division of labour? (C of S Intermediate, June 1967.)

(iii) Why do countries often import goods which they could manufacture
themselves? Illustrate your answer with particular reference to the trade
of your own country. (C of S Intermediate, November 1967.)

(iv) When considering its international trading policy a country must not
only compare its domestic costs with the price of foreign goods but
must also consider comparative costs. Discuss in terms of international
trade why comparative costs are important. (ACCA Section I, December
1967.)

(v) Explain the theory of comparative cost in relation to international
trade. (ACCA Section I, June 1969.)

8.2   *In Malanesia a unit of resources will produce either 100 yards of cloth
      or 20 units of steel. In Indolaysia a unit of resources will produce 90
      yards of cloth or 15 units of steel. Explain the effects of international
      trade on production of each of the commodities in each country.
      (U of L Advanced, January 1965.)*

Malanesia's absolute advantage

Evidently the factors of production in Malanesia are generally more
efficient than those in Indolaysia, since a unit of resources, whether it is
applied to the production of cloth or of steel, will produce more there, and as
a consequence Malanesia's standard of living will be the higher of the two
whether there is international trade or not. The fact that Malanesia's
superiority is less marked in the production of cloth than it is of steel,
however, means that it would be to the advantage of both countries if
specialization and trade took place.

Opportunity costs in Malanesia

In the absence of trade, the people in Malanesia could use each unit of
resources in such a way as to produce *either* 100 yards of cloth *or* 20
units of steel, or any combination of cloth and steel such that 5 more
yards of cloth could be obtained provided that 1 unit of steel were
sacrificed, or vice versa. In other words, the "opportunity cost ratio"
between cloth and steel in Malanesia in 5:1, and the range of choice open
to it can be illustrated thus —

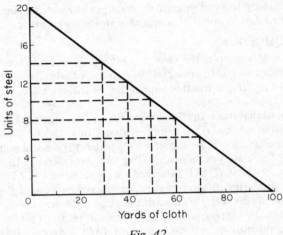

Fig. 42

For example, possible combinations of output in Malanesia would be —

> 70 yards of cloth *plus* 6 units of steel.
> 60 yards of cloth *plus* 8 units of steel.
> 50 yards of cloth *plus* 10 units of steel.
> 40 yards of cloth *plus* 12 units of steel.
> 30 yards of cloth *plus* 14 units of steel.

Opportunity costs in Indolaysia

Similarly, the opportunity cost ratio between cloth and steel in Indolaysia is 90:15, or 6:1, and possible combinations of output would be —

> 60 yards of cloth *plus* 5 units of steel.
> 54 yards of cloth *plus* 6 units of steel.
> 48 yards of cloth *plus* 7 units of steel.
> 42 yards of cloth *plus* 8 units of steel.
> 36 yards of cloth *plus* 9 units of steel.

as shown in Fig. 43.

Position before trade

Let us then suppose that, in the absence of trade, the people in each country choose the following combined outputs of cloth and steel as being the best possible use to which a unit of resources can be applied —

> Malanesia opts for 40 yards of cloth plus 12 units of steel.
> Indolaysia opts for 48 yards of cloth plus 7 units of steel.

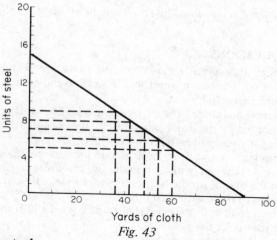

Fig. 43

Position after trade

Now, if both countries specialize, Malanesia in the production of steel and Indolaysia in the production of cloth, the former will be able to produce 20 units of steel from each unit of resources, and the latter 90 yards of cloth. But the difference in opportunity cost ratios between steel and cloth in the two countries will make it advantageous to Malanesia to offer 1 unit of steel if it can obtain more than 5 yards of cloth in exchange, whereas it will be advantageous to Indolaysia if it can obtain 1 unit of steel for anything less than 6 yards of cloth. Any ratio of exchange lying between 1:5 and 1:6 will therefore benefit both countries, as can be shown by assuming that trading takes place on the basis of 1 unit of steel against 5½ yards of cloth; if, for example, Malanesia exports 7½ units of steel to Indolaysia, and Indolaysia exports 41¼ yards of cloth to Malanesia, both countries will have slightly more of both commodities than those available to them when they were producing independently, namely —

> Malanesia will have 41¼ yards of cloth plus 12½ units of steel.
> Indolaysia will have 48¾ yards of cloth and 7½ units of steel.

Had the differences in opportunity cost ratios been greater, the gain would have been greater; if there had been no such difference, no purpose at all would have been served by specialization and trade.

The assumption of constant costs

The foregoing argument assumes that production of cloth and steel in both countries is carried on under conditions of constant costs, i.e. that variations in output have no effect on cost per unit. In so far as production took place under diminishing returns, trade would fall off as opportunity cost ratios tended towards equality; if on the other hand there were increasing returns to scale, unrestricted trade would be even more beneficial than the example suggests.

SIMILAR QUESTIONS

(i) "It is comparative advantage, not absolute advantage, which determines the pattern of trade between countries." Elucidate and discuss. (CIS Intermediate, December 1964.)

(ii) Can international trade between two countries be mutually profitable if one of them can produce all commodities more cheaply than the other? Give reasons for your answer. (CIS Intermediate, December 1966.)

(iii) Two countries, A and B, are both able to produce commodities x and y. In country A, however, a unit of productive resources can make $10\,x$ or $20\,y$, and in B a unit of productive resources can yield $10\,x$ or $15\,y$. If the countries begin to trade with each other:

    (*a*) In which good will A specialize? In which good will B specialize? Explain the reason for their choices.

    (*b*) What is the gain from specialization?

    (*c*) At what ratio of exchange between x and v will trade take place? (I of B Part I, April 1969.)

(iv) If a particular country can produce one commodity more efficiently than any other country can, why do other countries produce that commodity at all? (CIS Intermediate, June 1969.)

8.3   *Although the law of comparative advantage shows that free trade maximizes welfare, most nations in fact impose tariffs. What reasons are usually advanced in support of this policy, and to what extent are they justified? (I of B Part I, April 1967.)*

Tariffs provide employment

Perhaps the commonest argument which is advanced in favour of tariff protection is that if there is unemployment of any kind, and the country in question is importing goods which the unemployed could conceivably make, then it is in the general interest to keep the foreign goods out. Whether the unemployment is general, as in a depression, or whether it is in a declining industry, the advocates of protection would say it is better that the people concerned should be doing something rather than nothing. Such simple reasoning has one fundamental flaw, however, namely that if other countries are prevented from selling to you, they cannot buy from you either. Unemployment will therefore tend to reappear, first in the export industries and then by chain reaction in all the rest. What has happened in the past is that restrictions on imports by one country have had to be followed after a short interval by similar restrictions in other countries, and unemployment has got worse all round instead of better.

"Infant industries" deserve protection

The "infant industry" argument is often used by developing countries coming late on to the industrial scene. In such cases, it is maintained, existing industries in older countries already enjoying economies of scale make it impossible for would-be new industries in the developing country to sell their output, even in their home market, unless they are given a few years' freedom from competition in which to establish themselves. Such claims have a sound theoretical basis, but, as critics are fond of saying, these infants never seem to want to grow up, and continue to claim protection on one pretext or another long after the original justification for it has passed.

Tariffs protect high wages

Another recurring theme is that a "high wage country" needs to be protected against the import of goods produced by "sweated labour", in case domestic living standards should be driven down to those in the exporting country. This is rather like trying to talk yourself into a high standard of living, however; if a foreign country can genuinely undersell domestic producers, it is surely a sign that money wages in the importing country are too high in relation to the value of the goods being produced. If it can be shown that the imported goods are being "dumped", i.e. sold at a price which does not cover their full average cost per unit, then there are perfectly good reasons for discriminating against them, but so often the mere fact that goods are low in price is used as a pretext for invoking the anti-dumping laws.

Strategic industries must be protected

Making no attempt at justification on economic grounds, military advisers urge the protection of "strategic" industries, a category which can be made to extend from armaments themselves to iron and steel, shipbuilding, transport and so on right through to agriculture, or indeed almost anything outside sheer luxury goods. The economist as such is not qualified to pronounce on the merits of these arguments, beyond reminding policy-makers of the obvious fact that while this kind of protection may add to the nation's security, it can only detract from its standard of living.

Tariffs may improve the terms of trade

By contrast, a policy which aims at the crudest possible exploitation of economic advantage is a protective tariff designed to improve the terms of trade. This can be done either where a country is a very large buyer of goods which foreigners are dependent on selling to her, or a very large seller of goods which other countries depend on buying from her; either way, the price of imports is forced down so that the necessary amount of domestic currency may be earned by foreigners. As an exercise in the use of monopoly power this is undeniably effective, although its ethical basis is open to question, and the victims may succeed in finding other ways of solving their problems in the long run.

Gold reserve must be protected

Last, there is the plea that a balance of payments crisis has forced legislators into adopting a policy of tariff restriction in spite of themselves. This can, of course, easily happen; it is no good expecting a sudden increase in exports to redeem the situation in the short run, so that the only practicable thing to do to stop the gold reserve running out is to raise a barrier to imports. So, providing the appropriate explanations are given to foreign countries, coupled with an undertaking to remove the restrictions as soon as possible, no reasonable objection can be raised to protection on these grounds.

Summary

By and large, therefore, the detailed arguments in favour of tariffs have little to commend them on economic grounds except as strictly short-run expedients to assist a more balanced development of industry or to cope with a balance of payments crisis. Looked at more broadly, they may be a way of maintaining a greater degree of stability in the economy than if it were fully exposed to the vagaries of international competition, but in the long run the price of such stability is likely to be the retardation of progress.

SIMILAR QUESTIONS

(i) "The main justification of tariffs is to protect the industries of advanced nations from the unfair competition of backward ones." (U of L Advanced, Summer 1965.)

(ii) "Cheap imports threaten our industries." "Cheap imports have been a main contributor to our rising standard of living." Discuss. (CIS Intermediate, June 1966.)

8.4   *"Developing economies need trade rather than aid." Discuss. (CIS Final, December 1967.)*

The need for action

The whole issue of underdeveloped countries becomes more serious, both economically and politically, for while living standards in the advanced countries rise every year, theirs remain relatively stagnant. Whatever may be the reasons for this disparity in the rate of progress, it is in the mutual interest of all to redress the balance somehow, and this need not in the long run be at the expense of living standards in the advanced countries.

Initial investment

To say that "developing economies need trade rather than aid" presents the problem in the form of a false antithesis, however, as there is nothing in the one policy which precludes the other. At a very early stage of development, there may be very little which a backward country can offer as a trading partner to the highly industrialized nations; not only would there be the problem of squeezing out some margin for export from a productive capacity which might be barely sufficient to provide subsistence, but even the exploitation of mineral wealth or cash crop potential demands the initial investment of a certain amount of capital. This investment can only come from the outside, and the only question is whether it is financed by private enterprise or national and international agencies; while the only method adopted during the 19th century was the former, the political climate in recent years has thrown the main burden of investment on to international loans or outright gifts.

Problems created by aid

Naturally, the countries and international agencies providing this finance have been anxious to ensure that it is used to the best advantage, and this has led to a certain amount of interference in developing countries' affairs which has not always been welcome. Worse still, however, has been the emergence of a position where the developing countries have managed to achieve a surplus of some commodity for export, only to find themselves in competition with producers in the advanced countries. It is at this point that the argument about trade versus aid becomes relevant, but even so there should be no question of having to choose between one and the other.

Advanced countries' need to adapt

What seems indisputable is that nothing should be allowed to stand in the way of developing countries in their quest for export markets. They will presumably make a start in the field of primary products or simple manufactured goods, and in certain cases, e.g. cotton textiles, these are bound to compete with domestic producers in the advanced countries, but it would be defeating the whole object of the investment to restrict their entry by tariffs or quotas. It should not be beyond the capability of technologically advanced countries to devise some more rewarding use for their own resources than making goods of this kind; not only would failure to do so delay progress in the developing countries, but it would prevent the latter from meeting the interest and capital repayments on their loans. Nor should it be forgotten that in protecting one group of industrialists the advanced countries would be damaging the interests of others, i.e. the exporters who would be denied the opportunity of selling products which it would otherwise be within the developing countries' capacity to buy.

Trade and aid complementary?

Meanwhile, there would be no reason to terminate investment in developing countries; rather should their success in raising the level of their economic performance be regarded as justification for further investment, perhaps in more sophisticated fields, at least to a point where their "take-off" into Rostow's phase of self-sustaining domestic investment became assured. International trade and international investment may have to complement one another if the world's full productive potential is to be realized, and there is no reason in theory why both should not be pursued to the greatest possible extent.

SIMILAR QUESTIONS

(i) Is the development of economically backward countries the more likely to be encouraged by additional investment from abroad, or by increased willingness to trade freely with them? (CIS Final, June 1964.)
(ii) "Industrialized economies should not give overseas aid to developing economies because, in the long run, it will only transform them into trading rivals." Do you agree? (CIS Final, December 1968.)

8.5 *Distinguish carefully between the* terms of trade *and the* balance of trade. *How are they related? (CIS Intermediate, June 1969.)*

Definition of terms of trade

A country's terms of trade reflect changes in the general level of its export prices in relation to the prices of its imports. Hence, the terms of trade are usually expressed in the form of an Index Number, calculated as follows —

$$\frac{\text{Unit price of exports}}{\text{Unit price of imports}} \times 100.$$

Any upwards movement in the Index is then said to be "favourable", and any downwards movement "unfavourable".

Effect on balance of trade uncertain

It must not be assumed, however, that a favourable movement in the terms of trade will necessarily have a beneficial effect on the balance of trade, or indeed that there is any easily definable connection between the two. Obviously, a country's terms of trade will be improved either by a fall in the price of its imports or by a rise in the price of its exports, but the net result in regard to the total amount of foreign currency spent or earned respectively will depend on the elasticity of demand in either case.

Improvement in the terms of trade (1)

Should the improvement in the terms of trade be due to a *fall in the price of imports,* the probability is that the balance of trade would also benefit. For the most part, imports are likely to consist of goods which cannot be produced in the home country, i.e. for which there is no close substitute, and demand would therefore tend to be inelastic. Hence a general reduction in the price level of imports would lead to a less-than-proportional extension in demand, and the total amount of foreign currency required to purchase them would decrease.

Improvement in the terms of trade (2)

If, on the other hand, more favourable terms of trade were due to a *rise in the price of exports,* it is extremely doubtful whether the balance of trade would benefit. In exceptional cases, the rise in price might indicate an improved bargaining position on the part of the exporting country such as that which Britain enjoyed when she emerged as the principal supplier of manufactured goods during the 19th century, in which case foreign currency earnings would be increased by exacting higher prices. More usually, however, a rise in the price of a country's export goods merely reflects the rise in the general level of its costs caused by inflationary pressure: since the rest of the world is free to choose between one country's products and another's, a rise in export prices is therefore likely to be followed by a more-than-proportional contraction in demand, and hence a reduction in foreign currency earnings.

It is true that there are many other factors affecting demand, e.g. salesmanship, delivery dates, after-sales service, quality, etc., but price remains the biggest single influence, and one which, unlike the others, operates in only one direction over the whole field of products. In general, therefore, it is reasonable to assume that the demand for all countries' exports will tend to be elastic, so that while a rise in their price will improve the terms of trade in the strictly technical sense it may well lead to a deterioration in the balance of trade.

Effect of devaluation

A significant commentary on the importance attaching to this question is provided by the decision to devalue the domestic currency which is often taken by a country in Balance of Payments difficulties. In effect, this lowers the price of exports and raises the price of imports, thus making the terms of trade less favourable, but it is evidently assumed that the increase in earnings from exports, coupled with some reduction in the foreign exchange cost of imports, will help the Balance of Payments through an improvement in the balance of trade.

SIMILAR QUESTIONS

(i) Explain the difference between a worsening of the terms of trade, and an adverse movement in the balance of payments of a country. Which, in your opinion, is likely to be economically more disadvantageous for Great Britain? (CIS Final, December 1964.)

(ii) Define the terms of trade. Is an "improvement" in them necessarily advantageous? (C of S Intermediate, November 1966.)

(iii) Is a favourable movement in a country's international terms of trade necessarily advantageous to that country? (C of S Final, June 1967.)

(iv) Can the terms of trade ever be *too* favourable? (CIS Intermediate, December 1968.)

(v) Show the possible effects of a change in the terms of trade on the balance of payments. (CIS Final, June 1970.)

8.6 *"All double-entry book-keeping systems must provide an equality of debit and credit entries. There can therefore be no deficit on the balance of payments." Discuss. (CIS Intermediate, December 1968.)*

Receipts and payments

While a country's balance of payments is commonly said to be "adverse" or "favourable", the statement contained in the question serves to remind us that there are two parties to every monetary transaction, i.e. one who pays and one who receives, and that in a strict bookkeeping sense the two sides of the national "cash book" must somehow be made to balance, even if earnings from exports fail to cover the cost of imports.

Current account transactions

In Britain's case, the income received from selling goods abroad normally falls a long way short of the amount needed to pay for imports, but the "trade gap", as it is popularly called, could well be closed by a surplus on payments for "invisible" items, which include such things as insurance, shipping, civil aviation, travel, other services, interest, profit and dividends and private remittances. Unfortunately, one further item of an "invisible" nature, namely the Government's overseas expenditure, has been sufficiently large in recent years to cancel out much of the advantage derived from the others, so that in 1964, for example, there was still a total deficit on our balance of payments current account of £374 m.

Capital movements

In order to arrive at the overall balance of payments position, however, movements of capital into and out of the country must be merged with current transactions. Overseas investment, whether on Government or private account, involves making payments for foreign-owned assets, and gives rise to a debit entry in the balance in just the same way as do payments for imports; conversely, the purchase of assets in the UK by foreigners represents a credit item. It so happens that in 1964 the balance of payments on capital account was also adverse to the extent of £371 m., so that, allowing £1 m. for a "balancing item" of unknown origin, the "basic" balance of payments figure for that year showed an overall deficit of no less than £744 m.

Monetary movements

Thus the events of 1964 well illustrate the underlying significance of the quotation which forms the subject of this question. The money to settle the obligations incurred by Britain during that year had to be found by one means or another, and the published records show that the total amount needed was raised by borrowing £263 m. from various foreign banks, drawing £359 m. from the International Monetary Fund, and running down our reserves of gold and foreign currency by £122 m. This brought us so near the end of our ability to find further means of payment that some brake had to be applied to overseas expenditure; in the late autumn of that year, a 15 per cent surcharge was applied to a wide range of import duties, and severe restrictions were imposed on the export of capital.

The balance of payments must always balance

Had these measures failed to abate the demand for foreign currency, our reserves would have had to be supplemented by the liquidation of British-owned assets, whether in the UK or abroad – there is simply no escaping the obligation to find the money required to meet one's debts as they fall due. In this sense, therefore, it is correct to say that there can be no deficit on the balance of payments.

SIMILAR QUESTIONS

(i) How may the Government finance a deficit on the balance of payments in the short term? (ICWA Part I, June 1966.)
(ii) "The balance of payments always balances." Explain and discuss. (U of L Advanced, Summer 1966.)
(iii) What are the chief constituents of a country's "balance of payments"? In what sense can this balance be said to be in "deficit"? (CIS Intermediate, December 1967.)
(iv) What are the differences between the balance of trade and the balance of payments? Why is it important to distinguish between them? (C of S Intermediate, November 1968.)

8.7 *What are the functions of the International Monetary Fund? (U of L Advanced, Summer 1966.)*

Origins and purpose of the IMF

When the Allied nations met at Bretton Woods, USA, in 1944, their main objective was the creation of conditions in the postwar world favourable to the expansion of international trade. The 1930's had shown that one of the great stumbling blocks to a high level of trading was the difficulty experienced by all countries from time to time in financing balance of payments deficits; since for every creditor there must be a debtor, at any given time about half the nations of the world were drawing upon their reserves of gold and foreign currency to meet their current deficits. As most countries' reserves tended to be rather small in relation to turnover, they were frequently compelled to limit the value of imports by one means or another, thus shifting the deficit on to their trading partners, who in turn adopted protective measures and so on. Clearly, what was needed was an all-round extension of international purchasing power to enable countries in temporary balance of payments difficulties to "ride out the storm" without harming the interests of others, and this is mainly what the IMF was designed to do.

The IMF agreement

The basis of the original agreement was as follows —

(*a*) All member countries accepted a normal "par value" for their currencies vis-à-vis the others, and undertook to maintain it within plus or minus 1 per cent.

(*b*) All agreed to make contributions to a common fund according to a quota figure based on the size of their national economies, 25 per cent of which was payable in gold and 75 per cent in each member's own currency.

(*c*) Every member acquired the right to call upon the Fund for whatever currencies it needed up to a total of 25 per cent of its quota in any one year for a period not exceeding five years, paying interest on its drawings and putting an equivalent amount of its own currency into the Fund until repayment was made.

(*d*) Since initial par values might prove to be unrealistic in the light of postwar trading conditions, provision was made for devaluation of any members currency —

(i) By up to 10 per cent without reference to the Fund authorities;

(ii) By 10 per cent or more after consultation and agreement with the other members, in cases where a fundamental disequilibrium existed.

(*e*) In recognition of the fact that creditor countries were in a sense just as much responsible for balance of payments crises as debtor countries, a clause was included which gave the latter the right to discriminate against the exports of a persistent creditor once the Fund had officially declared its currency to be "scarce".

Post-war difficulties

While the Fund may not have done all that was expected of it, there can be no doubt that it has played an important part in helping the growth of world trade. At first, comparatively little use was made of the Fund; while the authorities could hardly contest the right of a debtor country to draw the first 25 per cent, or "tranche", of its quota (since this was covered by its own gold contribution), it became a matter for debate whether further tranches should be granted automatically, or whether some more positive action on the debtor's part was needed to prevent a continuing deficit. Moreover, the Fund exercised its right to discourage undue dependence on its facilities by exacting a higher rate of interest on drawings the larger they were and the longer they were outstanding.

For about the first ten years of the Fund's existence, there was also widespread disregard of its rules. All countries were extremely short of US dollars during this period, but dollars were never officially declared to be a scarce currency; Britain and her sterling area associates devalued the £ by about 40 per cent in 1949 without consulting the Fund authorities; almost all countries continued to operate a fairly rigorous form of exchange control, and so on.

Recent developments

Subsequently, however, there have been a number of more favourable developments. The device known as a "stand-by credit" was evolved in the early 1950's, whereby a country is publicly assured by the Fund that certain sums will be made available to it if and when required, thus helping to check speculation against its currency, and quotas were increased by 50 per cent in 1959 and again by 25 per cent in 1966. Furthermore, the Fund's rules have been eased slightly for underdeveloped countries, and some members have been allowed to draw amounts above the normal ceiling in exceptional cases. As a result, the total of outstanding drawings and unused stand-bys had increased from about $750 m. in 1950 to over $5,000 m. in 1967: during the same period, world trade grew in value from $55 billion to nearly $200 billion, although international gold reserves only rose from $33 billion to $40 billion.

The most recent development is the agreement by member countries to the creation of "special drawing rights" as from the beginning of 1970, which will in effect make a permanent addition of nearly $10 billion to the world's liquid assets over the ensuing three years. While this will undoubtedly help to ease the problem of international payments, no agreement has yet been reached on the fundamental question of how exchange rates shall be determined. Many are in favour of abandoning the system of fixed parities altogether, i.e. of allowing the value of each currency to find its own level in the foreign exchange markets, while others favour some less extreme remedy along the lines of a continuous but controlled adjustment. If the IMF could evolve some workable solution to this problem it would undoubtedly be the greatest contribution it had ever made to the expansion of world trade.

SIMILAR QUESTIONS

(i) What is the "world liquidity problem"? (CIS Final, June 1964.)
(ii) What do you understand by the "problem of international liquidity"? (ICA Final, May 1968.)

8.8 *What is meant by a country's balance of payments being "unfavourable"? Need an unfavourable balance of payments always give cause for alarm? (CIS Intermediate, June 1964.)*

An "unfavourable" balance of payments

Any statement made about a country's balance of payments normally relates to a specified period of time, e.g. a particular month or year; to say that there had been an unfavourable balance would mean that, taking the period in question as a whole, the amount of foreign currency accruing to the country from all sources had fallen short of its total disbursements. The inevitable corollary of this state of affairs would be an outflow of gold equal to the difference between the two amounts, since gold remains the sole means of settling international debts when all other methods of obtaining foreign currencies have been exhausted, i.e. exporting goods, selling services, negotiating for loans and attracting investments.

Amount and duration of deficit

As to whether an adverse balance of payments need give cause for alarm, much will depend first of all on the size of the deficiency in relation to the gold reserves of the country in question. If it is a relatively insignificant amount, then obviously no one is going to regard it as a very serious matter; it goes without saying that all the countries of the world cannot simultaneously achieve a surplus in their balance of payments, and random variations in any one country's monthly figures may result in deficits and surpluses cancelling one another out over a period of a year or so. Indeed, it is a well recognized feature of the United Kingdom's balance of payments that a deficit tends to develop during the autumn months of every year, but in the ordinary course of events this tendency is reversed in the spring.

Current and capital account items

In order to assess the real significance of changes in any country's balance of payments position, however, it is necessary to analyse more closely the components of its receipts and expenditures. Apart from the overriding question of whether a country has enough reserves of gold to meet an overall deficit in any given period, the most important aspect of the matter is whether it is managing to pay its way from month to month, i.e. whether its earnings from visible and invisible exports are sufficient to cover its liabilities for visible and invisible imports. In other words, one should look at the state of the balance of payments on current account as distinct from the balance of payments overall; in the same way that a favourable balance overall can be obtained by recourse to foreign loans or the sale of domestic assets, so an unfavourable balance for the time being would result from a country having made its currency available to others for long-term loans, or used part of its reserves for the purchase of capital assets abroad. Like any other kind of investment, such a decision implies the willingness and the ability to forgo current benefits for the sake of future income, and is by no means a cause for alarm.

"Hot money" and interest rates

Movements of short-term capital, or "hot money", have an equally disturbing effect on a country's balance of payments figures from one month to another; whether an outflow of such capital should be a matter for serious concern depends to a large extent on the circumstances in which it takes place. There is always a good deal of money invested in the financial capitals of the world on a strictly short-term basis, and it is quite normal for a change in the structure of international interest rates to give rise to a movement of these funds away from centres where the return on them happens to be low for the time being, and vice versa. Temporary factors arising from management of the domestic economy may make it desirable for a government to maintain a lower rate of interest than that obtainable elsewhere, and if the outflow of short-term money can be attributed solely to the desire to secure a better return, and the gold reserve is clearly capable of sustaining a temporary drain, no great harm is done. The real danger signal is a flight of "hot money" when the rate of interest is high, having perhaps been deliberately raised as a means of helping to correct an adverse balance of payments; this can only be interpreted as a sign that foreign holders of the domestic currency are now less concerned about securing a high return on their money than they are about the possibility of a reduction in the value of their capital should devaluation occur. Once such a speculative movement against the domestic currency has started, it is difficult to stop, and a country could even be forced into a devaluation which was not really justified by the broad underlying facts of its trading position.

World liquidity problem

When all has been said about the technical possibilities involved, however, an adverse balance of payments must on the whole give more cause for concern than a favourable one. In spite of the existence of the International Monetary Fund, and the degree of co-operation which exists between the various Central Banks, the fact remains that the growth in international trade has placed a well-nigh intolerable strain on the world's liquid assets; as a consequence no country has the necessary reserves to sustain an adverse balance of payments for very long, whatever may be the justification for it. Whilst we remain tied to the present system, therefore, maintenance of a favourable balance of payments, even in the short term, assumes a practical importance out of all relation to its theoretical significance.

8.9 *Consider the arguments for and against exchange rate devaluation for a country in Balance of Payments difficulties. (CIS Intermediate, June 1967.)*

Benefit not certain

It is generally assumed that devaluation will have a beneficial effect on the balance of payments, but it is by no means certain that this will be the case, especially in the longer run.

Foreign currency the sole criterion

It must be remembered that balance of payments difficulties relate solely to the question of foreign currency; while there may be many other problems in the field of international trade, the only thing which is relevant in this particular context is whether the amount of foreign currency received is greater or less than the amount of foreign currency going out of the country.

Exports in the short period

Leaving aside for the time being payments on capital account, and confining the argument to the short period, the *supply* of foreign currency arises mainly from the sale of exports, and the fact that devaluation has the effect of making domestic goods cheaper for foreigners to buy will certainly extend the demand for them. For this to increase total foreign currency earnings, however, two conditions must be satisfied —

(*a*) The elasticity of demand for exports must be greater than unity, i.e. the increase in volume of demand must be more than sufficient to off-set the fall in unit price. The chances of this condition being fulfilled are in general, fairly high, as it is likely that the bulk of goods exported by one country will be more or less acceptable substitutes for similar goods exported by other countries; in the case of the United Kingdom, for example, it was recently estimated that the overall elasticity of demand for exports was between 3 and 5.

(*b*) In addition, it must be physically possible to increase the volume of exports to satisfy the new level of demand. This can only be done by increasing total production or by diverting sales from the home to the export market, so that in a state of full employment it follows that the greater part of the adjustment must be made by the latter method. This makes it necessary for the government to institute measures to restrain home market demand at the same time as devaluation is effected, otherwise the whole object of the exercise is defeated — at the worst, the result could be an unchanged volume of exports at lower prices.

Imports in the short period

Still speaking in terms of payments on current account in the short period, the *demand* for foreign currency arises mainly from the purchase of imports, and devaluation will have the effect of raising their prices in terms of the domestic currency. Although the demand for imports may well be fairly inelastic, their volume will shrink to some extent, and, assuming their price in terms of foreign currency remains the same, there will be a beneficial effect on the balance of payments.

The need for long-term adjustments

Provided that the restrictive measures referred to above have the desired influence on home market demand, the combined effect of an increase in the supply of foreign currency and a decrease in the demand for it would seem to ensure an improvement in the balance of payments situation. If we now move away from the short run position, however, the outcome is by no means so certain. Going back to the state of affairs before devaluation, the chronic shortage of foreign currency must have been caused by the country in question persistently tending to consume more than it produced, which is only another way of saying that it was suffering from inflation. Now, the effect of devaluation of itself is to make the inflation worse, as the supply of goods to the home market is reduced both by the increase in exports and the reduction in imports. The prices of imported goods will rise at once in terms of the domestic currency, and if money incomes are allowed to rise as well any benefits arising from devaluation will soon disappear. In short, if the community manages to maintain its former level of consumption, and production does not increase, nothing will really have changed except the foreign exchange rate and the domestic price level, and the country will soon find itself in the same balance of payments difficulties as before.

Devaluation only "buys time"

Looking at the problem in these broad terms, devaluation seems a fairly pointless procedure; if the only things that will correct a balance of payments deficit are a reduction in consumption or an increase in production, why not proceed directly to one or both of these objectives, and avoid the risk of retaliatory action which devaluation of any one country's currency engenders? The most that can be said in favour of devaluation is that it provides a stimulus to action and a short "breathing space" for the results of that action to manifest themselves, but the basic remedies were never lacking and must ultimately be taken if the deficit is to be eliminated.

The confidence factor

Finally, the question of payments on capital account must not be forgotten. The main issue here is one of confidence, and all the careful calculations of gain or loss on current account through changes in the price levels of exports and imports can be swept aside by a speculative movement out of a currency once investors of short-term capital have a suspicion that there is a possibility of devaluation. This is why politicians are always at great pains to deny that it is even being considered up to the very moment when it is in fact done, but the world has learned to discount such protestations, and the pressure of selling may reach a point where the only thing which will stop it is the event which it anticipates. If the extent of the devaluation is then large enough to assuage any doubts about the restoration of equilibrium, there should be a reverse movement of dealings on the foreign exchange market, but unfortunately when a country has resorted to devaluation once as a means of solving its balance of payments problems speculators are readier to believe that it will do so again, and crises tend to occur with less and less justification from the point of view of trading prospects.

Devaluation a last resort?

All in all, there is a great deal to be said for trying to achieve equilibrium in the balance of payments without resort to devaluation, but if other kinds of remedial action are not taken at a sufficiently early stage there may come a point where it is practically unavoidable.

SIMILAR QUESTIONS

(i) Explain why the recent devaluation of the £ sterling had to be accompanied by restrictions on Government expenditure and a "tough" Budget. (ICA Final, May 1968.)

(ii) What additional policies should accompany devaluation to make it effective, and why? (C of S Intermediate, June 1968.)

(iii) "Devaluation, under full employment conditions, only results in a deterioration of the terms of trade of the devaluing country." Examine this view. (CIS Final, June 1968.)

(iv) Explain carefully the "elasticities" to be considered when contemplating the devaluation of a country's currency. (CIS Intermediate, December 1968.)

(v) Why should devaluation help a country's balance of trade? Are there conditions when it may not do so? (CIS Intermediate, June 1970.)

8.10 *Outline the "purchasing power parity" theory of foreign exchange. How far is it a satisfactory explanation of exchange rates? (I of B Part I, April 1968.)*

Outline of theory

The Purchasing Power Parity Theory of exchange rates is usually associated with the name of Professor Cassel, writing during the 1920's, but its origins date back to the controversy between the "banking" and "currency" schools among economists about 100 years earlier. Presupposing freedom from any kind of government intervention in the foreign exchange market, the theory asserted that a pattern of exchange rates would be established whereby the internal and external purchasing powers of all currencies would be equated. For example, if £1 in the UK would buy goods to the same value as $5.00 in the United States, then any tendency for the rate between pounds and dollars to depart from £1 = $5.00 in the foreign exchange market would automatically be corrected by an increase in exports from the country whose currency was being sold too cheaply.

Weaknesses of theory

Quite apart from the fact that no country today does allow complete freedom in the purchase and sale of its currency, the Purchasing Power Parity Theory never provided a very satisfactory explanation for the level of foreign exchange rates at any given time, for the following reasons —

(a) *Difficulties of comparison.* Differences in the assortment of goods available for purchase, and the different social customs, climate and so on in any two countries being compared, make any assessment of "equal money's worth" very difficult, if not impossible.

(b) *Goods not traded.* In so far as transactions in the foreign exchange market are prompted by the need for domestic and foreign currencies to pay for exports and imports respectively, it is only goods actually entering into international trade which contribute to the formation of exchange rates. It may well be, however, that the prices of such goods are unrepresentative of prices as a whole in the countries of their origin; some goods by their very nature, e.g. houses, inland transport, etc., cannot possibly be exported, and their prices may be lower or higher than those which can. There is, of course, a tendency for competition in the factor market to eliminate such differences, but the degree of immobility may be such that they exist for considerable periods of time; it would be quite possible, for example, for wages and prices in those parts of the economy enjoying natural immunity from foreign competition to remain persistently higher than wages and prices in the "unsheltered" sectors.

(*c*) *Government policies.* Without going so far as to control dealings in the foreign exchange market, a government can create lasting differences between the prices for similar goods in different countries. For example, while overt subsidization of exports is ruled out by international trading agreements, some indirect method is often adopted to make their prices lower than they are on the home market, e.g. low interest rates on export credits, remission of indirect taxes; conversely, a protective tariff is commonly used to raise the price of imported goods above that in their countries of origin. In both cases, the effect is to create an artificially high foreign exchange value for the domestic currency.

(*d*) *Elasticity of demand.* According to the theory, any fall in a country's general price level should raise the foreign exchange value of its currency *via* an increase in its exports, but if the demand for exports were inelastic the increased volume would not be sufficient to compensate for the lower unit price, and the foreign exchange rate would actually fall. This possibility is admittedly rather extreme, but obviously the degree of elasticity of demand for exports will govern the extent of the alteration in the exchange rate as well as changes in the domestic price level.

(*e*) *Capital movements.* Finally, transactions in the foreign exchange market include the import and export of capital, which bear no relationship to the level of prices of traded goods. It would be quite possible, for example, for a favourable balance of payments on current account, caused by relatively low domestic prices, to be more than offset by an export of capital, and vice-versa; in each case, the movement in the exchange rate would be contrary to that indicated by the theory.

Broad validity of theory

In spite of all these adverse criticisms, however, the Purchasing Power Parity Theory remains broadly true of the level of exchange rates in the long run. Even with the power which a government has to ration purchases of foreign currency by exchange control, it is impossible to postpone indefinitely the effects of a prolonged inflation on the international value of the domestic currency; loss of gold will eventually force a devaluation in order to restore some sort of parity between its internal and external purchasing powers.

8.11 *What do you understand by the General Agreement on Tariffs and Trade? What are the objects of GATT? (ICA Final, November 1967.)*

Origins and objects of GATT

Talks were already in progress among the Allied nations before the end of World War II about international arrangements to facilitate trade and payments in the postwar period. The International Bank for Reconstruction and Development and the International Monetary Fund were a direct outcome of these negotiations, but plans for a third body, the International Trade Organization, came to nothing, as its charter would have committed member nations to an unconditional return to free trade, and this proved unacceptable to the United States Congress.

The desire to do something to prevent a return to the state of near-anarchy which prevailed in international trade during the 1930's remained, however, and further talks resulted in 23 nations signing the General Agreement on Tariffs and Trade at Geneva in 1947. The approach was now much more pragmatic: countries subscribing to this agreement merely undertook to meet together from time to time and explore the possibilities of

(*a*) reducing trade barriers;

(*b*) eliminating discrimination wherever possible, and

(*c*) preventing any new restrictions being placed on trade.

Operations of GATT

Much of the success which has resulted from the meetings of GATT members has been due to this informal approach. Delegates from the various countries have simply met together at different times and places and conducted a series of bi-lateral negotiations in which each side has exacted the maximum concessions it could from the other on a reciprocal basis. This alone would have been beneficial, but the scope of each agreement has been greatly enlarged by acceptance thoughout of the "most favoured nation" principle, i.e. concessions granted to one country are automatically extended to all the others. Moreover, although GATT has basic principles which are opposed to quotas, dumping, discrimination and restrictive devices generally, its practice has been to examine individual cases on their merits, and to grant waivers on an "ad hoc" basis whilst continuing to work towards its general objectives.

Achievements of GATT

After the initial discussions at Geneva had been concluded, further "rounds" of negotiations took place at intervals of three to four years, all of which resulted in useful progress towards greater freedom of trade. An even more ambitious series of talks began in 1963, however, following the initiative of the late President Kennedy in securing provisional approval of the US Congress for a cut of up to 50 per cent in the American tariff in return for similar concessions by her trading partners, and, in spite of many difficulties, these culminated in a remarkably successful agreement in May 1967, the terms of which may be summarized as follows —

(*a*) An average reduction of 35 per cent in the tariff for industrial goods, extending to 50 per cent in the case of many products, e.g. cars, to be spread over the ensuing five years;

(*b*) new anti-dumping regulations;

(*c*) free delivery of 4½ m. tons of grain to developing countries, to be financed by the major grain-trading countries; and

(*d*) agreement in an increase in world price of hard wheat.

The "Kennedy Round" did not have the same degree of success in agricultural products as it did in manufactured goods, but it may have laid the foundations for further progress in subsequent negotiations. Even so, an agreement which will help to liberalize about a quarter of the world's trade must be regarded as highly satisfactory.

Critical summary

It is possible to offer three criticisms, namely —

(*a*) Insistence on "most favoured nation" treatment has sometimes led to no concessions being given at all.

(*b*) Countries which started with high tariffs, e.g. the USA, have had the most effective bargaining positions.

(*c*) No significant penetration has yet been made of the "iron curtain" separating communist states from the rest of the world.

There has nevertheless been widespread support for the aims and policies of GATT, and it has proved a valuable adjunct to the International Monetary Fund in promoting freedom of trade over the greater part of the world.

9
Industrial organization and finance

This last section deals with a somewhat miscellaneous assortment of topics, ranging from the nature of a limited liability company to the desirability of "take-over" bids, but the student is again reminded that the examiner will be looking for something more than purely descriptive matter or journalistic comment. In other words, all these questions must be treated primarily as exercises in applied economics; while it is important to know, for example, *how* the Stock Exchange works, the main point to stress is what economic *purpose* it serves.

Many questions are confined to the scope of the individual firm, e.g. how a company gets its capital, what influences the form in which it is raised, what are the respective advantages of large and small firms, and so on, right up to the problems of nationalized industries. On the other hand, some questions deal with inter-firm relationships, e.g. the nature and origins of industrial and financial groups, the work of Trade Associations, and problems affecting whole industries such as those found in the development areas.

Indeed, perhaps the kind of question which occurs with the greatest frequency is that which relates to the problem of industrial location. This is therefore a topic which should receive careful attention, bearing in mind particularly how the relative importance of the various locating factors has changed and continues to change with improvements in transport and communications, the declining use of coal as a source of power, new techniques of production and the emergence of completely new industries.

In spite of what has been said above about the importance of treating questions in this section primarily from the point of view of economics, the professional student should not be afraid to use his knowledge of company law, accountancy, or whatever it may be, whenever it is relevant and helpful — after all, the division of the syllabus into "subjects" is at best rather arbitrary, and there is no reason for keeping one's knowledge in watertight compartments. To what extent the other disciplines should be invoked when answering questions on the economics paper must in the last analysis be a matter for individual judgement, but if done with discretion it reveals to the examiner that which he is most pleased to see, namely that the student has applied his whole intelligence to the problem set before him.

9.1   *What is a public limited liability company? What are the advantages and disadvantages of this form of organization? (U of L Advanced, January 1965.)*

Definition

A limited liability company is a kind of business unit which a number of people agree to form by each contributing shares towards its initial capital under the conditions laid down in the various Companies Acts. These and any subsequent shareholders thereby become the owners of the company, having the right to direct its policy and derive an income from its profits, but since the company becomes a separate legal entity their liability for its debts is limited to the amount of share capital they have agreed to subscribe.

A public, as distinct from a private, limited company –

(*a*) Must have at least seven shareholders;

(*b*) Is entitled to appeal to the public at large for capital, whether by way of additional shares or by loan; and

(*c*) must not impose any limitation on the freedom of its members to dispose of their shareholdings in any way they see fit.

Advantages

The unique advantages enjoyed by public limited companies have made them the most important kind of business unit in the United Kingdom. Principally, these advantages are –

(*a*) Very *large amounts of capital* can be amassed from the contributions of many small investors. By offering various kinds of shares and debentures, the directors are able to appeal to different sections of the public willing to assume different degrees of risk within the limit set by the proportion of capital which they own.

(*b*) From the investor's point of view, "limited liability" means that they can *spread their risks* by participating simultaneously in many different kinds of enterprise without increasing their overall commitment.

(*c*) The large limited company gives ample scope for the exercise of *management skills* by experts who lack capital of their own, while at the same time allowing people who do have funds to employ them advantageously in projects which they themselves would be incapable of directing.

(*d*) Unlike a "sole trader" business or a partnership, the existence of a limited company is not bound up with the survival of any particular owner; so long as the total number of shareholders does not fall below the statutory minimum the *company goes on for ever.*

Disadvantages

In spite of the manifest advantages enjoyed by the public limited company for the conduct of large-scale businesses, this form of organization suffers from a number of weaknesses which successive amendments to the Companies Act have been unable to eradicate, namely —

(*a*) Divorce of *ownership* from day-to-day *control* means that most shareholders are not concerned about the way directors and managers run the company, provided that it pays satisfactory dividends.

(*b*) The *duties of directors* are difficult to define. Although they are elected by, and can in the last resort be removed by, shareholders, they may feel justified in pursuing policies which run counter to shareholders' wishes when these conflict with, say, the interests of their workers or that of the country as a whole.

(*c*) The underlying *identity of interest* which exists between workers and owners in the success of the business is hard to demonstrate to the satisfaction of the former. Management therefore has difficulty in securing the willing co-operation of labour in measures designed to increase productivity or reduce costs.

(*d*) The complicated organizational structure which management finds it necessary to create in order to secure *co-ordination and control* of a large company gives rise to heavy overhead costs and lack of flexibility.

(*e*) Although it is perhaps more a political than an economic question, it may be thought undesirable for an institution devoted primarily to *maximizing profit* to be the community's principal kind of wealth-producing agency.

9.2 *Describe the main methods of raising capital available to a firm, and indicate the factors which might influence choice among them.*
(*CIS Intermediate, June 1962.*)

There are a large number of ways in which a limited company can raise capital. While these may differ considerably in detail, they can conveniently be grouped under three main headings, of which the first two relate to permanent capital and the third to temporary finance.

Share capital

The existence of a body of investors who are willing to become shareholders is the essential prerequisite for the formation of any limited company. The "founder members" of a company, i.e. those who undertake to contribute its original share capital, are in effect declaring their confidence in the ability of the company to make a profit from the use of their money, and their willingness to allow the size of their reward to be governed by it, commensurate with the number of shares they have each agreed to take. By implication, they are also committed to the loss of their entire investment if the company has to be wound up in circumstances where the whole of the assets are absorbed by the prior claims of creditors.

It is this willingness to assume the risk of failure for the sake of an indeterminate reward which is the main characteristic of the *ordinary shareholder,* and raising more capital by issuing further shares of the same kind avoids burdening the company with any fixed claim on its revenue. On the other hand, since every new ordinary share means the creation of another vote at general meetings, this method of increasing capital involves a progressive reduction in the control which the founder members have over company policy, to the point where they may be outvoted altogether.

They may therefore decide to raise more capital by the issue of *preference shares,* which enjoy priority as to the distribution of dividend up to a stipulated percentage of their nominal value, but which in view of this privilege do not normally carry voting rights unless dividends have fallen into arrears. Thus, provided the company does well, ordinary shareholders get "the best of both worlds" — they retain 100 per cent control over company policy, and may even receive a higher rate of dividend than the preference shareholders.

Share capital can also be increased without recourse to sources outside the company by directors consistently failing to distribute the whole of profit in annual dividends. The money withheld is then used to purchase new assets, and ultimately a free, or "bonus", issue of shares is made to the existing shareholders in recognition of the fact that the value of their stake in the company has increased.

Loan capital

As an alternative to the creation of new shares of either kind, existing shareholders may consider it advantageous to raise more capital by inviting long-term loans. Such loans are normally evidenced by the issue of a document known as a "debenture", which not only embodies a contractual obligation by the company to pay interest at a fixed rate but also as a general rule creates a charge, or "mortgage", on the assets. Not only are debenture holders thus guaranteed a specified income, but they have first claim on the assets in the event of winding-up; in short, their position as creditors is as secure as the law can make it.

While the decision to raise capital by an issue of debentures calls for careful consideration, it has obvious attractions for a company which can anticipate fairly stable trading conditions; there can of course be no question of debenture holders having voting rights, and in consideration of the security which they enjoy it is usual for them to be satisfied with a relatively low rate of return. During a period of inflation, however, when the real value of a fixed money income is falling, it may be necessary to attract investors by offering them the option to *convert* their holdings of debentures into *ordinary shares* at some future date, and this kind of issue has become increasingly common in recent years.

The *proportions* in which permanent capital can be raised as between ordinary shares, preference shares and debentures can be varied within wide limits, but —

(*a*) it is usual for the company's Articles to stipulate that the amount of debenture capital shall not exceed the amount of share capital;

(*b*) prospective new shareholders may be frightened off by the existence of too many "prior charges" on the company's income and assets;

(*c*) ordinary shareholders' reward becomes very "highly geared" to changes in the company's income when an unduly large proportion of the total capital is in the form of debentures and preference shares.

Temporary finance

There are two major reasons why a firm may desire to commit itself to raising capital on a short-term basis only —

(*a*) The need for additional finance may be of predictably *short duration*. For example, most businesses experience some kind of seasonal fluctuation either in their revenues or their costs, and there would be no point in putting a permanent burden on the company's income for the use of money which it only required intermittently. In such cases, bank loans or promissory notes would be an appropriate means of securing temporary finance.

(*b*) The *current cost* of raising capital might be abnormally high, so that it would be advisable to raise money by borrowing on "unsecured notes" for say two or three years only in the hope that better terms would be available when the time came to redeem them.

SIMILAR QUESTIONS

(i) What sources of long-term capital are available in the United Kingdom? (ICWA Part I, December 1964.)

(ii) What do you understand by share capital and loan capital? What factors might cause a firm to decide to finance expension by one form rather than the other? (CIS Intermediate, June 1965.)

(iii) Describe and compare the advantages to firms of issuing (a) ordinary shares, and (b) fixed interest securities. (C of S Intermediate, June 1968).

(iv) Explain and evaluate the role of ordinary shares in financing the activities of business firms. (U of L Advanced, January 1966.)

9.3 *Describe the organization and functions of the Stock Exchange.*
   (I of B Part I, September 1966.)

Function of the Stock Exchange

The existence of a market in titles to business assets is an essential feature of an economy where industry and commerce rely for the most part on private sources for the provision of capital. Continuity of operation demands that capital once committed to a business shall remain invested during the lifetime of the enterprise, hence the law naturally demands that investors may not ask a company to buy back its own shares.

   While there is nothing in principle to stop would-be sellers of shares from finding their own buyers, e.g. through the medium of advertising, the likelihood of an individual seller immediately finding a potential buyer who requires the type and number of shares he wishes to dispose of by such means is fairly remote. Even so, conclusion of the deal might be hampered by widely differing ideas about the value of the shares, and they would finally have to make arrangements acceptable to both parties for payment and delivery, also for having the transfer of ownership recorded by the company concerned where necessary. If they were faced with the uncertainty and expense of this procedure when they wanted to sell shares, few investors would be persuaded to part with their money in the first place; such a situation obviously calls for the intervention of "middlemen" to make a market, and that is in essence the function of dealers on the Stock Exchange.

   Before going on to outline the organization of the Stock Exchange, it should be added that as soon as an organized market in securities had been established the Government found it much easier to borrow by means of long-term bond issues. In this case, the bonds were not necessarily representative of any real assets, but the Government's promise to pay interest and eventually to repay the capital sum involved were backed by the taxable capacity of the whole community, and, measured by the total amount of money which changes hands, the value of transactions in "gilt-edged" stocks now exceeds all the rest put together.

Organization of the Stock Exchange

The conduct of business on the "floor" of the Stock Exchange is strictly limited to members. These consist of "brokers" and "jobbers", whose respective roles are as follows —

   (1) *Brokers.* A broker is an agent who buys or sells securities on behalf of members of the public. He will give advice to his clients if called upon to do so, but is eventually bound to act as instructed by them in the negotiation of a buying or selling order, receiving a commission, or "brokerage", as a reward for his services. The procedure on receipt of, say, an order to buy a certain kind of share is for the broker to —

(*a*) go on to the floor of the Exchange and get the lowest quotation he can from a jobber, without disclosing whether he wishes to buy or to sell;

(*b*) strike a verbal bargain there and then to buy the shares his client wants;

(*c*) submit an account to this client showing the amount due, including brokerage, transfer fee, etc;

(*d*) pay the amount due on settlement day;

(*e*) arrange for the transfer of ownership to be entered in the share register of the company concerned, and for them to issue a new share certificate.

(2) *Jobbers*. It is jobbers who make the market in shares by their willingness either to buy or to sell at any time. Jobbers take up positions on the floor of the Exchange in informal groups specializing in certain kinds of shares, and when approached by a broker each member of the group quotes a double price, one for buying and one for selling, before being told which he may be called upon to do. He naturally hopes to make a profit out of the difference between these prices, called the "jobber's turn", but there is no guarantee that he will do so. A jobber who misjudges the trend of the market and puts his prices too high will only make bargains with brokers wishing to sell, whereas one who pitches his prices too low will only attract buying brokers; as he wants to finish the account period with buying and selling contracts in balance, he may well have to adjust his prices so that in the end he is forced to sell shares for less than he agreed to pay for them, or buy in shares for more than he contracted to sell them for.

There are now approximately 3,500 members of the Stock Exchange, of whom about 500 are jobbers organized into no more than about 30 firms. The marked contraction in the number of jobbing firms in recent years reflects the growing difficulty of raising sufficient capital to finance their operations. For the same reason, the Stock Exchange Council is now prepared to abandon its traditional rule that no firm should seek the protection of limited liability for its members.

Stock exchange council

Finally, one of the most useful functions performed by the Stock Exchange is the general supervision which the Council exercises over the business ethics of quoted companies. In many ways the Council's code of conduct is more exacting than company law itself, and any breach of its rules would be penalized by the withdrawal of quotation rights.

SIMILAR QUESTION

(i) Describe the functions of the Stock Exchange. (ICWA Part I, June 1967.)

9.4 *What is the function of the New Issue Market, and how does the market operate? (ICWA Part I. May 1968.)*

Nature of the "Market"

The New Issue Market is operated by a loosely-knit group of merchant bankers in the City of London who have acquired great experience in matters concerned with the raising of new capital, so much so that many have come to be known simply as "issuing houses".

Type of issue

Given that a company needs to raise more capital, and that the amount has been decided upon, a number of questions have to be answered before proceeding to the flotation of a new issue, and it is at this stage that the advice of the issuing house can be most valuable. For example, in what form should the new capital be raised? There are so many variations of loan and share capital that it needs an expert to point out the advantages and disadvantages of each, both from the company's point of view and that of the prospective investor. Broadly speaking, the choice will be determined from the company's angle by the degree of risk involved in the enterprise for which the new capital is required, the amount of "gearing" which already exists between the company's income and rewards to equity capital, the length of time for which the money is required, and so on; from the point of view of market appeal, the issue will need to strike the right balance between those who are looking for high income and those who are more concerned with security.

Terms of issue

Having determined the form of the new issue, the question of the terms on which it will be offered has to be considered. Assuming, for example, that a debenture stock has been decided upon, the return it guarantees to investors should be enough to ensure that the issue is fully subscribed, but not so high as to impose an unnecessary burden on the company's finances. With so wide a choice of equally safe investments on the market, even a difference of ¼ per cent in interest rate one way or the other is going to have a significant effect on the volume of applications — indeed, still finer adjustments are possible by offering the stock at a point or two above or below par.

Timing of an issue

The question of terms is bound up to some extent with the timing of the issue. Should the issuing house consider that a general downwards movement in the interest rates was imminent, they would no doubt recommend postponement of the issue for the time being, with recourse to some form of temporary finance if the company's investment plans could not be delayed. There are also periods when the market has been saturated with new issues of a similar kind, so that it would be advisable to allow some time for it to recover.

Issue procedure

Once these important preliminary decisions have been made, the issuing house takes over the entire responsibility for seeing that the company gets the money it wants. The issuing house will either *buy* the whole issue outright, and re-sell it to the public at a slightly higher price by means of an "offer for sale", or it will *sponsor* an issue by the company by advertising their prospectus, taking a fee for its services and for "underwriting" the issue, i.e. guaranteeing to take up any part of it for which no applications are received. (Normally, some or indeed all of this risk is passed on by re-insuring with sub-underwriters.) Whatever happens, therefore, the company's interests are protected; if the issue should be under-subscribed, e.g. because of some adverse change in market conditions subsequent to fixing the terms, either the issuing house or the sub-underwriters will be left holding the balance, which they will have to dispose of as and when they please at the best price they can get.

"Placings"

It is sometimes possible to avoid a good deal of the trouble and expense involved in a public issue by means of a "placing" on the Stock Exchange. In such case, clients of the issuing house or of their stockbrokers are allowed to subscribe direct for the greater part of the issue, but some proportion must be made available to the general public through the medium of jobbers. Applications for "placings" must receive the approval of the Stock Exchange Committee on Quotations, and the procedure laid down by them as to advertising, supplying jobbers with shares, etc., must be strictly complied with.

"Introductions"

A somewhat similar procedure, known as an "introduction", may be followed if the shares of a private company are already widely held, but it is desired to secure a quotation for them on the Stock Exchange, e.g. for the purpose of assessing death duty. In this case, there is normally no question of new shares being issued, but there must of course be an undertaking by existing holders to release a certain proportion of their shares to jobbers so as to form a basis for market dealings.

Issuing house and client

The relationship between an issuing house and its client is not usually confined to arranging a single issue in one of the ways described; it is common practice for the issuing house to take a continuing interest in the financial affairs of the company concerned so as to be able to give further assistance whenever it is needed. In particular, issuing houses have played an important rôle in recent years in advising companies on the complicated financial arrangements involved in mergers and take-over bids.

9.5   *What is meant by (a) horizontal integration, and (b) vertical integration? Why do firms combine in each of these ways? (C of S Intermediate, June 1967.)*

Definitions

Horizontal integration denotes a combination of firms making the same kind of product or performing similar processes, i.e. operating at the same stage of an industry, whereas vertical integration indicates a combination of firms making different products or performing different processes which stand in some kind of sequential relationship with one another at different stages of an industry. Using the textile industry for the purpose of illustration, a number of spinning firms combining their manufacturing facilities would be an example of horizontal integration, while an association between a spinning firm, a weaving firm and a clothing manufacturer would be an example of vertical integration.

Horizontal integration

In its pure form, horizontal integration does not increase the range of a group's activities in any way. Its primary object is usually to eliminate competition between the members of a group, the most powerful pressure to do so occurring at the time of a recession in trade. Output is then reduced in order to support the price, and so long as all the plants in the combine can manage to cover their marginal costs all will survive until trade recovers. Opportunity may subsequently be taken to install single large plants to replace small ones as they become obsolete, with some benefit to consumers from economies of scale, but the underlying motive remains monopolistic in character.

Backwards and forwards integration

Vertical integration presents a much more varied picture. Starting from any given stage in the evolution of the product, integration may be backwards or forwards. Backwards integration implies the acquisition by a firm of its sources of supply, e.g. a manufacturer of iron and steel going into ore and coal mining; the general tendency is for this kind of vertical integration to occur in times of boom, when there is a danger that supplies might be exhausted or diverted to competitors. Forwards integration denotes a movement into the stages which use the firm's product, e.g. the manufacturer of iron and steel might take up the fabrication of girders, the construction of bridges, etc. There is, indeed, no reason why forward integration should stop short at manufacturing; the desire to ensure that his products maintain or improve their share of the market, especially in times of depression, may well induce the manufacturer to go into the field of distribution. For example, a well-known producer of meat and meat extract with cattle ranches abroad also owns a shipping line, cold storage facilities and a chain of retail butchers' shops.

Benefits of vertical integration

It is a mistake to imagine that the combination of firms at different stages of an industry makes for a lowering of costs in the sense that it eliminates profit margins at intermediate stages of production and distribution. A manufacturer who undertakes his own distribution, for example, will need to find more capital to finance this new activity and employ more staff to run it, and every addition to the size of his undertaking will need a corresponding addition to his profits in order to justify its existence. These incursions into other fields are more often undertaken with a view to securing greater *control* than anything else; sometimes it is to ensure continuity of supplies, sometimes to safeguard the quality of the materials used in manufacture or the condtion of the finished product at the point of sale, sometimes merely to obtain knowledge of the costs and problems involved in independent suppliers' and distributors' activities so as to be able to bargain more effectively with them. It may, however, be cost saving in the sense that the volume and flow of inputs and outputs can be regulated throughout the sequence of operations so that surpluses and bottlenecks are eliminated. In the special case of industries where the application of heat represents an important element in cost, the saving of fuel effected by running processes "end on", e.g. in a steel strip mill, may result in considerable economies.

Finally, although the administration of a vertical combination of firms tends to be more complicated than that of a horizontal combination, there may yet be a reduction in costs because of economies of scale in management.

SIMILAR QUESTIONS

(i) Why, and in what ways, do industrial companies seek to combine? (ICWA Part I, December 1964.)

(ii) What forms can vertical integration take? Why do firms seek to expand or combine in these ways? (C of S Intermediate, May 1969.)

9.6   *"The advantages of large-scale production are so great that soon there will be no small firms." Comment. (U of L Advanced, January 1967.)*

A superficial view

The benefits to be derived from economies of scale in many kinds of production are so spectacular, and are moreover the subject of so much public attention, that one is inclined at first sight to concur with the statement contained in the question. We are constantly being reminded that larger blast furnaces and rolling mills can produce cheaper steel, larger generating plant can provide cheaper electricity, larger ships can operate at lower cost per ton-mile, and so on, and it is demonstrably true that in these fields the optimum size of operating unit climbs steadily upwards. Similarly, the main weight of the economic case for Britain's joining the European Economic Community rests upon the argument that an enlarged market will give our industries greater scope for exploiting economies of scale.

The statistical evidence

It is something of a surprise to find, therefore, that statistical evidence does not support the view that small firms are being inexorably squeezed out of existence by large ones. Adopting the percentage total number of workers in an industry employed by the three largest firms in it as the criterion of the degree of concentration into larger units, even industries like chemicals, electrical engineering and vehicles (where giant firms predominate) only showed a figure ranging from about 40 per cent to 50 per cent in a 1961 survey; at the other end of the scale, building and contracting, clothing and footwear were in the range 12–14 per cent. Moreover, these figures do not differ significantly from those obtained in 1951. More recent statistics which might show a change are not yet to hand.

Survival of small firms (1)

The first reason for the survival of small firms is that in certain circumstances they may have *cost advantages* which are denied to large firms. Economies of scale in the technical field normally involve the use of large, specific plant; firms thus equipped may well incur greater costs per unit than their less highly-capitalized rivals during a period of slack demand, and they usually find it more difficult to adapt their products to constantly changing market conditions.

Survival of small firms (2)

Again, many *markets* simply are not large enough to warrant the existence of a large firm. Since personal transport costs time and money, the village shop will always find enough customers to pay its way, and the demand for artificial limbs is happily too small to engage the attention of mass-production experts. Even where there are many customers, small firms are better fitted to the task of supplying them if individual requirements vary.

Survival of small firms (3)

It is also misleading to imagine that small and large firms always meet in head-on competition just because they are members of the same industry. There is a tendency in many industries for integration and *disintegration of processes* to proceed at the same time; for every firm which seeks a cost advantage in making its own components, another decides to throw the burden of design and tooling costs on to a specialist manufacturer, so that the activities of large and small firms are often complementary rather than competitive. The existence of such specialist suppliers, together with joint research and common information services, also means that *external economies of scale* are available to all firms in an industry, whether they be large or small.

Survival of small firms (4)

Finally, the multiplicity of small firms may also be explained by the fact that their numbers are not readily eroded by a constant tendency to earn *subnormal profits*. A small-scale entrepreneur may so value the interest which he derives from running his own business and the freedom of action which it allows him that he is satisfied with a niggardly and uncertain financial reward. And, even though a high proportion of small firms do actually fail in any given year, it seems that there is always an adequate supply of new recruits eager to fill the gaps in their ranks.

SIMILAR QUESTIONS

(i) Why do small firms continue to exist in industries characterized by large-scale production? (CIS Intermediate, December 1966.)
(ii) Outline the economic advantages obtained by large business enterprises. In view of these advantages, how do you account for the survival of the small business? (I of B Part I, September 1967.)
(iii) Discuss the economies of large-scale production, and explain why some small firms still exist. (ACCA Section I, June 1968.)
(iv) Are large firms necessarily more efficient than small ones? (C of S Final, May 1969.)

9.7   *If specialization leads to the reduction of costs of production, how do you account for the existence of many multi-product plants? (CIS Final, December 1966.)*

While it is undoubtedly true of the vast majority of manufacturing processes that concentration of effort into the mass production of a single line will reduce costs, there are many factors which militate against firms specializing on one line to the exclusion of all others.

Costs other than manufacturing

First, the cost of manufacturing is by no means the only cost a firm has to meet. Quite frequently the cost of distribution far outweighs that of production, and in the case of a firm with a fairly simple product already being made on an optimum scale it would help to reduce the overall cost if a number of other simple lines could be added so as to utilize the distribution facilities more intensively. Similarly, the cost of management and finance per unit of output might well benefit from increasing the size of the firm's turnover by introducing new products.

Seasonal factors

Another very common reason for running a number of different product lines is the fact that demands may be seasonal. If, therefore, the various lines can be produced by the same workers with little or no modification to plant, there is an obvious gain to be secured through being able to work to capacity all the year round. Or it may be that the supply of the raw material, e.g. fruit or vegetables, is markedly seasonal, in which case the same argument applies. Reasoning along these lines, it is not difficult to see why a firm which starts by selling tinned beans finishes up by producing "57 varieties" of food in cans.

Risk spreading

Alternatively, the decision to manufacture a number of different lines may be prompted by the desire to spread risks in some way. It is very unusual for even a non-technical product to have an indefinitely long life; it is more typical for a new line to require some time to build up to maximum demand, to carry on at about that level for a further period, then eventually for demand to taper off. Consequently, a firm may well be engaged in the simultaneous production of an old line which still has some useful potential, a current "best seller", and a new product which it is hoped will become a best seller in its turn. Or again, the firm may simply decide to manufacture a number of different lines as an insurance against purely random fluctuations in demand for individual items.

Allied products

Sometimes the successful exploitation of one product leads naturally into the manufacture of allied products. This may happen in two ways —

(*a*) The first product forms the basis of a group of lines whose uses complement one another, e.g. the manufacturer of a farm tractor seizes the opportunity of setting up as the supplier of a complete range of implements for ploughing, sowing, reaping, etc., in conjunction with the tractor.

(*b*) The manufacturer's main product generates a miscellaneous assortment of by-products, and rather than waste them, or allow someone else to acquire them cheaply, he decides to process them himself. Thus a firm whose main business is producing petrol from crude oil is induced to enter into the manufacture of insecticides, detergents, synthetic rubber, etc.

Conclusions

In the real world, therefore, single product firms are becoming something of a rarity, in spite of continuing advances in the design of specialized plant. The various reasons why firms decide to develop on multi-product lines such as those mentioned above operate in most fields against the advantages of complete specialization, and on the whole seem to outweigh them.

SIMILAR QUESTION

(i) "Specialization is the key to economic efficiency." "Diversification of activities is characteristic of the progressive modern firm." Discuss. (CIS Intermediate, June 1966.)

9.8 *Are take-over bids desirable or not? Give reasons for your answer.* (*CIS Final, June 1965.*)

Criteria difficult to establish

It is not possible to give an answer to this question in general terms, as the great variety and complexity of situations in which take-over bids can occur make it necessary to know a good deal about the circumstances in each particular case before expressing an opinion one way or the other. Even so, the final verdict is likely to rest upon matters of opinion rather than fact, as it generally involves weighing opposing considerations, and most of the arguments usually advanced in favour of take-overs can only be justified by the subsequent course of events.

"Take-over bids" and "mergers"

It is necessary first of all to recognize that the very expression "making a take-over bid" has an emotional content tending to prejudice public opinion against it, in contrast to "agreeing to a merger" which sounds much more rational and acceptable. In essence, however, the only difference between the two is the way in which the union of the firms in question is brought about, and much of the antipathy towards take-over bids must therefore be attributed to the unfavourable publicity resulting from the struggle for control which takes place between the contending parties.

Since bidders are now prevented by law from purchasing more than 10 per cent of the shares of the company they intend to take over without disclosing their true identity, they are mainly limited to making an overt appeal to existing shareholders to sell their holdings at a figure above their present market value. This places the directors of the threatened company in a somewhat difficult position if they want to resist the bid; they must try somehow to convince shareholders that their assets are worth even more than the bidder is offering for them, and at the same time explain why the present market value of the shares is as low as it is. This leads naturally to all kinds of conflicting statements and estimates being made by both sides, which may result either in an inflated price being paid for the shares or in a perfectly reasonable bid being withdrawn.

Increase in profits not conclusive

When considered in a broader context, however, a successful takeover bid on reasonable terms is no different in principle from a merger, and the only real point at issue would seem to be whether or not a fusion of the two firms' interests resulted in a more productive use of resources. Clearly, the bidders would only attempt to acquire control if they considered that the assets they were buying could be made to yield a greater profit than that being obtained by the existing management; if, therefore, the anticipated increase in profits was realized this would on the face of it appear to justify the change in ownership regardless of how it was brought about. To accept such evidence as conclusive would be unwise, however; while the private interests of shareholders would presumably have benefited, the public interest might well have suffered if the higher profits were achieved merely as a result of increased control over the market. In other words, an amalgamation of firms having as its primary objective the creation of some kind of monopoly must be looked at very critically indeed, and one would need to have a considerable amount of information about the new group's policies, both before and after the merger, before being able to say whether it was desirable or not.

Influence of international trade

The whole position is further complicated in an "open" economy by the existence of international trade. With the growth in both imports and exports (now amounting to nearly 25 per cent of the GNP), and persistent difficulty in balancing our overseas payments, the government's attitude towards large groupings of industrial assets has tended to become more favourable. There are undoubted cost advantages to be gain vis-à-vis foreign competitors, both on the home and export markets, from rationalizing the activities of rival British firms, e.g. by cutting out duplication of research, overlapping production facilities, etc., and by substituting single large plants for a number of smaller plants, and provided that no tariff protection is given to such groups, the benefits to the economy would appear to outweigh the danger of monopoly exploitation.

Effect on employees

There remains the question of how take-overs, and mergers for that matter, affect the interests of the employees concerned. A union of two firms which did not result in significant economies in the use of manpower would fail in one of its major purposes, so that some redundancy following a take-over is normally to be expected. Individual hardship can be alleviated by giving as much notice as possible of dismissal, help with finding another job, and payment of a lump sum, so that if the change takes place against a background of full employment the consequences need not be too serious. All these measures are in line with government policy, and the authorities can also give direct help by setting up temporary employment exchanges on the spot. Those likely to fare worst are the older, long-service workers, and members of the management team who find that there is no place for them in a new "streamlined" organization structure, but it should not be impossible for society to devise some way of protecting everyone from undue hardship if a take-over is judged to be in the general interest.

SIMILAR QUESTIONS

(i) "The taking-over by one company of another is always in the interest of the shareholders of the latter, but rarely in the interest of the country as a whole." Discuss this statement. (CIS Final, December 1965.)
(ii) Many financial commentators have recently expressed the view that the number of mergers in British industry will increase. What advantages may stem from such mergers? Illustrate you answer by reference to recent cases. (ICA Final, May 1968.)
(iii) What information do you require in order to decide whether a merger between two firms in the same industry is economically advantageous? (C of S Final, November 1968.)
(iv) Do mergers always produce economies of scale? (CIS Final, December 1968.)
(v) "Since mergers create unemployment and reduce competition they should be discouraged." Do you agree? (CIS Final, June 1969.)

9.9 *What factors affect the location of industry? Illustrate your answer by examples of industries with which you are familiar. (ACCA Section I, December 1966.)*

There would be no location problems for manufacturers if transport and communications did not involve time and money. If materials, power, men and finished products could be moved about without expense or delay, and if customers and suppliers, managers and subordinates, could communicate with one another by telepathy, it would not matter where a factory was sited. But since such costs and delays do exist, it becomes necessary to evaluate the net advantages of possible alternative sites, and the following factors will have varying degrees of relevance.

Labour supply

The availability and type of labour in the immediate vicinity of the site must be assessed. Different industries vary widely in their requirements: some need large amounts of labour with no particular skill, whereas others demand relatively small numbers of highly-trained people; some look to women to fill the majority of the jobs, while others must rely mainly on men, and so on.

In circumstances where a site is advantageous from other points of view, something can be done to adapt workers to traditional processes by training schemes; alternatively, it is sometimes possible to adapt processes so that they can be performed by unskilled workers. In the main, however, firms tend to go where the requisite number of workers with the appropriate skills already exist, even if this means bidding some of them away from their existing employment.

Power supply

Although coal is still the biggest single source of power in the UK, its influence as a locating factor is negligible compared with what it was in the early days of the industrial revolution; even the iron and steel industry has found it progressively more advantageous to locate on orefields rather than coalfields as smelting processes have become more efficient.

The widespread availability of electricity has done much to free light industry from locational problems as far as power supply is concerned, but it has introduced a factor of its own in determining the sites of aluminium smelting plants, whose unparalleled demands for current virtually tie them to sources of cheap and abundant hydro-electricity, e.g. Kitimat in British Columbia.

Oil has been largely responsible to date for the trend away from coal, and since it is all imported into the UK the tendency is to favour industrial locations near the points of entry. The building of pipelines may modify this influence to some extent, but oil products will presumably always be cheaper near the main ports and refineries.

The advent of North Sea gas will reduce still further industry's dependence on coal, with a tendency to favour east coast locations.

Raw materials

This is a powerful locating factor where the raw material accounts for a high proportion of total cost, and especially when it loses a lot of its weight or bulk in processing, e.g. the shift in location of iron smelting referred to above has been accelerated by the need to work leaner ores. Conversely, where bulk is increased, as in the assembly of steel plates into car bodies, planks of timber into furniture, etc., it becomes more advantageous to be near the market for the finished goods.

Where raw materials are derived from a number of different sources, it is often best to locate a factory at some convenient assembly point, e.g. Rotterdam.

Markets

Proximity to major markets not only reduces the cost and risk of damage in making deliveries, but helps in maintaining close and easy contact with customers. A quicker and better appreciation of competitors' activities can also be obtained, and less capital need be employed in building up depots and local stocks of finished goods.

Clothing manufacture, especially where fashion is important, is typical of the industries which are attracted to major centres of population, e.g. London, Paris.

Transport

Since it is cost and time which are really significant, suitable transport facilities may offset the disadvantage of being some distance away from raw materials and/or markets. Waterborne freight charges are far lower per ton-mile than for other forms of transport, and when allied to the operating economy of large ships (e.g. oil tankers, ore carriers, car transporters) may make haulage half way across the world a practical proposition. Even the cost of mixed sea/land transport is now being considerably reduced by "containerization", and motorways facilitate the operation of fast, heavy road vehicles.

Natural environment

Some industries require a particular kind of climate for economical or effective working. The traditional example of this is Lancashire, where the humid atmosphere helped to prevent the yarn from breaking in the early days of cotton spinning, though it is doubtful whether this would exert much influence under modern conditions.

Water supply is, however, of growing importance. The nature of the water has always been significant — soft water is usually preferred as it makes cleansing cheaper and produces less deposit in boiler tubes and piping generally. More especially, however, the quantity of water available is becoming a key factor in some industries which need large amounts for cooling purposes, and in such cases there is a growing tendency to avoid locations in eastern England.

The cultivation of industrial crops is, of course, largely dependent on climatic conditions, and very often the processing of such crops is now established in the regions which favour their production, e.g. cotton goods in the southern United States, jute cloth in Bengal.

SIMILAR QUESTIONS
(i) Why are certain industries highly localized while others are widely dispersed? (CIS Intermediate, June 1965.)
(ii) Why are some industries more concentrated geographically than others? (C of S Intermediate, November 1968.)

9.10 *What factors would you consider in assessing whether a particular firm might or might not be established successfully in a Development Area? (U of L Advanced, Summer 1965.)*

Definition
"Development Area" is the description officially applied to those parts of the UK formerly known as depressed areas, where unemployment during the slump of the 1930's was most heavily concentrated, and which even today display rates of unemployment two or three times the national average. The precise number and demarcation of such areas changes from time to time, but parts of NE England, Wales, the Clyde region and Northern Ireland figure consistently among them.

Government policy and powers
It has been the declared intention of successive Governments for many years to encourage industrialists to set up factories of diverse kinds in these areas, and in order to give effect to their policy they have statutory powers of two kinds. First, would-be builders of factories anywhere in the country are obliged to get an Industrial Development Certificate from the Board of Trade, and applications relating to areas where the board considers that the labour force is already fully employed can be refused. Second, under the Local Employment Act, they have power to offer a variety of inducements to firms to go to Development Areas: the Treasury are able to make loans available for capital investment at low rates of interest, or can even allow outright grants in extreme cases; new factories are built with all necessary services laid on and offered at low rentals; Government training centres are set up where local labour can acquire new skills; favourable rating assessments can be negotiated to ease the burden of overhead costs, and so on. From the purely financial aspect, therefore, a decision will depend on the amount of aid available to the firm in question under these various headings, and whether it is considered sufficient to offset the disadvantages which a location in one of the Development areas is commonly assumed to possess.

Evaluation of disadvantages

We must now turn, therefore, to the crux of the problem, namely an evaluation of these disadvantages. If there were no costs or delays attaching to the movement of raw materials, labour, power or finished products, and instantaneous communications could be maintained with suppliers and customers, objections to setting up factories in Development Areas would largely disappear. In weighing up the chances of success, therefore, one would have to pay particular attention to costs arising under these headings.

(*a*) As regards the acquisition of *raw materials*, a development area location would not be a great disadvantage if their value were small in relation to the value of the finished product; this would be true of an industry which, by the application of much skill and/or capital, transformed small physical quantities of material into objects of great value, as in watchmaking. In this connection, it must be remembered that actual distance from the source of materials is not the sole determinant of transport costs; if advantage could be taken of the low cost per ton-mile of water transport, or if for reasons of any kind inward freight rates were favourable, then this would again help to reduce the cost of a Development Area location.

For some firms, e.g. car manufacturers, it is not so much access to raw materials which must be considered, but the proximity of other firms supplying the many components and accessories which are required to produce the complete assembly. Some 60 per cent or more of the value of the typical car is accounted for by "bought-out" supplies, so that any extra cost or delay which might be incurred in obtaining them would obviously weigh very heavily against going to a Development Area.

(*b*) As for *labour cost,* the first point that needs to be emphasized is that, while the overall supply of labour may be good, labour is not a homogeneous factor. Much will therefore depend on the nature of the industry's requirements as compared with the sex ratio, age structure and skills of the local working population, not to mention its attitude towards "foreigners" running the local factories and to work in general. There is a tendency for the labour force in Development Areas to include rather a large proportion of older men, and in some places, e.g. Wales, wives are not so ready to enter the employment market as they are in other parts of the country. It is, of course, unlikely that the necessary skills will exist ready-made, and the practical question is usually whether they can be easily acquired, perhaps at one of the previously-mentioned Government training centres. Alternatively, the possibility of altering the manufacturing process itself (in general, by investing in more capital equipment as a substitute for skill) could be investigated. Trade Union policies may also have an important bearing on labour costs — insistence on the "rate for the job", whether it is done in Dagenham or some remote part of Scotland, could be a considerable deterrent to moving into a Development Area.

(*c*) On the score of *power costs,* Development Areas might compare quite favourably with other parts of the country, as their location is strongly linked to coalmining, and coal remains the major source of industrial power. This advantage would operate most strongly where the coal was consumed in its raw state, e.g. to raise steam in a factory's boiler plant, but even electric power is available at somewhat lower rates the nearer one gets to the coalfields as most electricity is still generated in thermal power stations.

(*d*) Perhaps the majority of objections which are heard to Development Area locations are on the grounds of their remoteness from the larger and faster-growing *markets* of the south-eastern part of the UK, and to a lesser extent the continent of Europe. It is not so much a question of the additional transport cost involved in moving finished products as the general difficulty in maintaining continuous two-way contact with customers and keeping in touch with what competitors are doing; unfavourable circumstances of this sort are not easy to evaluate, but they are none the less real, and may swing the balance of advantage against Development Areas when the final decision has to be made.

(*e*) An even more intangible factor is the *general atmosphere* of obsolescence and neglect which pervades towns in the heart of Development Areas; the ebbing tide of industry and population stretching back over the years has left behind abandoned factories and derelict houses, which, combined with the lack of any recent building and a low rate of investment in public amenities, creates an unfavourable impression on the mind of anyone visiting such an area for the first time. Any doubts which responsible executives may have in their business capacity about setting up a factory there tend to be reinforced by personal misgivings about the desirability of moving into such surroundings with their wives and families; the very fact that local councils in Development Areas stress the other side of the picture (e.g. the proximity of open moorlands, golf courses and so on) in their advertisements only underlines the significance of considerations lying mainly outside the scope of pure economics, but which may nevertheless exert an important influence on management in deciding which way the balance of advantage lies.

Summary

Looking at the whole picture, assessment of all the relevant factors involved in moving into a Development area is a very complex matter, and any decision to do so must to some extent be an act of faith in the ultimate success on the Government's efforts to restore full economic life to these parts of the country.

SIMILAR QUESTIONS

(i) A major manufacturing company has been asked by the Board of Trade to consider erecting its proposed plant extension in one of the Development

Areas. The board of the company has asked your advice. What facts and considerations would you take into account in advising the board? (ICA Final, November 1965.)

(ii) Discuss the factors which determine the location of business firms. Consider each of these factors and analyse how it would be possible to change the location of firms by the introduction of grants for selected areas. (ACCA Section I, December 1968.)

9.11 *Discuss the contention that the efficient development of an inland transport system is not possible under competitive conditions.* (*CIS Final, June 1965.*)

Analogy with a centrally planned economy

The arguments for and against a completely planned transport system are in many ways similar to those relating to a centrally planned economy. In both cases, there are obvious wastes involved in allowing individual entrepreneurs to pursue their own diverse interests, and these wastes are if anything easier to demonstrate in the field of transport than they are in the economy as a whole.

Advantages of a planned transport system

The basic economic principles which govern the efficiency of transport services are set out below, and in each case it seems that they would be better served by having some kind of central planning than by unrestricted competition.

(*a*) *Utilization of capacity.* A vehicle travelling empty costs nearly as much to run as one which is full, and occupies the same amount of track, road or air space. On the simple law of averages an organization which had a monopoly of transport services would stand a better chance of keeping its vehicles full in whichever direction they were travelling, and should therefore be able to operate at a lower overall cost per ton-mile.

(*b*) *Size of vehicles.* All forms of transport show important economies of scale, so that one large vehicle can operate more cheaply than a number of smaller ones of equivalent total capacity. Duplication of carriers would therefore raise costs unless the volume of traffic was large enough to enable all firms to operate vehicles of the maximum practicable size.

(*c*) *Type of vehicle.* Some goods require quick delivery, some are particularly susceptible to damage, some are heavy or bulky in relation to their value whereas others are light and small, etc. Ideally, therefore, every consignment should be carried by the kind of vehicle best fitted to deal with it, but this would hardly be likely to happen when independent rail, road, water and air services were competing for traffic. Once operating capacity has been created, marginal cost is usually so low that ratecutting is resorted to to keep it full, and an uneconomic pattern of vehicle allocation is likely to result.

(*d*) *Idle time.* A vehicle at rest, for whatever reason, represents unproductive capital, and the greater the investment in it the more serious the waste becomes. Some idle time is, of course, inevitable, e.g. during loading and unloading, but a large transport undertaking handling a continuous flow of vehicles would find it more economical to mechanize these processes. The need for servicing is the other major reason why vehicles are compelled to remain at rest, and this too can best be organized by having large fleets of vehicles serviced on a rota basis; not only can servicing itself be made more efficient, but routine preventive maintenance can reduce loss of operating time caused by breakdowns.

(*e*) *Through booking.* It is often necessary for a consignment to travel over different sections of the transport network, using different forms of vehicle. The dovetailing of timetables would be easier to arrange under a common transport authority, also the issue of a through ticket against a single payment.

(*f*) *Speed.* Some costs rise as the speed of a vehicle rises, e.g. fuel consumption, wear and tear, but others show a considerable reduction per ton-mile. For example, the more journeys that can be accomplished in a given time the greater the amount of effective work done by both vehicle and crew, so minimum operating cost demands that high speeds should be maintained consistent with safety. Attempts by competing firms to "cream the traffic" over busy routes and at peak periods tend to reduce average speeds, whereas a central authority should be better able to minimize congestion by co-ordination of services.

(*g*) *Uneconomic services.* Private enterprise would not be attracted to the provision of services over low-density routes to outlying districts or areas of declining trade, but the wider public interest might well require such services to be maintained, even if they made losses. Such losses could, of course, be borne by a publicly-owned transport system by subsidizing them out of the proceeds of the most profitable services.

Disadvantages of a planned system
While all the above points appear to favour a centrally planned transport system, it is doubtful whether a single authority could in fact achieve all the economies which were theoretically possible.

(*a*) The sheer complexity of the overall requirements and their ever-changing nature would involve *administrative problems* exceeding those of any other industry, and once profit had been abandoned as a criterion of efficiency, unsatisfactory though it may be, it is difficult to see what could replace it.

(*b*) As in all planned systems, there would be a danger of *consumers' demands* being subordinated to the requirements of the planners; no arbitration procedure could be as swift and effective an antidote to this as freedom to choose another supplier.

(*c*) It would not be practicable to eliminate competition in the field of passenger transport from *private cars,* not to prohibit the carriage of goods in *traders' own vehicles.* To this extent, therefore, a fully co-ordinated system of all forms of inland transport would be impossible.

SIMILAR QUESTIONS

(i) Consider the view that the efficient development of transport is not possible under competitive conditions. (CIS Final, December 1965.)
(ii) How, if at all, should competition between rail and road transport be regulated? (C of S Final, November 1968.)

9.12 *Does economic theory indicate any rules which should govern the policies pursued by the nationalized industries? (CIS Final, December 1964.)*

The "perfect competition" model

While a strong case can be made out against the mere existence of privately-owned monopolies, economic theory does not provide any equally clear positive guidance for the operation of public monopolies. The difficulty arises from the fact that the economist's main concern is to contrast the evils of private monopoly with the virtues of perfect competition: omitting the supporting argument, his analysis is usually presented with the aid of two diagrams showing the fundamental differences which emerge when it is sought to maximize profit in each case —

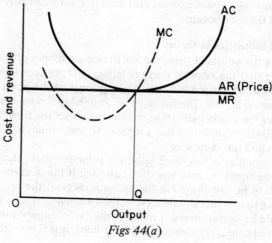

Figs 44(*a*)

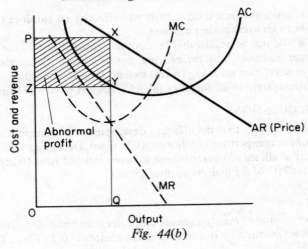

Fig. 44(b)

The conclusions are that, as compared with a firm in a perfectly competitive market —

(a) monopolies deliberately restrict their output;
(b) monopoly price is greater than marginal cost;
(c) monopolies make abnormal profits, and
(d) monopolies do not achieve the optimum scale of output.

While these conclusions may or may not be entirely valid, some industries by their very nature can only be operated as monopolies, and the fact that they are entrusted to public ownership does not automatically provide an answer to all these criticisms.

Nationalized industries in theory

(a) Taking the points in turn, the restriction on monopoly output arises from the fact that the *demand curve* is falling, and, since marginal cost is necessarily positive, output is bound to stop short of the point where marginal revenue is zero. The question of ownership has no bearing whatever on either the market situation or the cost structure, however, and unless a nationalized industry was prepared to lose money it would restrict its output in just the same way.

(b) The second criticism turns upon the principle that price and marginal cost should be equal in every line of production if the community's resources are to be distributed in the optimum way; if the reward to any factor in a particular line should exceed its marginal cost, this is a sign that society would be better served if more of the factor moved into that use and away from others. Proceeding on these lines, it is therefore arguable that the output of a nationalized industry should be increased to the point where marginal cost and price were equal, viz. $MC = AR$ just as if it were operating in a perfect market. Leaving aside the practical difficulty of quantifying marginal cost, this would certainly meet one criticism, but equating MC and AR on the monopoly diagram would not, except by sheer coincidence, result in normal profit being earned, nor in average cost being minimized.

(c) and (d) Similarly, the abnormal profit could be eliminated by fixing output where $AC = AR$, or the lowest average cost achieved by fixing output where $AC = MC$, but in each case the solution of one problem would only be at the expense of the other two. In short, there is no combination of output and price which would enable a monopoly, regardless of ownership, to equal the theoretical ideal of perfect competition.

Nationalized industries in practice

(a) If one looks at the policies pursued by nationalized industries in practice, the picture is equally confused. First of all it was laid down in the various enabling Acts that each nationalized industry should aim to "*cover its costs*, taking one year with another" — presumably this would justify seeking to equate AC and AR, though whether the former was meant to include the economist's concept of a normal rate of profit was not explicitly stated. This point has now been made somewhat clearer by the setting of "target" percentages for the *return on invested capital* in each case, but there can be no way of telling whether such a rate of profit, if achieved, is the result of efficient working or the exercise of monopoly power.

(b) Nationalized industries are, of course, criticized when they make losses, but the fact that the electricity authority is able to show better financial results than, say, the railways, is no proof of superior efficiency or greater dedication to the public interest. Indeed, when the nationalized industries behave in a *purely "commercial" way,* as they are often exhorted to do, the result is virtually indistinguishable from private monopoly, except that excess profits are not paid out to private shareholders. The Gas Council, for example, has not only made full use of its bargaining power to beat down the price of North Sea gas, but it also seems determined to sell the product for "what the traffic will bear"; similarly, the price structure announced by the British Steel Corporation is a very fair example of "differential charging", a practice for which private monopolies have often been criticized in the past.

Summary

It therefore seems impossible to secure all the alleged benefits of perfect competition where such a state of affairs does not in fact exist. Whether the public interest is best served by selling at *marginal cost* without regard to the resulting deficit or surplus, whether each Board should aim to *"break even"*, or whether they should make some arbitrarily *specified return* on their capital, remains open to debate; in any event, none of these policies will ensure that the nationalized industries are being operated at maximum efficiency.

SIMILAR QUESTIONS

(i) Discuss the proposition that the nationalized industries should be run on "commercial principles". Explain what you understand by this proposal and illustrate your answer by reference to the affairs of ONE of the nationalized industries. (ICA Final, November 1965.)

(ii) How should any one nationalized industry price its products? (C of S Final, 1969.)

(iii) Discuss the advantages and disadvantages of the public ownership of major industries in the United Kingdom. (ICWA Part I, June 1966.)

10
Objective tests

This last section contains a selection of questions of the kind used in
"objective tests", which seem fairly certain to become a feature of most
examination syllabuses in economics in the near future, starting with the
University of London and Associated Examining Board papers in Summer,
1971.

The selection has been confined to the two types of question which seem
most likely to be encountered, namely —

(*a*) *Multiple choice,* i.e. those to which only one of the suggested answers is
correct, and

(*b*) *Multiple completion,* i.e. those to which none, one or more of the
suggested answers may be correct.

In either case, the candidate is asked simply to choose which of the five
suggested answers, or combination thereof, he thinks is the correct one; no
explanation for the choice is asked for, and none should be given. The
typical paper may include some 70 or so questions to be answered in 1½
hours, so there is little time for dawdling, and yet it is essential that the
candidate should read each question carefully and be sure that he understands it before committing himself to a choice. Obviously, if there are five
choices, one of which must be right, pure guesswork will give approximately 20 per cent of correct answers, but there may be a marking scheme
which discounts random successes of this kind. Even when no such scheme
is used, however, it is unlikely that guessing will make any appreciable
difference to a candidate's relative score.

As the name denotes, objective tests are designed to eliminate variations
in the standard of marking among different examiners, and they also
favour the student who knows his subject fairly well but has no gift for
self-expression. They are not well suited to examining certain parts of an
Economics syllabus, however, i.e. those in which it is difficult to frame
questions with five fairly plausible answers, some of which are undoubtedly
right and others just as certainly wrong; nor is the ability to present an
argument in a tidy and logical manner a virtue lightly to be dismissed as
mere juggling with words. For these reasons it is unlikely that objective

217

tests will ever completely supersede the traditional essay paper, but between the two the examiners will no doubt be able to form a better judgement of a candidate's overall ability than by means of one kind of test alone.

In order to help the student test his own scores on these questions, the answers have been grouped together at the end of the Section.

Questions

1 The diagram represents the demand schedules for two different commodities. At which of the five points A, B, C, D, and E is demand most elastic?

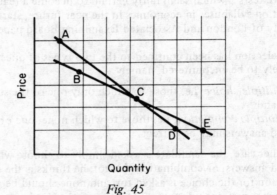

Fig. 45

2 Which one of the following measures would be *in*consistent with a policy of deflation?

(*a*) Purchase of long-term securities by the Bank of England.

(*b*) Increase in "special deposits".

(*c*) Imposing a ceiling on bank advances.

(*d*) Increase in Bank Rate.

(*e*) Increase in deposit required for hire-purchase transactions.

3 Which of the following statements MUST be true?

(*a*) If average revenue is falling, marginal revenue is less than average revenue.

(*b*) If average cost is falling, marginal cost is falling.

(*c*) If average cost is at a minimum, marginal cost is rising.

(*d*) If marginal cost and marginal revenue are equal, average cost and average revenue are also equal.

(*e*) If marginal cost is constant, and some element of fixed cost is present, average cost is falling.

1. None.   2. *a, c* and *e*.   3. *a, b* and *d*.   4. *b, c* and *d*.
                           5. All.

4 With reference to the Law of Diminishing Returns, which one of the following statements is NOT true?

(*a*) The law is valid no matter which factor is considered as being fixed in quantity.

(*b*) Diminishing returns to the variable factor set in once its average product per unit starts to fall.

(*c*) When the average product of the fixed factor is maximized, the marginal product of the variable factor is nil.

(*d*) The marginal product of the variable factor reaches a maximum before its average product.

(*e*) It would be wrong to try to maximize the average product of the variable factor unless the fixed factor were a free good.

5 Which of the following would contribute to a rise in prices?
    (*a*) An increase in imports.
    (*b*) Devaluation.
    (*c*) A fall in savings.
    (*d*) An increase in the note issue.
    (*e*) A budget deficit.

1. *a, b* and *c*.   2. *b, d* and *e*.   3. *a, c* and *e*.   4. *c, d* and *e*.   5. *b, c* and *e*.

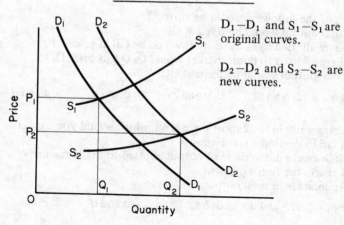

$D_1 - D_1$ and $S_1 - S_1$ are original curves.

$D_2 - D_2$ and $S_2 - S_2$ are new curves.

Fig. 46

6 Which of the following do you think the preceding diagram is meant
to represent?
   (*a*) The discovery of a new source of oil.
   (*b*) The long-run effect of an increase in demand for cars.
   (*c*) The introduction of a new, high-yielding variety of wheat.
   (*d*) A reduction in price to encourage bigger sales of washing machines.
   (*e*) The seasonal fluctuation in demand for holiday accommodation.

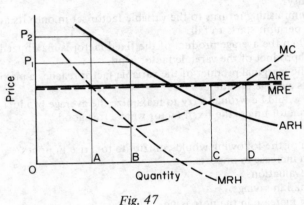

Fig. 47

The above diagram illustrates a firm selling on home and export markets,
ARH denoting average revenue in the home market, etc.

7 Which of the following would be correct?
   (*a*) Total output would be fixed at OD.
   (*b*) Share allotted to home market would be OB at price OP$_1$.
   (*c*) Share allotted to home market would be OA at price OP$_2$.
   (*d*) Total output would be fixed at OC.

1. *a* and *b*.   2. *b* and *c*.   3. *a* and *c*.   4. *c* and *d*.   5. *a* and *d*.

8 Assuming a rise in the export price level, which would you expect –
   (*a*) A fall in the home market price.
   (*b*) An increase in the share of output allotted to the home market.
   (*c*) A rise in the firm's profits.
   (*d*) An increase in total output.

1. *a* and *c*.   2. *b* and *d*.   3. *b* and *c*.   4. *a* and *d*.   5. *c* and *d*.

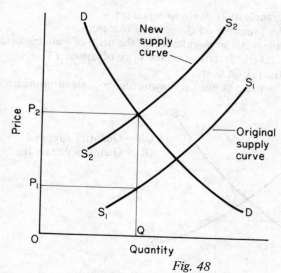

Fig. 48

9 Which of the following do you think the above diagram represents?
   (a) An extension in the supply of a commodity.
   (b) An increase in the demand for a commodity.
   (c) A decrease in the demand for a commodity.
   (d) An increase in the supply of a commodity.
   (e) A rise in price caused by a tax on a commodity.

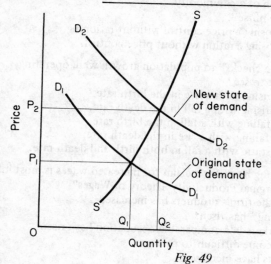

Fig. 49

10 The preceding diagram is most likely to represent —
  (a) The effect of a bad summer on the price of tomatoes.
  (b) The effect of an increase in population on the price of building land.
  (c) The long-run effect of advertising on the price of colour TV sets.
  (d) An increase in the tax on beer.
  (e) An increase in the price of meat following higher costs of production.

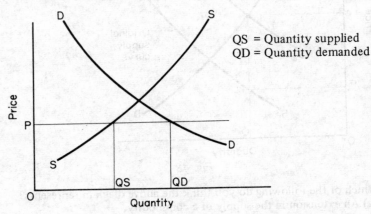

QS = Quantity supplied
QD = Quantity demanded

Fig. 50

11 The above diagram is most likely to represent —
  (a) Overproduction of a commodity.
  (b) Underconsumption of a commodity.
  (c) "Rationing by the purse".
  (d) The effect of imposing a price control without rationing.
  (e) The effect of imposing a ration without price control.

12 If Malthus's "positive checks" to population growth were operating, which would you expect to see?
  (a) Total population rising with a rise in the birth rate.
  (b) Total population rising with a fall in the death rate.
  (c) Total population falling with a fall in the birth rate.
  (d) Total population falling with a rise in the death rate.
  (e) Total population static with a fall in both birth and death rate.

13 Which of the following bases for a claim for increased wages is most in accordance with the Marginal Productivity Theory of Wages?
  (a) The demand for the firm's products has increased.
  (b) The "cost of living" has risen.
  (c) The wages of workers in a comparable occupation have risen.
  (d) The work has become difficult to perform.
  (e) The firm's exports have increased.

14 Which of the following statements are true?

(*a*) Elasticity of demand is governed by substitution.

(*b*) If demand is inelastic, a change in price will not affect the quantity sold.

(*c*) If total revenue falls when price increases, demand is elastic.

1. *b* only.   2. *a* and *b*.   3. *a* and *c*.   4. *b* and *c*.   5. All.

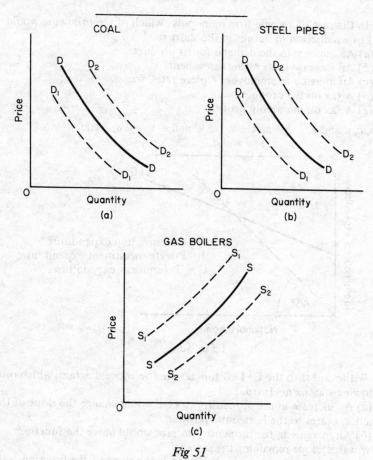

Fig 51

15 In the above diagram D—D and S—S represent original demand or supply schedules as the case may be for the products shown. What would you expect the position of the schedules to be subsequent to the discovery of large quantities of natural gas in the country concerned?

	COAL	STEEL PIPES	GAS BOILERS
(a)	D_1-D_1	D_2-D_2	S_1-S_1
(b)	D_1-D_1	D_2-D_2	S_2-S_2
(c)	D_1-D_1	$D -D$	S_2-S_2
(d)	$D -D$	D_2-D_2	S_2-S_2
(e)	D_1-D_1	D_2-D_2	$S -S$

16 In the case of a single-firm monopoly, which of the following would lead to a reduction in output in the short run?

(a) An increase in the demand for its product.

(b) An increase in its rating assessment.

(c) An increase in employees' "piece rate" wages.

(d) A tax on the product.

(e) A tax on monopoly profits.

1. *b, c, d* and *e*.   2. *c* and *d*.   3. *d* and *e*.   4. *a, c* and *e*.
                          5. *b, c* and *d*.

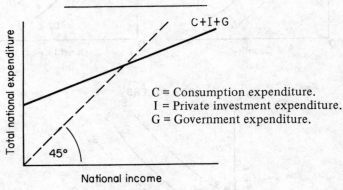

C = Consumption expenditure.
I = Private investment expenditure.
G = Government expenditure.

Fig. 52

17 With respect to the C+I+G function in the above diagram, which of the following statements is true?

(a) An increase in the propensity to save would change the slope of the function nearer to the horizontal position.

(b) An increase in the propensity to save would move the function downwards, slope remaining the same.

(c) An increase in exports would change the slope of the function nearer to 45°

(d) An increase in imports would not affect the slope or position of the function.

(e) An increase in the marginal efficiency of capital would move the function upwards, slope remaining the same.

1. *a* and *e* only.   2. *b* and *c* only.   3. *a, d* and *e*,   4. *b, c* and *e*.
            5. All of these.

18 Which of the following statements are *necessarily* true?

(*a*) An improvement in the terms of trade will improve the balance of payments.

(*b*) An improvement in the terms of trade will improve the balance of trade.

(*c*) A rise in the price of exports will improve the terms of trade.

(*d*) Provided that equilibrium in the balance of payments is maintained, an improvement in the terms of trade will raise the standard of living.

(*e*) Devaluation will make the terms of trade worse.

1. *a, c* and *d*.   2. *b, c* and *e*.   3. *a, c* and *e*.   4. *b, c* and *d*.   5. *c, d* and *e*.

19 Given the following information, what is the Gross Domestic Product at factor cost?

	£M
Consumer expenditure at market prices	24,000
Public authorities' current expenditure	6,400
Gross domestic investment in fixed capital and stocks	7,000
Export of goods and services	7,000
Import of goods and services	7,200
Net property income from abroad	200
Taxes on expenditure	5,600
Subsidies	600
Capital consumption	3,000

1. £32,400 m. 2. £32,200 m. 3. £29,600 m. 4. £29,400 m. 5. £29,200 m.

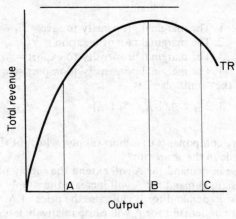

Fig. 53

20 The preceding diagram shows the way in which a firm's total revenue varies with output. Which of the following deductions would be justified?

(a) That output A was too small for maximum profit.

(b) That profit was maximized at output B.

(c) That output C was too large for maximum profit.

(d) That demand was inelastic at output A.

(e) That elasticity of demand was unity at output B.

1. *a*, *b* and *c*.   2. *b* and *d*.   3. *a*, *d* and *e*.   4. *c* and *e*.   5. *a*, *b*, *c* and *e*.

21 A commodity is produced in the home country, but is also imported subject to a low rate of duty. If the duty is increased, which of the following consequences will *necessarily* result —

(a) There will be an increase in customs revenue.

(b) The price of imported supplies will rise by the amount that the duty has increased.

(c) Home producers will find it easier to make profits.

1. None of these. 2. *a* and *c*.   3. *a* and *b*.   4. *c* only.   5. All.

22 In which one of the following circumstances would reducing the price of the product be most likely to increase a firm's profit?

(a) Inelastic demand, low fixed cost, working to capacity.

(b) Elastic demand, high fixed cost, working below capacity.

(c) Elastic demand, low fixed cost, working to capacity.

(d) Inelastic demand, high fixed cost, working below capacity.

(e) Inelastic demand, high fixed cost, working to capacity.

(f) Elastic demand, high fixed cost, working to capacity.

23 Given that — 1. The marginal propensity to save = $\frac{1}{4}$
2. The marginal rate of taxation = $\frac{1}{3}$
3. The marginal propensity to export = $\frac{1}{6}$
4. The marginal propensity to import = $\frac{1}{6}$.

Then the size of the "multiplier" is —

1. 4   2. 3   3. $2\frac{2}{5}$ 4. $1\frac{1}{3}$ 5. $1\frac{1}{11}$

24 If A and B are components of a joint supply, which of the following statements are true in the short run?

(a) An increase in demand for A will extend the supply of B.

(b) An increase in demand for A will increase the supply of B.

(c) An increase in demand for B will raise the price of A.

(d) An increase in demand for A will cause relatively less of B to be produced.

(*e*) A tax on B will cause relatively more of A to be produced.

1. *b, d* and *e*.   2. *a, b* and *d*.   3. *c, d* and *e*.   4. *b, c* and *e*.   5. *b* and *e* only.

25 If A and B are components of a joint demand, which of the following statements are true in the short run?

(*a*) An increase in demand for A + B will increase the supply of both of them.

(*b*) An increase in demand for A + B will raise the price of both of them.

(*c*) A discovery which increases the supply of A will raise the price of B.

(*d*) A tax on A will decrease the supply of B.

(*e*) A subsidy on B will extend the supply of A.

1. *a, b* and *c*.   2. *a, c* and *e*.   3. *b, c and d*.   4. *b, c* and *e*.   5. *c, d* and *e*.

26 With reference to the Index of Retail Prices, which of the following statements is always true?

(*a*) A rise in the index indicates a fall in the value of money.

(*b*) A rise in the index indicates a fall in the standard of living.

(*c*) A weighted average is used in arriving at the overall index figure.

(*d*) A change in Purchase Tax is reflected by a change in the index.

(*e*) A change in social security contributions is reflected by a change in the index.

1. *a, b* and *c*.   2. *b, c* and *d*.   3. *c, d* and *e*.   4. *a, c* and *d*.   5. *a, d* and *e*.

27 Which of the following assets of a commercial bank would be used in calculating its liquidity ratio?

(*a*) Cheques in course of collection.

(*b*) Treasury Bills.

(*c*) Commercial bills.

(*d*) Special deposits.

(*e*) Consols.

1. *a, b* and *c*.   2. *a, b, c* and *d*.   3. *b* and *c* only.   4. *b, c* and *d*.   5. All.

28 Which of the following would be conducive to an increase in credit creation by a particular commercial bank?

(*a*) An increase in special deposits.

(*b*) An increase in credit creation by the other commercial banks.

(*c*) Failure of another bank to pay its depositors.

(*d*) More widespread agreement to paying wages by cheque.

(*e*) More workers being paid monthly instead of weekly.

1. *a, b* and *d*.   2. *b, c* and *d*.   3. *a, d* and *e*.   4. *b, d* and *e*.   5. All.

29 Which of the following would contribute to "cost push" inflation?

(*a*) A rise in the import price index.

(*b*) A fall in interest rates.

(*c*) Devaluation.

(*d*) Higher productivity without higher wages.

(*e*) Higher wages without higher productivity.

1. *a, b* and *e*.   2. *a, c* and *e*.   3. *b, c* and *e*.   4. *a, b* and *c*.   5. *b, c* and *d*.

30 Which of the following circumstances are conducive to wide geographical dispersal of an industry?

(*a*) Goods are perishable.

(*b*) Goods are small in relation to their value.

(*c*) Finished goods are bulkier than raw materials.

(*d*) Much weight is lost in production process.

(*e*) Finished product contains a high percentage of water.

1. *a, b* and *d*.   2. *a, c* and *e*.   3. *b, c* and *e*.   4. *b, d* and *e*.   5. *c, d* and *e*.

In the four questions which follow, imagine that the Government is considering a variety of policy measures, including —

(*a*) An increase in income tax.

(*b*) An increase in selective employment tax.

(*c*) An increase in import duties on manufactured goods.

(*d*) An increase in Purchase Tax.

(*e*) An increase in food subsidies.

31 Which of the following combinations would be most deflationary?

1. *a, c* and *e*.   2. *b, c* and *e*.   3. *b, c* and *d*.   4. *a, b* and *d*.   5. *c, d* and *e*.

32 Which combination would contribute most to a more equal distribution of the national income?

1. *a* and *b*.   2. *a* and *c*.   3. *a* and *e*.   4. *b* and *d*.   5. *c* and *e*.

33 Which combination would be most likely to encourage exports?

1. *b* and *d*.   2. *a* and *b*.   3. *b* and *c*.   4. *c* and *e*.   5. *d* and *e*.

34 Which combination would be most likely to stimulate investment in manufacturing industry?

1. *a* and *b*.   2. *b* and *c*.   3. *a* and *c*.   4. *b* and *d*.   5. *c* and *e*.

---

35 You are given the following information about the costs and revenues of a firm —

Output	Units of Total Revenue	Units of Total Cost (including normal profit)
0	0	15
1	5	18
2	10	20·2
3	15	21·5
4	20	22
5	25	22·3
6	30	23·4
7	35	25·9
8	40	30
9	45	36·5
10	50	47

With which of the following statements would you agree?
(*a*) The firm is producing under imperfect competition.
(*b*) The firm's most profitable output is 8 units.
(*c*) The optimum size of output is 8 units.
(*d*) The industry is in a state of disequilibrium.
(*e*) Marginal cost is at a minimum when output is 5 units.

1. *a*, *b* and *d*. 2. *b*, *c* and *d*. 3. *a*, *d* and *e*. 4. *b*, *d* and *e*. 5. *c*, *d* and *e*.

---

36 Which of the following would explain why a firm was operating at less than its optimum scale of output?
(*a*) It had a monopoly of the supply of its product.
(*b*) It was operating in an imperfect market.
(*c*) It was operating in a perfect market in a state of equilibrium.
(*d*) It was operating in a perfect market in which demand had recently increased.
(*e*) It was operating in a perfect market in which demand had recently decreased.

1. *a*, *b* and *c*. 2. *a*, *b* and *d*. 3. *b*, *c* and *e*. 4. *a*, *b* and *e*. 5. *a*, *c* and *e*.

37 Which one of the following situations would *not* be likely to increase the bargaining power of a trade union in wage negotiations?
(*a*) Inelastic demand for the firm's product.
(*b*) Industry is highly capitalized.
(*c*) The firm has just merged with a competitor.
(*d*) Employers have agreed to the "closed shop" principle.
(*e*) Ratio of labour employed to capital difficult to alter.

38 Which of the following would you expect to increase liquidity preference?
(*a*) Expectation of a rise in the price index.

(b) Expectation of a rise in long-term interest rates.

(c) More widespread adoption of banks "credit card" schemes.

(d) More comprehensive arrangements for social security.

(e) The approach of Christmas.

1. *a, b* and *d*.   2. *b, c* and *d*.   3. *a, c* and *e*.   4. *b, c* and *e*.   5. *b* and *e* only.

39 With which of the following statements would you agree?

(a) There is no point in advertising if competition is perfect.

(b) There is no point in a monopolist advertising his product.

(c) Advertising tends to make the demand for a product more elastic.

(d) Advertising has no effect on elasticity of supply in the short run.

(e) Advertising may sell more goods, but in the long run it must raise the price of the product.

1. *a* and *c*.   2. *b* and *c*.   3. *a* and *d*.   4. *b* and *d*.   5. *c* and *e*.

40 Which of the following would be likely to result from legislation obliging employers to pay the same wages to men and women for the same kind of work?

(a) A rise in women's real wages.

(b) A rise in employers' costs.

(c) A marginal displacement of male labour in jobs which both sexes are able to perform.

(d) An increase in the tendency for some jobs to be regarded as "man's work" and others as "women's work".

(e) An increase in the number of women in employment.

1. *a, b* and *c*.   2. *a, b* and *d*.   3. *a, b* and *e*.   4. *b, c* and *d*.   5. *b, d* and *e*.

41 In which *one* of the following cases can it safely be said that the supplier will bear the whole of a tax on his output?

(a) Demand is more elastic than supply.

(b) Supply is more elastic than demand.

(c) Production is subject to diminishing returns.

(d) There are increasing returns to scale.

(e) The supplier's receipts consist entirely of economic rent.

42 Which of the following should be included in arriving at the value of the national income?

(a) Consumers' hire-purchase debt interest.

(b) Undistributed profits of companies.

(c) Family allowances.

(d) Money won on football pools.

(e) Rentable value of owner-occupied houses.

1. All.   2. *c* and *d* only.   3. *b* and *e* only.   4. *a* and *e* only.   5. None.

43 Which of the following was *not* one of the original "canons of taxation" put forward by Adam Smith?

(*a*) A tax should be convenient to pay.

(*b*) A tax should be impossible to evade.

(*c*) The burden of a tax should be equitably shared.

(*d*) A tax should be easy to understand.

(*e*) A tax should be economical to collect.

Apart from raising revenue, a tax may have one or more of the following objectives —

(*a*) To reduce consumption generally.

(*b*) To reduce consumption of luxury goods.

(*c*) To distribute the national income more equally.

(*d*) To improve health.

(*e*) To improve the balance of payments.

Which effects do you think the following might have?

44 Income tax.

1. *a* and *c* only.   2. *a*, *c* and *e*.   3. *a* and *e* only.   4. *b* and *c* only.
5. *b*, *c* and *e*.

45 Purchase Tax.

1. *a*, *c* and *e*.   2. *b*, *d* and *e*.   3. *b* and *e* only.   4. *c* and *e* only.   5. *e* only.

46 Tobacco duty.

1. *b*, *c* and *d*.   2. *b*, *c* and *e*.   3. *c* and *d* only.   4. *c*, *d* and *e*.   5. *d* and *e* only.

47 Estate duty.

1. *b*, *c* and *e*.   2. *b* and *e* only.   3. *c* and *e* only.   4. *b* and *c* only.
5. *e* only.

---

48 Indirect taxes are usually said to be preferable to direct taxes for all except *one* of the following reasons.

(*a*) They are more adaptable to requirements of Government policy.

(*b*) They are fairer.

(*c*) They do less harm to incentive.

(*d*) They are more difficult to evade.

(*e*) They are more convenient to pay.

The market for secondhand cars would be influenced in some way by all of the following —

(*a*) A rise in national income per head.
(*b*) An increase in purchase tax on new cars.
(*c*) A rise in railway fares.
(*d*) A fine spring.
(*e*) Tightening-up of regulations on road-worthiness.

49 Which of these would *not* tend to raise the price of secondhand cars?

50 Which of these would tend to increase the demand for secondhand cars?
1. *a* and *b* only. 2. *a*, *b* and *c*. 3. *b* and *c* only. 4. *a*, *b*, *c* and *d*.
5. All of these.

51 Which of these would tend to increase the level of dealers' stocks of secondhand cars?

1. None of these. 2. *a*, *b* and *c*. 3. *b*, *c* and *d*. 4. *c*, *d* and *e*. 5. *e* only.

52 Which of the following are direct taxes?
(*a*) Surtax.
(*b*) Car licence.
(*c*) Purchase Tax.
(*d*) Capital Gains Tax.
(*e*) Stamp duty on cheques.

1. All of these. 2. *a*, *b* and *c*. 3. *a*, *b* and *d*. 4. *b*, *d* and *e*. None of these.

53 Which of the following are specific taxes?
(*a*) Income Tax.
(*b*) Tobacco duty.
(*c*) Petrol tax.
(*d*) Purchase tax.
(*e*) TV licence.

1. *a*, *b* and *c*. 2. *b*, *c* and *e*. 3. *c* and *d* only. 4. *c* and *e* only.
5. *d* and *e* only.

54 Calculate personal disposable income from the following —

	£M
Income from employment (including self-employment)	26,000
Trading surpluses of public enterprises	1,000
Total profits of private sector companies, before tax	5,000
Company taxation	2,500
Undistributed profits	1,500
Taxes on income	8,000

| Indirect taxes | 3,000 |
| Personal savings | 2,000 |

1. £14,000 m. 2. £15,000 m. 3. £18,000 m. 4. £19,000 m. 5. £20,000 m.

Unemployment can be reduced by one or more of the following Government policies —

(a) Reduction in the standard rate of income tax.
(b) Industrial Training Boards
(c) Better Employment Exchange facilities.
(d) The "regulator".

Which *one* of these would you consider most appropriate for —

55 Transitional unemployment.

56 Structural unemployment.

57 Persistent general unemployment.

58 Cyclical unemployment.

59 Which of the following would tend to increase the number of workers in employment —
(a) An increase in the propensity to save.
(b) An increase in liquidity preference.
(c) A rise in export earnings.
(d) An increase in the efficiency of capital equipment.
(e) An increase in the velocity of circulation of money.

1. *a, b* and *d*. 2. *a, c* and *e*. 3. *b, c* and *e*. 4. *c, d* and *e*. 5. *c* and *e* only.

60 Which of the following would tend to increase private savings?
(a) More equal distribution of the national income.
(b) An increase in the national income.
(c) A fall in the general level of prices.
(d) Easier terms for house mortgages.
(e) More comprehensive social security.

1. *a, b* and *c*. 2. *b, c* and *d*. 3. *b* and *c* only. 4. *b, d* and *e*. 5. All of these.

61 Which of the following would tend to increase savings by businesses?
(a) An increase in the national income.
(b) A fall in the general level of prices.

(*c*) An increase in the tax on distributed profits.

(*d*) A "dividend freeze".

(*e*) An increase in Corporation Tax.

1. *a*, *b* and *c*.   2. *a*, *c* and *d*.   3. *a* and *c* only.   4. *a* and *d* only.   5. All of these.

62 Which of the following would an economist classify as investment for the purpose of UK national accounting?

(*a*) A purchase of shares in a British company on the London Stock Exchange by a UK national.

(*b*) A purchase by a UK national of shares in an American company from a US national.

(*c*) Government expenditure on atomic research.

(*d*) An increase in the book value of stocks and work-in-progress caused by rising prices.

(*e*) Money savings used to purchase newly-issued share capital.

1. *a*, *b* and *e*.   2. *c* only.   3. *a*, *b*, *d* and *e*.   4. *b*, *c* and *e*.   5. All of these.

63 Which of the following is likely to raise the rent payable by farmers in the long run?

(*a*) A fall in the birth rate.

(*b*) An increase in food subsidies.

(*c*) A reduction in the tariff on imported foodstuffs.

(*d*) An improvement in productivity per acre.

(*e*) An increase in the amount of land allocated to builders.

1. *a*, *b* and *d*.   2. *b*, *c* and *d*.   3. *b*, *d* and *e*.   4. *c*, *d* and *e*.   5. *a*, *d* and *e*.

64 Which of the following is NOT a normal function of profit in a state of perfect competition?

(*a*) An inducement to entrepreneurs to accept the risks inseparable from forecasting.

(*b*) An indication to entrepreneurs as to which industries should be expanded and which allowed to contract.

(*c*) A source of funds for expansion of successful businesses.

(*d*) A payment to entrepreneurs for services rendered in organizing the work of the other factors.

(*e*) A means whereby inefficient producers are driven out of business.

65 Which of the following are legal tender?

(*a*) A Scottish bank note.

(*b*) A half-crown piece.

(*c*) £1·50 worth of "silver" (cupro-nickel) coins.

(*d*) A banker's draft.
(*e*) A Postal Order.

1. *a, c* and *e*.   2. *b* and *d*.   3. *a* only.   4. *c* only.   5. *e* only.

66 Which one of the following *cannot* be influenced by Budgetary policy?
(*a*) Power of private monopolies
(*b*) General level of prices.
(*c*) Regional distribution of employment.
(*d*) Balance of trade.
(*e*) Distribution of the national income.

67 Which one of the following cost/revenue situations always indicates a normal rate of profit, no more and no less?
(*a*) Marginal cost = marginal revenue.
(*b*)Average cost = marginal cost.
(*c*) Marginal cost = average revenue.
(*d*) Average cost = marginal revenue.
(*e*) Average cost = average revenue.

68 Which one of the following would indicate a population of optimum size?
(*a*) Birth rate = death rate.
(*b*) Net migration = 0.
(*c*) GNP per head at a maximum.
(*d*) GNP per square mile at a maximum.
(*e*) Balance of payments in equilibrium.

69 Which of the following might be compatible with each other, at least in the short run?
(*a*) Equilibrium in balance of payments (current account).
(*b*) Prices rising faster than world prices.
(*c*) A fixed exchange rate.

1. No two of these.   2. *a* and *b* only.   3. *b* and *c* only.   4. *a* and *c* only.
5. Any two of these.

70. A firm's "close-down" point is reached when –
(*a*) Average revenue fails to cover average total cost.
(*b*) Average revenue fails to cover average variable cost.
(*c*) Average revenue fails to cover average fixed cost.
(*d*) Average revenue fails to cover marginal cost.
(*e*) Marginal revenue fails to cover marginal cost.

71 The following diagram shows price and output of a commodity before (1) and after (2) the imposition of a tax.

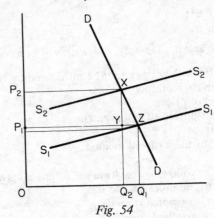

Fig. 54

Which of the following statements are correct?
(a) Buyers pay most of the tax.
(b) Price rises by the full amount of the tax.
(c) Total revenue from the tax is $P_1 P_2 XY$.
(d) Loss of consumer surplus is XYZ.
(e) Conditions of demand for the commodity have been changed
by the tax.

1. *a, b* and *d*.   2. *a, c* and *d*.   3. *a, d* and *e*.   4. *a* and *d* only.   5. *a* and *e* only.

72 Which of the following would be conducive to increased mobility of labour?
(a) A national minimum wage.
(b) A reduction in the marginal rate of tax on earned income.
(c) Transferability of pension rights.
(d) Wages tied to the "cost of living" index.
(e) Demolition of old houses.

1. *a, b* and *c*.   2. *b, c* and *d*.   3. *c, d* and *e*.   4. None of these.
5. *b* and *c* only.

Answers to objective test questions

1 . . . **A**	25 . . . **4**	49 . . . (*e*)
2 . . . (*a*)	26 . . . **4**	50 . . . **4**
3 . . . **2**	27 . . . **3**	51 . . . **5**
4 . . . (*b*)	28 . . . **4**	52 . . . **3**
5 . . . **5**	29 . . . **2**	53 . . . **2**
6 . . . (*b*)	30 . . . **2**	54 . . . **4**
7 . . . **3**	31 . . . **4**	55 . . . (*c*)
8 . . . **5**	32 . . . **3**	56 . . . (*b*)
9 . . . (*e*)	33 . . . **1**	57 . . . (*a*)
10 . . . (*b*)	34 . . . **2**	58 . . . (*d*)
11 . . . (*d*)	35 . . . **4**	59 . . . **5**
12 . . . (*d*)	36 . . . **4**	60 . . . **3**
13 . . . (*a*)	37 . . . (*c*)	61 . . . **2**
14 . . . **3**	38 . . . **5**	62 . . . **4**
15 . . . (*b*)	39 . . . **3**	63 . . . **3**
16 . . . **2**	40 . . . **2**	64 . . . (*d*)
17 . . . **1**	41 . . . (*e*)	65 . . . **4**
18 . . . **5**	42 . . . **3**	66 . . . (*a*)
19 . . . **2**	43 . . . (*b*)	67 . . . (*e*)
20 . . . **4**	44 . . . **2**	68 . . . (*c*)
21 . . . **4**	45 . . . **3**	69 . . . **5**
22 . . . (*b*)	46 . . . **5**	70 . . . (*b*)
23 . . . **4**	47 . . . **4**	71 . . . **4**
24 . . . **1**	48 . . . **(b)**	72 . . . **5**